THE RECOVERING ALCOHOLIC

SOCIOLOGICAL
OBSERVATIONS

Series Editor: **JOHN M. JOHNSON,** Arizona State University

"This series seeks its inspiration primarily from its subject matter and the nature of its observational setting. It draws on all academic disciplines and a wide variety of theoretical and methodological perspectives. The series has a commitment to substantive problems and issues and favors research and analysis which seek to blend actual observations of human actions in daily life with broader theoretical, comparative, and historical perspectives. SOCIOLOGICAL OBSERVATIONS aims to use all of our available intellectual resources to better understand all facets of human experience and the nature of our society."

—John M. Johnson

THE RECOVERING ALCOHOLIC

Norman K. Denzin

SAGE PUBLICATIONS
The Publishers of Professional Social Science
Newbury Park Beverly Hills London New Delhi

For information address:

SAGE Publications, Inc.
2111 West Hillcrest Drive
Newbury Park, California 91320

SAGE Publications Inc.   SAGE Publications Ltd.
275 South Beverly Drive   28 Banner Street
Beverly Hills   London EC1Y 8QE
California 90212   England

SAGE PUBLICATIONS India Pvt. Ltd.
M-32 Market
Greater Kailash I
New Delhi 110 048 India

Printed in the United States of America

Library of Congress Cataloging-in-Publication Data

Main entry under title:

Denzin, Norman K.
    The recovering alcoholic.

    (Sociological observations ; v. 19)
    Includes index.
        1. Alcoholics—Rehabilitation—United States.
2. Alcoholism—Treatment—United States. 3. Alcoholics
Anonymous. I. Title. II. Series: Sociological
observation ; 19. [DNLM: 1. Alcoholics Anonymous.
2. Alcoholism—rehabilitation. WM 274 D199r]
HV5279.D44   1986   616.86'1'0019   86-6525
ISBN 0-8039-2746-0
ISBN 0-8039-2747-9 (pbk.)

Contents

Foreword

John M. Johnson
Arizona State University, Tempe

The Recovering Alcoholic is the second volume of Professor Norman Denzin's trilogy about the nature of drinking, alcoholism, the inner structures of alcoholic experience, and the processes of alcoholic recovery. Taken together, they represent a profound statement about white male culture, and what it means to be alive for many Americans in the latter part of the twentieth century. The theoretical importance of these volumes resides in Professor Denzin's ability to move from the phenomenological level of analysis, the realities of individual, subjective experience, to the larger contexts of group, social interaction, and culture. Even though alcoholism is a dis-ease experienced at the most personal and subjective level by individuals, it is impossible to separate alcoholism from the group, interactional, and cultural contexts that provide its meaning for individuals.

The first volume of Professor Denzin's trilogy, *The Alcoholic Self*, published by Sage Publications earlier in 1986, details the inner structures of alcoholic experience. The analysis is at one and the same time phenomenological and structural. It is phenomenological in that it lays bare the inner logic and inner experience of alcoholism. Many individuals joined with Professor Denzin in this search, and the work recognizes the truth contained in each individual's experience with alcohol. It is structural in that it ties these personal experiences to the larger contexts in which they have emerged. From *The Alcoholic Self* we learn that using alcohol is part of the experience of being a normal American at this point in time, and is associated by individuals with their selfhood, freedom, and locations in the status order. The story about alcoholism, then, is a story about a relationship between individuals and social structure. From Professor Denzin's view, this relationship involves a dis-ease of time, a dis-ease of emotionality, and a dis-ease of self for those who experience it in daily life. Alcoholics use alcohol in an attempt to make peace with their sense of the relationship between past, present, and future. Use of alcohol reflects a lack of inner peace with their existence in the here and now of their lives. Alcoholism additionally involves a dis-ease of emotionality, wherein alcohol is used to gain control over negative emotions such as guilt, fear, resentment, anger, and hostility. Alcoholism produces what Professor Denzin terms an *alcoholically-divided self*, an experienced separation between the alcoholic subject and its place in the social and spiritual order. Alcoholics use alcohol to gain, recognize, and assert their power in the world, to become "the captains of their ship," a value deeply ingrained in American culture. Alcoholics seek self-control. Each believes that he or she is in control of the world that surrounds the self, and in this control is experienced a sense of pride, which leads the individual to take the next drink, even when the individual knows that he or she will probably lose control of self. It is this pride in self that ties the alcoholic self to a competitive relationship with alcohol. To understand the present volume, it is important to understand this inner logic of alcoholism and what Professor Denzin presents as the Six Theses of Alcoholism. Readers are encouraged to review *The Alcoholic Self* in order to more fully appreciate the present work.

In *The Recovering Alcoholic*, Professor Denzin tells us how individuals join with others to recover from their dis-ease. Whereas the study of active alcoholism reveals what is taken for granted and driven deep inside the consciousness of ordinary Americans, the study of the recovery process makes problematic what other cultural members take for granted in their daily lives. The social and spiritual poverty of alcoholism contains the seeds for its own recovery. The process begins with the alcoholic's surrender to his or her self-pride, bad faith, and imaginary ideals. The recovery process is a group process, and through participation in Alcoholics Anonymous (AA) we learn how participation in the storytelling rituals and traditions of AA produces a new definition and sense of self that flows from the group structures of the AA collective. The treatment process is predicated on the assumption that the pretreatment style of sobriety drove the alcoholic to drink, and from this provides a reinterpretation of the alcoholic's taken-for-granted ideas concerning self, emotionality, temporality, others, alcohol, and alcoholism. AA members are similar to others who undergo a group socialization process, such as mental patients, military recruits, prisoners, and college students. They socialize one another, and collectively develop adaptive strategies for dealing with problematic situations. They develop their own meanings for the cultural problematics they are presented with. They develop a "medicalization" or "treatmentization" of their worldview. AA members teach and support each other in the development of a new sense of self-pride, one founded on a recognition of their alcoholism, and their personal achievement of recovery. This book details how all this occurs in the daily lives of alcoholic subjects. It shows how AA gets inside the self of the alcoholic, and how spiritual regeneration occurs as a collective accomplishment.

Although formally open to all alcoholics regardless of social rank, status, or position, the recovery processes outlined by Professor Denzin are implicitly structured by gender and race. The pretreatment style of sobriety that drove the alcoholic to drink is one that is, for the most part, grounded in the values of a culture dominated by whites and males, even for women and minority alcoholics. The rituals of talking and story-telling that occur in AA groups involve a shift from male to female emotionality and emotional expression, and so perhaps it is not surprising to learn that 7 of 10 AA participants will experience one or more "slips" or relapses into alcoholism as they undergo the treatment process. Members of minority groups show an even greater tendency to relapse, and Professor Denzin's work shows how this tendency is tied to the group ideology and processes. Slips and relapses are at the heart of the recovery process, and are related to the identity the alcoholic forms about himself or herself as an alcoholic.

American society is secular, democratic, and competitive. At no institutional level is there a formal ontology, theory, or perspective on the self and its rightful place in the social and spiritual order. This produces for many individuals a subject-object dualism, an experienced separation between the active, knowing, sentient subject and his or her social experiences within this culture at this point in time. Recovering alcoholics seek a more authentic, truer sense of this relationship, and so this book may be read as a story of their spiritual search and success.

Preface

My topic is the recovering alcoholic self. The recovering alcoholic, who I define as a once-active alcoholic who no longer drinks, undergoes radical transformations in identity as the drinking self of the past is let go of. In the 1980s recovery from alcoholism involves socialization processes that often begin in treatment centers and then move to Alcoholics Anonymous. In these contexts, which I call the social worlds of recovery, the alcoholic discovers a new, nondrinking self that may find its place in a preexisting society of recovering selves. The recovering self, like the alcoholic self, is a group and interactional phenomenon.

The rather large literature on treatment for alcoholism does not contain any sustained, in-depth analysis of the lived experiences of the recovering alcoholic self. This book, the second of three volumes on alcoholism in American society, addresses this void.[1] This study begins, then, where *The Alcoholic Self* (Denzin, 1986a) ended; that is, with the alcoholic who has surrendered, however superficially, to alcoholism. This individual is pushed and sometimes pulled either directly into a treatment center for alcoholism, or into Alcoholics Anonymous. He may find that he has no true desire to stop drinking, or to recover, yet others force these options upon him. Whether he likes it or not he is asked to recover from alcoholism. Hence he finds himself moved along a trajectory of experience that includes treatment and then participation in A.A. This twin trajectory of social experience constitutes the focus of my analysis. The following question structures my inquiry: "How is the recovering self of the alcoholic lived into existence?" This is an interactional and phenomenological study of the institutional and group socialization practices that create and shape the recovering alcoholic self.

My research sites are twofold: substance abuse or alcoholism treatment centers and Alcoholics Anonymous. My methods are inter-pretive and ethnographic (see Denzin, 1986a, chap. 1). I do not study, except incidentally, the recovery process that occurs outside these socialization contexts. I am mindful, however, that alcoholics do recover—that is, stop drinking—in ways other than those that I study in this work. Some seek counseling. Some join self-help and therapy groups that are not based on Alcoholics Anonymous's 12 Steps. Others recover with spouses or significant others. Others just stop drinking. Some enter spiritual programs, or related 12 Step Programs (for example, Emotions Anonymous, Grow, Narcotics Anonymous, Women for Sobriety), and so on (see Wholey, 1984). The recovery experiences of such persons are not well understood.

This work may be controversial or problematic for certain experts in the field of alcoholism studies. It is, in a sense, "pro-Alcoholics Anonymous." I am of the opinion that one's biases should be immediately placed in front of the reader. I have seen A.A. work and I have seen individuals die from "alcoholism" after they were taught how to become normal social drinkers.

I understand alcoholism to be a *dis-ease* of conduct. It is an uneasiness of self, time, emotionality, and social relationships with others. The alcoholic self dealt with this uneasiness of being by drinking. At some point in her drinking career a line was crossed that no longer made drinking an option. The individual became an alcoholic. She lost the ability to abstain from drinking for any continuous period of time. And when the first drink was taken, the drinker was unable to stop with just one drink.

The recovering alcoholic reverses this process. He or she learns how to resolve this uneasiness of living by not drinking. This learning process occurs, as just indicated, in treatment centers and in Alcoholics Anonymous. The recovering alcoholic becomes an individual who (1) incorporates the identity of recovering alcoholic into his or her self-conception; (2) having once been an active, drinking alcoholic, becomes a nondrinker, and (3) for the purposes of this study calls himself or herself a member of Alcoholics Anonymous.

The recovering alcoholic self undergoes transformations in experience that produce situational and long-term commitments to the identity of "recovering alcoholic." This new identity will include central components of the A.A. program of recovery, that is, if the alcoholic commits himself to A.A. This means he will become an A.A. member. It is this individual that I study in this work.

The recovering alcoholic is, in a sense, an outsider to the broader drinking culture of American society. Previously a drinking member in the public and private situations of that culture, the alcoholic was nearly destroyed by alcohol. In the pursuit of a desired self that was to be given in the drinking act, alcoholics found that their drunken comportment produced the label of alcoholic. They became failed drinkers; stigmatized deviants who had lost control over themselves and over alcohol. As recovering alcoholics, ex-drinkers thus look somewhat askance at the society that defined them as alcoholic. Some even feel betrayed, for they pursued a prescribed mode of valued self-expression that nearly killed them.

Having once internalized society's commonsense reasons for drinking, the recovering alcoholic now learns an interpretive theory that makes the drinking of alcohol a tabooed, or forbidden, self-act. The recovering alcoholic, once a deviant drinker, carries the history of this past self within a new selfhood that allows for the appearance of "being normal" within a society of other "normals." By studying the recovering alcoholic self we gain insight, then, into another side of being normal, but deviant at the same time.

The Recovering Alcoholic addresses a behaviorist bias in much of the current literature on alcoholism and the recovery process. That literature is often preoccupied with behavior modification techniques that are intended to transform the alcoholic into a social drinker. It does not offer an interpretation of the phenomenon of recovery as lived from the inside by the alcoholic self. My intentions are to present the inner side of this process as seen from the point of view of the recovering alcoholic self.

This book is directed to four audiences. First, as with *The Alcoholic Self*, it is addressed to those social theorists who are concerned with the vanishing subject in modern, postcapitalist society. The recovering alcoholic is a universal instance of a subjectivity that refuses to be obliterated by the forces of the postmodern world. Second, this work is addressed to social psychologists, sociologists, psychologists, anthropologists, medical scientists, and other practitioners who are concerned with alcoholism and the recovery process. Third, it is aimed at practitioners in the field who confront the problematics of recovery on a routine, regular basis. It is also intended for alcoholics who are recovering from alcoholism.

CONTENTS AND ORGANIZATION

My work is organized into seven chapters. Chapter 1 examines the empirical materials and the theoretical approach my analysis rests upon. The Six Theses of Recovery (see Denzin, 1986a, chaps. 1 and 5) are briefly presented and discussed. Chapters 2 and 3 deal with the treatment experiences of alcoholics who become residents or clients in substance abuse treatment centers. Chapters 4, 5, and 6 deal with the social worlds of recovery as experienced in Alcoholics Anonymous. They deal, in order, with the A.A. group, slips and relapses, and the restructuring of self that occurs once the individual becomes committed to building a "recovering alcoholic self." Chapter 7 offers a set of reflections on alcoholism, recovery, and American society.

NOTE

1. Volume one of this study is titled *The Alcoholic Self* (Sage Publications, 1987). Volume three is titled *Treating Alcoholism* (Sage Publications, 1987).

Acknowledgments

I would like to thank Carl Kingery for suggesting this project, Katherine Ryan for her insights throughout, Norbert Wiley for our discussions of the ritual self, Nathan Stevens for his assistance with the index, and John Johnson for his assistance in conceptualizing this volume and its companion, *The Alcoholic Self*.

Recovery:	Act of recovering. The regaining of something lost or taken away. To regain the strength, composure, balance, etc., of (oneself). Time required for recovery [*American College Dictionary*].
Recovering Alcoholic:	An alcoholic who has stopped drinking and regained a sense of self previously lost to alcohol.

1

INTRODUCTION
Interpreting Recovery

> I used to have to drink every day. Now I don't have to. I'm an alcoholic, sure, but I'm a recovering alcoholic [Recovering alcoholic, sober 8 years, male, 35 years old; occupation, lawyer].

In 1985 Alcoholics Anonymous counted a worldwide membership of slightly over 1.2 million persons. Over 585,000 of these individuals reside in the United States. An estimated 59,000 A.A. groups provide a point of contact for the alcoholic and A.A.'s program of recovery.

In 1983 the National Institute on Alcohol Abuse and Alcoholism reported 4,465 treatment units for alcohol addiction, including 745 hospitals, 923 halfway houses, and 2,423 outpatient treatment facilities (Alcoholics Anonymous, 1983: 44). Nearly a decade ago Baekeland and Lundwall (1977: 162) estimated that about 350,000 alcoholics were receiving treatment for alcoholism. The growth in treatment facilities since 1977 and the increase in A.A.'s membership since 1977 suggest that in 1985 perhaps over 800,000 individuals a year in the United States are receiving direct hospitalization or indirect A.A. and outpatient treatment for alcoholism. Although these figures are surely subject to wide variation (and interpretation), they suggest that "treatment" for alcoholism is becoming a commonplace occurrence in American society.

It is my purpose to analyze this experience of recovery as it has recently become institutionalized within our society. I assume that each alcoholic who seeks treatment is a *universal singular*; that is, a single instance of a process that is experienced by any alcoholic who seeks to recover from alcoholism. The universal singularity of every alcoholic's experience suggests that although recovery is different for every alcoholic, the broad outlines of the experience are the same. It is my intention to fill in this broad outline of experience. I will bring before the reader the generic, or basic, features of the phenomenon called recovery as it is experienced in treatment centers and in Alcoholics Anonymous.

My emphasis on the universal singularity of any alcoholic's recovery is not meant to overlook important variations in the recovery process, many of which are set by structural and cultural factors. That is, the recovery process will vary and have greater or lesser degrees of success (if success is measured by not drinking), depending on the age, race, ethnicity, gender, religion, education, and wealth of the alcoholic. White males over 35 have a greater chance of recovery than do black men in the same age group. White males have a greater chance for recovery than do females, white or black. Persons in the 18-25-year age bracket, male or female, have lower recovery rates than do persons over 35. Wealth, a higher education, and a high-status occupation also appear to stand in the way of recovery. These structural constraints introduce important variations in the recovery process and hence cannot be ignored (see Gomberg, 1982: 337-354, for a review of these factors).

The existence of such a large number of treatment facilities for alcoholism and the expanding membership in A.A. suggest that "treatment" for alcoholism is becoming a big business in the American health care and insurance system. These occurrences are due, in part, to changes in federal and state law that have followed since the Comprehensive Alcohol Abuse and Alcoholism Prevention and Rehabilitation Act of 1970 and its revisions of 1976. This act decriminalized public intoxication and mandated federal assistance to community-based treatment programs for alcoholism. The processes through which one becomes a recovering alcoholic in the United States today can be directly and indirectly traced to the structural changes that have occurred within the American legal and medical institutions since 1976.

The phenomenon of recovery from alcoholism as a primary illness (as well as from other addictions) is embedded inside an expanding social world I term the *world of recovery*. The boundaries of this social world are set by the limits of communication and shared experience. The explosion in treatment centers for alcoholism has widened the experiential net from which this social world draws its membership. This membership crosscuts sexual, marital, economic, educational, racial, cultural, religious, age, and national boundaries. The social worlds of recovery exist within and alongside the private and public social structures of American society. That is, recovering alcoholics have reinserted themselves into virtually every institutional niche our society makes available to any adult interactant. Neither hidden nor entirely private, this social world nonetheless is only completely visible to those who share in the experience of recovery (see Goffman, 1963b, on the visibility of the stigmatized, and Strauss, 1978: 119-128, on social worlds). To study the social worlds of recovery is to study the processes by which all social worlds grow, segment, splinter, differentiate, institutionalize, become legitimate, intersect, and change to fit the growing needs and interests of their membership (Strauss, 1982: 171-190).

This, then, is a study in *adult socialization* and *identity transformation* or conversion, terms I understand to refer to the process by which the self of the person actively enters into the acquisition of new self-images, new languages of self, new relations with others, and new bonds or ties to the social order (see Becker, 1960, 1964; Berger and Luckmann, 1967; James, 1904/1961; Lofland, 1977; Lofland and Stark, 1965; Rudy, 1986; Travisano, 1981).

This is also a study in deviance, for alcoholics, as indicated previously, regard themselves as deviants and clearly different from "normals" (Beauchamp, 1980; Becker, 1973; Madsen, 1974). An inquiry into family and group interactions is also involved, because recovery occurs within groups and alcoholism affects families (Ablon, 1976; Bateson, 1972a; Jackson, 1962; Kurtz, 1979; Maxwell, 1984; Steinglass, 1977; Steinglass and Robertson, 1983; Trice, 1957).

An examination in medical and psychiatric sociology is also required, for the experiences of many recovering alcoholics involve interactions with the medical establishment, including physicians, psychiatrists, clinical psychologists, social workers, and substance abuse and treatment counselors (see Solomon, 1983). Alcoholism has, since 1955, been designated as a form of physical, as well as mental, illness by the American Medical Association. The 1980 edition of the American Psychiatric Association's Diagnostic and Statistical Manual of Mental Disorders (DSM-III) contains two general categories under which alcohol-related problems are found: Alcoholic Organic Mental Disorders and Substance Use Disorders (American Psychiatric Association, 1980; Solomon, 1983: 68-69).

If alcoholism is a form of mental illness, it is a disorder that is given special meaning by alcoholics (A.A., 1953, 1976), social scientists (Bateson, 1972a; Cahalan, 1970; Goffman, 1967; Lemert, 1967; MacAndrew and Edgerton, 1969; MacAndrew and Garfinkel, 1962), psychiatrists (Laing, 1965; Menninger, 1938; Solomon, 1983; Szasz, 1961, 1975; Tiebout, 1944, 1949, 1953, 1954), medical practitioners (Royce, 1981), and anthropologists (Madsen, 1974).

Without attempting to resolve the controversies over whether or not alcoholism is (1) a disease (Beauchamp, 1980; Cahalan, 1970; Jellinek, 1960) and (2) a form of mental illness (Solomon, 1983), I will take the position that the active and recovering alcoholic lives an emotionally divided self (Denzin, 1984a, 1986a; James, 1904/1961; Scheler, 1916/1973; see following discussion).

THE SIX THESES OF RECOVERY

Six interpretive positions organize my understanding of the recovery process. I term these the *Six Theses of Recovery* (see Denzin, 1986a, chaps. 1 and 5, for a statement of these theses as they apply to alcoholism). The first is the *Thesis of the Temporality of Self*. This thesis asserts that alcoholism is a dis-ease of time; that is, the alcoholic knows himself or herself through past, present, and future experiences with alcohol. Fearful of time and its passage, the alcoholic drank in order to deal with this fear. Locked inside the past, or projected far into the future, the alcoholic was unable to live in the present. Recovery involves a recovery of time without the use of alcohol. Treatment and Alcoholics Anonymous teach the alcoholic to live in the present and to clear away the wreckage of his or her past. A One Day At A Time program is taught.

The second thesis concerns the alcoholic's self and his or her relations with others. It is termed the *Rational Structures of Self*. It argues that the alcoholic must restructure the alcohol-centered relationships that were lived when he or she was drinking. In becoming sober the alcoholic comes to interact with others without the effects of alcohol. He or she learns new modes of self-presentation, self-feeling, and interacting. Recovery involves a radical rebuilding of the alcoholic's relationships with others.

The third thesis is the *Emotionality of Self* thesis. It assumes that alcoholism is a dis-ease of emotion and self-feeling. The alcoholically divided self experienced negative, contrasting emotions on a daily basis. These emotions became part of the alcoholic's social relationships with others. Recovery turns on the relearning of emotional feeling. It also involves relinquising the negative emotions of the previously divided self. Emotional repair is at the heart of recovery.

The fourth thesis is the *Thesis of Bad Faith*. The alcoholic and his or her other attempted to escape or deny alcoholism. Lying, self-deception, and denial were part of daily existence. Recovery involves the shattering of the structures of bad faith that organize the alcoholic's self-system and his or her relations with others (see Sartre, 1943/1956 on bad faith and Denzin, 1984a: 198-199). The *Thesis of Self-Control* is the fifth thesis. Following Bateson (1972a: 312, and Jellinek, 1960) this thesis argues that the alcoholic believes he is in control of himself and the world that he lives in. Denial of alcoholism is coupled with this belief in self-control. The alcoholic drank in order to assert control over his world. As he becomes sober alcohol is no longer used as a means of self-control. A.A. and the treatment process locate the alcoholic in an interactional structure that is larger than he is. This collective structure, as Durkheim (1912/1961), Mead (1934), and Sartre (1960/1976) might argue, envelopes the alcoholic and makes him part of something larger than himself. Self-control then becomes a matter of shared, social control. The alcoholic finds his self-structure lodged in a collectivity that is larger than he is.

The sixth thesis, the *Thesis of Surrender*, extends the fifth thesis. As long as the alcoholic surrenders to a collective force that is outside himself his recovery will be maintained. A refusal to surrender, or a taking back of the act of surrender (Denzin, 1986a: chap. 7), signals the alcoholic's desire to once again become "the captain of his soul" (Bateson, 1972a; Jellinek, 1960). This was the position he occupied during his days of active alcoholism.

THE RECOVERING SELF

As with my analysis of the alcoholic self (Denzin, 1986a: chaps. 1 and 5), a basic premise organizes the Six Theses of Recovery. The alcoholic self drank to escape an inner emptiness and fear of self. This emptiness was manifested in a fundamental instability of self-experience. Alcohol was used as a crutch; as a means of finding a valued self-feeling that would transcend the inner lack that was felt on a regular basis. When she drank, the alcoholic modified her self-feelings, but these feelings were based on the effects of alcohol in her consciousness. The self that she lived tended toward narcissism and madness (Lacan, 1977; Laing, 1965). Divided against itself, it dwelled in the imaginary, inner worlds alcohol produced. Uneasy in their sexuality, uncertain about who they are, alcoholics run from themselves, seeking a hiding place within the private consciousness of alcoholic drinking. Cut off from others, unable to project themselves into the position of others, alcoholics live solitary lives.

Recovery sets in motion a process that potentially reverses this mode of existence. Treatment places the alcoholic in the company of large numbers of other alcoholics who are also experiencing treatment for their solitary illness (Whitney, 1965). A.A. involves interaction in a group context. Treatment and A.A. thus constitute interactional contexts in which the self, if symbolic interaction is going to occur, must take the attitude of others.

In order for the alcoholic self to recover it must come out of itself. It must find a place for itself in a network of selves who are undergoing the same process. If the alcoholic refuses to surrender to this process his or her recovery will be transitory, and a "fleeting," or "uncommitted," alcoholic identity will be formed.

Recovery, then, requires a rebuilding of self. But before this rebuilding can begin, a deconstruction, or destruction of the alcoholically divided self, must occur. Hence, treatment involves a dismantling of the self-structures of the alcoholic. Once these structures are laid out in front of the alcoholic a rebuilding process is set in motion (see Lifton, 1961, and Lindesmith et al., 1977, for a discussion of these processes in other contexts). The process of rebuilding the self (see Chapter 6) involves the steps outlined previously in the Six Theses of Recovery.

These theses, and the basic argument that organizes them, are drawn from three sources: my reading of the scientific literature on recovery, A.A.'s theory of recovery, and my observations of recovering alcoholics in A.A. meetings and in treatment centers (see Denzin, 1986a: chap. 2). They offer an interpretive guide through the analysis that follows.

EMPIRICAL MATERIALS

This work may be read as a case study of the lives of those men and women who were drinking and recovering during the period of my fieldwork (1980-1985). While I present no life in its entirety, I present slices of life-stories, or stories of self that are given around the "tables" of

A.A. At the same time I present accounts of self that were given in the treatment centers that I studied. My methods are ethnographic, involving participant observation, open-ended interviewing, triangulation, and the study of biographical and autobiographical accounts of the recovery process (see Berryman, 1973; Merryman, 1984).

My research sites were, as indicated in the Preface, twofold: substance abuse or alcoholism treatment centers and the meetings of Alcoholics Anonymous. A brief discussion of each of these sites and my methods is required.

Treatment Centers

I studied three treatment centers that employed a multimethod approach to the treatment of alcoholism (Kissin, 1977: 44-46). Each of these centers utilized, in varying degrees, the following treatment modalities: (1) detoxification units; (2) inpatient, residential treatment of three to four weeks; (3) aftercare programs; (4) family counseling; (5) outpatient counseling; (6) ongoing group therapy, drawing upon a variety of human relations, group dynamic treatment approaches, including psychodrama, confrontational therapy Re-evaluation Counseling (Scheff, 1979), Reality Therapy (Glasser, 1965), group lectures, and the use of recovering alcoholics as therapists and group leaders; (7) individual psychiatric counseling; (8) pastoral counseling; (9) nutritional therapy; (10) recreational therapy; (11) occupational rehabilitation services; and (12) A.A. lectures and A.A. meetings.

All three centers also utilized, in varying degrees, the Twelve Steps of A.A. In each center the patient (client or resident) was taken through the first five Steps of A.A. The termination of treatment often coincided with Family Week and with the alcoholic having done a Fourth and Fifth Step (see Glossary).

These three centers offer a program of treatment that is typical of alcoholism treatment centers in the United States at this time (Kissin, 1977; Merryman, 1984). They did not, however, utilize the aversive therapy programs and the Individual Behavior Modification programs that attempt to resocialize alcoholics into becoming social drinkers (see Mello, 1983; Sobell and Sobell, 1978; Wholey, 1984).

I give these treatment centers the names *Westside Lodge, Northern Center*, and *Eastern*. They were all located within the eastern part of the United States in medium-to-large metropolitan areas. Westside had facilities for 20 patients. Northern could treat 60 patients at a time. Eastern had a 30-bed capacity. All three dealt with alcohol and drug abuse and all three treated males and females. Each had approximately a 3:1 staff-client ratio.

I have observed the workings of Westside and Eastern for four years. At Northern I followed a cohort of patients through a four-week treatment cycle. In all three centers I employed the previously outlined methods.

Alcoholics Anonymous

My materials on A.A. are drawn from a five-year period of study, primarily in a medium-sized community of 150,000 in the eastern part of the United States. I have observed the workings of A.A. in over 2000 open and closed meetings in this community, which is also where Westside and Eastern are located. The A.A. meeting and the A.A. group thus became a research site that permitted the study of alcoholics in treatment who (1) attended A.A. while in treatment and/or (2) became members of A.A. after leaving treatment.

Within the community that I studied there were 2 open meetings, 37 closed meetings, and 5 Al-Anon meetings weekly. There was a daily noon meeting and at least 1 meeting every night. There were also 7 Narcotics Anonymous meetings a week. Many of the alcoholics I studied, both in and out of treatment, attended A.A. and N.A. meetings on a regular basis.

There was also a social club for recovering alcoholics and their families that required 30 days of sobriety for membership. If a slip occurred a member was required to turn in his or her key, which would be returned when three months of sobriety had been attained. A member had to be sponsored by a club member in order to become a member. This club held monthly social gatherings, an annual dinner-dance, and monthly lotteries for which tickets could be purchased. A membership fee of $5.00 per month was charged all members. The club counted a membership of over 135. A monthly newsletter was sent to all members, reporting the happenings at the club, the first names of members, who their sponsors were, and a monthly report of A.A. birthdays, with the dry date of each person who had a birthday that month (see Glossary).

A 24-hour-a-day answering service was maintained by the A.A. and N.A. groups in the community. In total, there were 19 registered groups in the A.A. community, with a membership of over 300. There were special interest groups: two for women, one for gays and lesbians, and one young people's group. I observed over 700 individuals who came and went or visited A.A. meetings during my study (see Denzin, 1986a: chap. 1, for a fuller discussion of these features of my field setting and the methods I utilized).

The problematic that organized my field observations centered on the self-stories, or accounts of self that alcoholics produced at A.A. meetings. These stories typically, but not always, were organized around the topic of discussion given in any specific meeting (such as resentment, anger, First Step, relations with others, One Day At A Time). From these stories a picture of a recovering self could be gleaned. However, no alcoholic gives an entire recovery story at any given meeting. Hence, multiple observations of the same alcoholics over a continuous period of time is required if a picture of the recovering self is to be constructed. I therefore followed the same group of individuals over a five-year period, watching and observing their recovery stories as they were told around the A.A. tables.

At the same time I followed, as indicated above, individuals who underwent treatment and then became A.A. members. I was aided in my understanding of this process because members of my family are recovering alcoholics.

SITUATING THIS STUDY

In the interpretive analysis that follows I intend to remain as close as possible to the actual lived experiences of recovery. The center of consciousness that I work outward from is that of the alcoholic who goes through treatment and then becomes a regular member of A.A. I present an "ideal typical" (Weber, 1946) version of this experience, seeking to find the universal, or generic structures of recovery. Hence, it is a process, not individual experience, that I seek to understand. However, that process can only be captured by studying individuals and the interactions they confront. Because these events occur within institutional and group settings my study is necessarily sociological, as well as interpretive, phenomenological, and interactionist (Blumer, 1969).

As with my investigation of the alcoholic self and the existence that self lives (Denzin, 1986a), this inquiry should be evaluated by the following criteria. First, do my interpretations illuminate and reveal recovery as a lived experience? Second, are the interpretations based on thickly contextualized materials that are temporally, historically, and biographically grounded? Third, do the interpretations engulf and incorporate previous understandings of the recovery process? Fourth, do the interpretations cohere into a meaningful totality that produces understanding, however provisional and incomplete? If these criteria are met, I shall be pleased.

Part 1

TREATING THE ALCOHOLIC SELF
An Ethnography of the Treatment Process

2

THE PARADOXES OF TREATMENT
Introduction to the New Self

We admitted we were powerless over alcohol—that our lives had become unmanageable [A.A.'s First Step].

"Why do you think you're back in treatment?" He was not keen on the question, but he might as well give her the word. "One, I'm damned if I know, Louise. Two, I must have conned Gus Larson with my First Step; I don't see how" [Berryman, 1973: 13].

I want to die. I've been trying to drink myself to death. I've lost my wife. She filed for divorce yesterday. All I've got are those two kids of mine. I don't see how this is going to work. It can't. Oh maybe they'll dry me out, that'll be all. I'm a failure. I haven't done a dammed thing for 10 years. Actually I'd rather enjoyed drinking myself to death. But this last month nothing has worked. I can't even get drunk anymore. Do you think it'll work? [Field conversation with 46-year-old male in a detoxification unit, 10 June 1984. This man has just checked himself into a 30-day treatment program].

The alcoholically divided self enters treatment feeling helplessness, frustration, despair, and a sense of mixed hopefulness. He is probably (although not always) intoxicated, or in the process of withdrawal from alcohol. He has surrendered to alcoholism, perhaps not fully, or completely. His interpretive system has collapsed. No longer able to drink successfully, his alcoholism has produced a crisis situation that has precipitated forced or semivoluntary entry into treatment. He must confront anew the meaning of surrender to alcoholism (see Denzin, 1986a: chap. 6). But more important, he must learn *how* to be treated for the disease called alcoholism. This will involve a serious confrontation with A.A.'s First Step. Treatment is organized so as to accomplish this act of surrender. How that is achieved is the topic of this and the next chapter.

The Berryman quote, cited above, suggests that this act of surrender to the First Step may not be complete or successful. Hence, the alcoholic finds himself or herself back in another (or the same) treatment center. The second alcoholic, Fritz, quoted in the opening passage, is undergoing treatment for the first time. He is depressed and suicidal.

In this chapter I study the first phase of surrender and recovery as these two processes intertwine within the quasi-total institutional settings (Goffman, 1961a), that substance abuse centers offer the alcoholic who seeks treatment. My empirical materials are drawn from the following sources. First, I shall draw heavily on Merryman's (1984) study of the recovery process as experienced by a female alcoholic who underwent a four-week residential treatment program. Second, I shall utilize John Berryman's account of his own treatment as given in his *Recovery* (1973). Having gone through several treatment centers for alcoholism, Berryman offers a considerably different view of the recovery process than does Merryman. Third, I draw from my own observations of the treatment process as it occurs in the three treatment centers described in Chapter 1.

The *Six Theses of Recovery* (and alcoholism) organize my interpretation of the treatment process. I assume that central to treatment is the temporal recovery of self that has been lost to alcoholism. Further, I assume that a relational and emotional restructuring of self occurs in treatment. Treatment *treats* alcoholism as a *dis-ease* of emotionality, temporality, social relationships, and self. Treatment locates the self of the alcoholic in the center of the disease called alcoholism. Treatment confronts and exposes the alcoholic's systems of bad faith and denial. Treatment attempts to puncture the drinker's beliefs in self-control. That is, treatment directly addresses the problematics of power and control in the alcoholic's life.

I will take up in order the following topics: (1) the paradoxes of treatment—that is, what does treatment treat, who is doing the treating, and is the alcoholic cured of an illness or a disease when he or she leaves treatment, and (2) the linguistic, temporal, and interactional structures of a "typical" treatment program as these structures are presented to the recovering alcoholic in a three- to four-week program.

THE PARADOXES OF TREATMENT

There are five paradoxes of treatment that involve dilemmas the alcoholic must confront. They may be stated as follows: (1) alcoholism is an incurable illness and disease; (2) alcoholism is an illness and disease that stands for something else; (3) the treatment for alcoholism requires that the patient become the therapist—temporal work on the self is the work of treatment; (4) alcoholism is an emotional illness; and (5) the alcoholic is not unique; rather she suffers from an illness and disease that leads her to believe that she is unique.

These paradoxes set problematics (Becker, 1960, 1964) in front of the alcoholic. Situational adjustments of a group and individual nature are made to them as alcoholics proceed through treatment together. These paradoxes define part of the "culture" of treatment centers. How the alcoholic adjusts to them will determine how he or she will become part of the culture of treatment. It is necessary to discuss each paradox.

The first paradox suggests that the alcoholic must learn that he has an illness that cannot be cured. It can only be placed in remission by abstinence from alcohol. Hence, he does not have an ordinary illness. He is told that alcoholism is a physical, mental, and spiritual illness.

Berryman (1973: 145) offers the following conversation between two patients:

> "What is the disease picture then?" . . . "Well." Severance gulped coffee. "Progressive, fatal, incurable . . . it seems to be *loss of control.* Unpredictability. That's all. A social drinker knows when he can stop. Also, in a general way, his life-style does not arrange itself around the chemical as ours does."

This disease picture of alcoholism is placed before all patients, upon entry into a treatment center. Each of the centers I studied placed Jellinek's (1960, 1962) progressive stages of alcoholism model in front of its clients. In the three treatment centers I observed, alcoholics are given A.A.'s *Big Book* (A.A., 1976) as well as *Twelve Steps and Twelve Traditions* (A.A., 1953). They are told to read A.A.'s discussion of alcoholism as a mental, physical, and spiritual illness.

The second paradox the alcoholic is confronted with elaborates the disease conception of alcoholism. She is told that this illness she has is located inside her and in her relationship to the world. Alcohol is but a symptom of her illness. She drinks alcoholically because she is an alcoholic. She is at the center of her illness. Alcohol merely made her alcoholic. She drank so as to be able to confront the world she lived in. Hence, because she has an incurable illness, she will never again be able to put in her body the symptom that produces yet masks her illness. She must learn that she is powerless over alcohol. Alcohol is poison to her.

Third, because she is at the center of her illness, only she can treat what she has. That is, she is both the patient and the therapist for her illness. This position is phrased as follows by an alcoholism counselor speaking to Berryman and the members of his group in treatment:

> It's been decided on high . . . that you Repeaters need special treatment . . . this is your Group. . . . Group is not just here in this room two hours a day five days a week. . . . Treatment goes on every minute you're awake. . . . Every one of you is on trial; if you don't show definite progress by the end of three weeks, you're out. . . . You've all got to seek each each other out and level with each other and take the risk of confronting each other, namely, give each other hell. . . . Get to work on your Programmes [Berryman, 1973: 42-43].

Several points are important in this journal entry by Berryman. Each bears on the fact that in treatment patients are responsible for treating themselves. First, the group counselor tells the patients that it is "your group." Second, he tells them that treatment does not just occur in group. It occurs during every waking hour. Even when the patients are not in group they are expected to be undergoing treatment. Third, the counselor places every member of the group on trial, charging them to make progress. This reinforces the patient's self-responsibility for treatment. Fourth, he creates a group that extends beyond the temporal boundaries of two hours a day, five days a week. The patients are to become a "pledged" group (Sartre, 1960/1976: 419), fused around the omnipresent threats of not making progress in treatment and leaving treatment to drink again. The patients are told to form relationships with one another that will permit aggressive, confrontative, self-evaluative interactions. Fifth, the patients are told to develop their own "programs" of recovery. Of course they will have to forge their own definitions of what a program is, before they can develop one.

This third paradox reverses all previous understandings the alcoholic has held concerning illness and treatment. If she has internalized her society's norms concerning the sick role (Parsons and Fox, 1978), then she understands that when you are sick you go to a physician for treatment. Now she finds that she has come to a treatment center to treat herself. This will take some time to learn. She may feel that nothing is happening to her while she is in treatment. Berryman (1973:44) offers an exchange between two patients that clarifies this point.

"When did you come back in?"

"Sunday night. How about you?"

"How does it seem to be going?"

"I didn't get anywhere for ten days. . . . But I made a breakthrough last Friday."

The patient, then, must learn how to treat herself, and she must learn that her treatment will occur in a setting where everyone else has the same mandate. To treat herself, to build a treatment program for herself, to confront others, to be confronted by others, this is what treatment is. A reciprocity of sharing and confrontation underlies the recovery process.

The recovering alcoholic must, under the third paradox of treatment, learn to transcend her own self-centeredness. She must learn how to apply a group perspective to her recovery. She is taught the language of A.A., which is a group, not an individual language of self. Hence, although she is responsible for her own treatment, that treatment occurs within and derives from a group point of view. She must enter a group in order to treat herself.

Berryman's conversation reveals another central theme of treatment, and that is temporality. When the woman states, "I didn't get anywhere for ten days," she underscores perhaps the most basic feature of treatment. That is, treatment occurs within time (Roth, 1963). But treatment's time is the patient's time. This is time no longer experienced through the altered temporal consciousness that alcohol once gave the alcoholic. Hence, treatment passes slowly, then rapidly, as "breakthroughs" are experienced, then slowly again, as the patient waits for another breakthrough to occur. Because she produces her own breakthroughs, the patient realizes treatment only through her own temporality and her own being in time (see Heidegger, 1927/1962). Because she has previously led an inauthentic temporal existence—locked into the past, or running always from the future, never living in the now of the present—the patient expects others to work time for her. They will not do this, as Berryman's counselor pointed out to his group. Waiting for things to happen within time, the patient then experiences treatment as a waste of time. Berryman offers an instance of this critical point. He states: "Sometimes long periods seemed to drag without one word being spoken by anybody in the entire room" (Berryman, 1973: 15).

Merryman (1984: 104) offers another instance. His subject is speaking with her psychiatrist. He has asked how things are going. She indicates that not much is happening and she feels that her counselor is not helping her. He states: "Can she make treatment happen for you?"

The fourth paradox the alcoholic encounters involves a further elaboration of her illness. She is told that her illness is emotional. She learns that she has never expressed the emotions that have led her to drink. She is told that she must get in touch with her emotions, for if she does not she will drink again. A counselor in Northern phrased this position as follows:

> You have an emotional illness. Alcoholism is an emotional illness. You have all lived in an emotional prison. You are all afraid and lonely. You can't trust anybody, including yourself. You're trapped in your past. You're afraid to feel. You don't know how to feel. You're all sick as Hell! Now get to work" [field observation, April 14, 1981].

Merryman reports this comment made by a lecturer on alcohol addiction:

> In the real world we were never taught to identify our feelings—glad, sad, mad, hurt, lonely. But even if our heads didn't know we were having an emotion, our bodies were feeling a whole lot of things [Merryman, 1984: 98-99].

Berryman (1973: 71) offers an additional example. A counselor is speaking to a patient: "You've got to get in touch with your feelings. If you *knew* how resentful you are, maybe you wouldn't drink. You've got to learn to level with your feelings—get them out in the open."

The alcoholic is told that if he drinks again, he will court both death and insanity. Indeed his treatment center will inform him of the casualties of his illness, perhaps relaying the recent death of a former patient who has returned to drinking (Berryman, 1973: 59; Merryman, 1984: 344, 347).

These statements are meant to suggest to the alcoholic that he has buried his emotions beneath his alcoholism. He is told that he has never been in touch with the "real" self that he has buried inside. He is told that he drinks because of his emotions. Further, he is informed that he has lived in his body the emotions he has lacked words to express.

A psychiatrist in Northern is speaking to a patient:

> You don't even have the right words for your emotions. You talk about feeling, but you can't feel. Your body does. Listen to your body. Listen to your emotional reactions in your back, in your stomach. When you feel pain in your body your emotions are trying to tell you something (field observation, April 20, 1981).

The patient is told that he has an inadequate language of emotion. He is told that his body feels what he should feel with his head. His emotions are given an autonomy of force that is seen as expressing a level of reality he has not been in touch with. Treatment teaches a new language of emotions and emotionality to the alcoholic. He or she will learn to use such words as leveling, conning, resentment, and dry drunk (see Glossary). He or she will learn to make a distinction between primary and secondary emotions and will learn how to talk about an emotion and how to feel an emotion.

The Theory of Self in Treatment

Prior to treatment the alcoholic has lived a theory of self that hinged on the denial of alcoholism and the alcoholic pursuit of a fictional "I" that alcohol would hopefully bring into existence (Denzin, 1986a; Tiebout, 1954). He has experienced a division in his inner emotional life, perhaps attempting to hide, or mask from others large portions of who he is and who he has become. He has presented a self to others that is not the self he feels in his inner self-conversations. Treatment attempts to shatter this theory of self. The alcoholic is presented with an entirely different theory of how a person comes to know the "real" self that lies beneath the facades of everyday life. Treatment rests on a fourfold theory of self. In Northern it was presented to the patients in terms of the *Johari Window* (also see Merryman, 1984: 71). Introduced into the human relations field by Luft in 1961, the Johari Window addresses the problem of self-awareness. It appears as follows:

JOHARI WINDOW

	I	II
Known to Others	Open	Blind
Not Known to Others	III	IV
	Hidden	Unknown

In Northern this window was modified as follows: Quadrant I was labeled "Free," quadrant II "Secret," quadrant III "Blind," and quadrant IV "Unconscious." In human relations training for self-awareness, quadrant I represents behaviors known to self and others. Quadrant II, the Blind cell, represents behaviors known to others, but not the self. Quadrant 3, the Hidden cell, represents behaviors known to the self, but not others. The Unknown quadrant, IV, represents behaviors known neither by self or by others. "One important goal of human relations training is to increase the size of the public area (quadrant I) and to reduce the blind and hidden areas (quadrants 2 and 3)" (Goodstein, 1984: 161).

Patients at Northern were told that they were blind and self-deluded and did not know who they were. They were told that they would have to learn how to *level* with others about how they felt. In so doing they would perhaps be able to find the self they had hidden from others. The Patient Workbook given to all patients stated: "We level when we take the risk of being known by spontaneously reporting our feelings. For example, we are leveling when we let someone know that we are hurt, or afraid or angry."

In addition to leveling, patients are told they must learn how to confront others. Confrontation was defined at Northern as "presenting a person with himself by describing how I see him." Rather than pleasing others by telling them what they want to hear about themselves, patients are told to be direct. This directive was phrased as follows at Northern:

If we care about our fellow group members, and if we want them to be honest with us in return, we will present them with our picture of them. . . . Confrontation is most useful when spoken with concern and accompanied with examples of the confronted behavior or data. For example, "You seem hostile because of the sarcastic answers you give." "Your face is so red that you seem very angry." We are most useful as confronters when we are not so much trying to change another person as we are trying to help him see himself more accurately. Change, if it comes, comes later when a person chooses it and enlists the spiritual help that the Sixth and Seventh steps of the A.A. Program describes. Because of our egocentric *blindness* and self-delusion we are *all* dependent on others for that completed picture. Confrontation provides it [patient workbook, p. 4].

Leveling and confronting are reciprocal processes that refer, respectively, to self and other. Although based on the language of group therapy, these two terms relate directly to Cooley's (1902/1956) concept of the "looking-glass self" and Mead's "I" and "me" of social interaction. Treatment asks the alcoholic to seriously learn how to see himself from the point of view of others (me). And further, the patient is told to feel, not mask, those feelings of self that are derived from the reflected appraisals of others. He is also told that his inner "I" has been hidden from him. If he thinks he knows who he is he has deluded himself.

He is told that he has hidden behind the public self of heavy drinker. Indeed, by denying his alcoholism, he has presented himself to the world through the false sense of self alcohol has given him. The alcoholic is told that if he does not get in touch with the secret and buried selves of his past he will not recover. He is told that these structures of self are hidden behind the false emotions he presents to others. If the alcoholic does not penetrate this emotional facade he has placed in front of himself, he will not recover and uncover the deep, underlying reasons that lead him to drink. *The recovery of self through emotionality is the underlying premise of treatment.* Leveling and confrontation, coupled with group therapy and patient-to-patient interaction, are the mechanisms that treatment provides for this recovery of self.

This position is phrased as follows at Northern:

Most of us tend to think we already know ourselves and are afraid of looking bad, so it is hard for us to take the risk of being revealing and genuine. But what have we really got to lose? Remember how unsuccessful our previous attempts to change have been. Since we can't change something until we really see it, and accept its existence, we shoud ask ourselves, "Do I really accept something if I keep it a secret?" Risking openness is the key. When you are tempted to withdraw into silence, remember, that we are all in the same boat, and a common feeling of everyone, when introduced to group, is *fear*.

Try leveling with the feeling of fear for a start, and discover how that makes you feel. You will probably find, as others have, that when you report a feeling, you modify it. Keeping it a secret seems to increase its power. If we don't begin now to risk being genuine and self-revealing, when will we ever really do it?

The fourth paradox of treatment hinges on the fact that the alcoholic must undergo the painful exposure of these buried structures of self that she has kept hidden from herself and from others. Accordingly, not only must she undergo pain, but she must expose herself to others in ways that will cause embarrassment, anger, and fear. The protective structures of self that Goffman (1959) has identified, including the maintenance of fronts, impression management, collusion, the idealization of self-performances, the misrepresentation of self, mystification, secrecy, self-pride, and dramaturgical circumspection must all be set aside if the alcoholic is to recover the self she has lost to alcoholism. Similarly, treatment is organized so as to penetrate the feeling-rules individuals utilize so as to manage their emotionality in everyday life (Hochschild, 1983). Treatment attempts to lay bare the underlying emotional structures of the self. The valued presentations of self in treatment are predicated on a model of self that is distinctly not dramaturgical.

Treatment, then, rests on a theory of self that does not reside in the books of etiquette the patient has been taught to internalize and practice in everyday life. Rather, treatment presumes that a deep level of self exists beneath the surface levels of the self the alcoholic has hidden behind. Treatment assumes that the self, at the deep, inner, moral level of the person (Heidegger, 1982) is the real person. That person, the alcoholic is told, is afraid, immature, warped, distorted, and angry. Treatment attempts to bring this level of the person to the surface. It will give the alcoholic a set of tools (A.A.'s steps) by which the new (but old) self may be brought into sober existence.

The *fifth paradox of treatment* is the *paradox of uniqueness*. The alcoholic enters treatment under a unique set of circumstances. A multiplicity of events has produced a crisis situation in her life that has brought her into the treatment center. These events are uniquely hers. She brings to treatment a unique personal history. She drank in ways that were solely hers. The collapse of self she has experienced is, she believes, special and unique to her. She arrives in treatment deeply sunken inside herself, desperately holding onto the belief that she is unique and special. Merryman's female alcoholic expressed this belief in the following words: "Well, I'm not sure I'm an alcoholic. . . . I'm not like *any* of the people here" (Merryman, 1984: 63).

Treatment shatters the myth of self-uniqueness. A counselor at Eastern told her group:

> You're all a bunch of drunks. You're not special, you're not unique.
> You're all alcoholics. You all hid the booze, you lied to get it, you hurt

your families. You cheated others. You lied to yourself. You'll die of terminal uniqueness if you don't get to work! [field observation, February 20, 1983].

The alcoholic is required to surrender to the myth of self-uniqueness, so as to be able to recover the inner self alcohol has taken away. An A.A. lecturer at Western phrased this position in the following words:

> We're not bad people trying to get better. We're sick people trying to get well. We each have something unique to offer. We are each unique individuals. But we're all alike. We're alcoholics. We can't find what is special inside us until we accept how we are all alike. Then we start to get better. Then we start to find a power greater than ourselves outside ourselves [field observation, May 2, 1983].

To summarize, the treatment the alcoholic receives is self-induced and self-produced, yet it occurs within a group context. Others will facilitate her self-discoveries, but she must do the temporal work of treatment. This work will only begin when she stops believing in her self-uniqueness. Only she can start her treatment and only she can end it. Treatment provides the context of discovery for the recovery of self.

The alcoholic finds that she must cast aside her previous under- standings of what treatment for an illness involves. She will be given no pain killers or tranquilizers. If she receives any medication it will be given to her by the medical staff. She can no longer medicate herself. Any drugs she may have brought into treatment with her will be confiscated (see Merryman, 1984: 55, for a description of this "drug search" each patient undergoes upon admission into treatment).

Treatment presupposes a radical restructuring of self. This restruc- turing cuts to the very core of the open, blind, hidden, and unknown structures of the alcoholic's self. The alcoholic does not understand this process, or what it entails when she enters treatment crying out for help.

The work of treatment is biographical and historical. A new language of self and emotionality is given to the alcoholic as she attempts to discover, through the twin processes of leveling and confronting, the underlying reasons in her life that led her to drink. It is not enough for the alcoholic to get sober in treatment. She must uncover the reasons she has hidden from herself that could or will take her back to alcoholic drinking again. Treatment assumes, then, that once an alcoholic, always an alcoholic. Yet there are two kinds of alcoholics, active or drinking and recovering. Before I turn to the temporal and interactional structures of treatment that are presented to an alcoholic who enters a treatment center, it is necessary to examine briefly how the language and beliefs of A.A. are woven into the patient's treatment program.

THE TWELVE STEPS OF
ALCOHOLICS ANONYMOUS AND TREATMENT

In each of the treatment centers that I observed, patients were immediately exposed to the Twelve Steps of A.A. This was done through attendance at A.A. meetings, through lectures on A.A. by counselors and outside A.A. speakers, and by reading the A.A. literature. In Northern, alcoholics were given a patient workbook when they were admitted into treatment. I quote from the first page of that workbook:

WELCOME. . . .

to our treatment program—with all the fears and frustrations that accompany you here. We wish you to know that we care about you. We are here to support you and to assist you in arresting your illness.

We would like to introduce you to our program with the following message—from Chapter Five of "ALCOHOLICS ANONYMOUS":

"Rarely have we seen a person fail who has thoroughly followed our path. Those who do not recover are people who cannot or will not completely give themselves to this simple program, usually men and women who are constitutionally capable of being honest with themselves."

The "Steps" listed below are the foundation of our treatment program. You will find them easy to read, but far more difficult to understand and accept. With this, you will have help and as you accept, you will experience personal change and the start of recovery.

The Steps of A.A. (see Glossary; A.A., 1953, 1976) followed this statement. Patients were next informed that the chemical dependency program they were a part of was based on the philosophy of A.A. and that the disease they suffered from was a family illness. The patient handbook stated: "We use a multidisciplinary approach and treat the physical, emotional, social, mental and spiritual deterioration characteristic of this illness. . . . Here recovery is the patient's responsibility. Passive submission or compliance with treatment does not work." They were told that the entire family would have to be treated and that this was the purpose of "Family Week," which would occur in the last week of treatment.

Told that they and their family members were sick, the alcoholics at Northern were then reminded that their treatment would end in one short month. The prospects of maintaining a recovery program after treatment was next raised. Clients were urged to sign up for aftercare. This was an outpatient counseling program that would potentially involve the patient and his or her family for a minimum of one year in weekly therapy sessions.

The following points need to be taken from these directives that were issued to the patients at Northern. First, each of the paradoxes of treatment is addressed explicitly. The alcoholic is told that his illness can be arrested. He is told that his illness is a relational, or family, illness, and that it is physical, emotional, social, mental, and spiritual in nature. He is also told that his recovery is "almost entirely (his) responsibility." His illness is his personal problem. He will recover if he honestly expresses feelings toward other patients. This process inspires fear. He is told that he shares this fear with every other patient. In this statement the treatment center attempts to produce the interactional conditions that will promote the emergence of a "group" point of view. He is told that he may discover the "real you" that has been buried within his alcoholism.

By attempting to draw the family members of the alcoholic into treatment, Northern broadens the patient's understanding of his illness. At the same time it increases the cost of treatment. The alcoholic is told that extended treatment will last for at least one year. He is also encouraged to become involved in Alcoholics Anonymous. As this statement welcomes the patient to Northern, it suggests that he too can become a successful alumnus. This may well be the last thought the alcoholic has in his mind as he reads these words on his first day in treatment.

By presenting A.A.'s Twelve Steps on the first page of the patient's workbook, Northern anchors recovery in A.A. The quotation from chapter five of *Alcoholics Anonymous* (A.A., 1976: 58) suggests that Northern has the path to recovery. By coopting A.A.'s position, and weaving it into a treatment program that involves aftercare, Family Week, group counseling, leveling, and confrontation, Northern indicates how the modern treatment center depends upon A.A. for any success it might achieve in the field of alcohol rehabilitation. The alcoholic will soon learn that he must master A.A.'s first Five Steps before he "graduates" from Northern in "approximately one short month."

In short, a mutually beneficial partnership, or symbiotic relationship, exists between this treatment center and A.A. Indeed, this state of symbiosis underlies virtually any treatment program the alcoholic might enter. Although A.A. does not lend its name to any treatment center, affiliate with any treatment institution, or employ any treatment professionals, it willingly permits any treatment center that so desires to utilize its texts and program of recovery. This mutually beneficial relationship between A.A. and the modern treatment center permits A.A. to broaden its membership base, while giving treatment centers a successful program upon which they can base their appeal to the prospective alcoholic client. Because many treatment centers employ recovering alcoholics as counselors, or treatment directors, they are often led to rely upon A.A. for the production of these members.

THE LANGUAGES OF TREATMENT

Patients are presented with a complex and new vocabulary of terms that reference a language they must learn to speak and understand while they are in treatment. Not only must they come to understand the words and terms contained in A.A.'s Twelve Steps, but they must also master a language of group therapy. At Northern the following terms were presented to patients in their patient workbooks: communication, addiction, aftercare, Alcoholics Anonymous, black-out, chemical dependency, concerned person, confronting, congruence, treatment plan or program, controlling, defenses, delusion, dry drunk, troubled dysfunctional family (chemically dependent family), enabler, family disease, feeling, group therapy, halfway house, head tripping, intervention, letting go, leveling, locked in, nurturing family, primary disease, recovery program, self-growth, spirituality, treatment, tunnel vision, wholeness. (See the Glossary for a definition of these terms.) As given meaning, the words they define are intended to give the patient and her or his counselor a commonsense language that will permit the discovery of the "real" self of the alcoholic. They are terms that allow patients and staff to confront one another through a "group therapy" language. The use of these words sets the battleground for treatment, inasmuch as they will be used as weapons by patients as they "confront" and "level" with one another.

The following interaction, between two patients at Western, illustrates this point. The first speaker, A (a 45-year-old male, in treatment for three weeks), is confronting a new patient, C (also male, 35 years old), who has been on the unit for 6 days.

A to C: I don't like what you said in group this morning. You're not being honest with Ed. You know you don't like him. You know he reminds you of your father. Yet you told him you liked him and wanted to be his friend. You know you hate him. Come on, start leveling, get honest, you're still trying to please people and be everybody's friend. You enable yourself and Ed when you do this and you're trying to control his emotions to make him feel better. *How do you feel about you?* Get honest for Christ's sake! You know I'm only trying to help you, don't get mad [field observation, July 12, 1983].

If key terms on the above list of words were carefully defined, a large number of pivotal words that surrounded these terms were left undefined. No definitions were given to the following: blaming, placating, computing, distracting, disease, recognition, admittance, acceptance, principles of A.A., anger, rationalizing, denial, justifying, bullying, fear, intellectualizing, projection, grandiose, judgmental, intolerant, fixing, helping, hurt, sadness, rejection, joy, natural high, feeling person, cold emotional statement, high self-worth, using, defensive, compulsively, inner peace, serenity, calm, nurturing system.

Despite the fact that these words were not defined, their presence in the patient handbook sets an interpretive frame within which treatment occurs. They establish the context for an emotional language of self. That they are undefined indicates that "intellectual" definitions are not warranted. Patients must be able to feel their way into the meaning these terms have for them. Paradoxically, the emotional language of treatment requires an elaborate dictionary of meanings and definitions.

Two Languages of Emotionality

Two languages of emotionality exist side by side in treatment. The first is the *meta-language of emotionality*; a language about the language of emotions and treatment. This language includes such terms as *head-tripping, leveling,* and *confronting.* Second, there is the language of direct and indirect emotionality, expressed in the phrase "learn to communicate on a *feeling* level." At this feeling level, terms require no definition. At the meta-level definitions are required and are given. That is, the technical language of treatment in fact requires a definition of terms, including what a chemical dependent is, what a family disease is, and what a harmful dependency consists of. The meanings in this language must be conveyed before the language of emotionality that exists beneath and within it can be conveyed. That language will often be conveyed in words of vulgarity and profanity, with specific reference to biological functions.

Treatment, then, exists on two levels of meaning: the technical and the emotional. In order for the emotional work of treatment to be accomplished, the technical language must be communicated. It is that language that constitutes the framework inside of which emotional work occurs.

The language of direct and indirect emotionality is subdivided in treatment into two forms: the language *about* feelings and the language *of* feelings. A language of direct feeling is the language of anger, hurt, guilt, and resentment. A language about these feelings mediates the patient's thinking about the feeling and the direct expression of feeling. Merryman (1984: 100) illustrates this difference with the following dialogue. A counselor asks a patient what she is feeling:

> "I feel like I really want to sink right through the floor." A fellow patient replies: "Any sentence with a 'that' or a 'like' in it doesn't give a true feeling. Feelings are mad, glad, sad . . . "

This exchange reduces the expression of emotionality to the linguistic format the speaker uses when speaking of or about her emotions (see Wittgenstein, 1955). Words such as "like" or "that," which come before purely emotional words, are seen as diminishing the emotional feeling that is felt by the speaker. Such bracketing is regarded as undesirable. The patient is taught to select carefully the words she uses when she expresses her feelings.

The emotional languages of treatment (meta, of, and about) are given greater detail by the following list of words patients are presented with as they construct their treatment programs. These terms were given to patients at Northern as potential problem areas in their lives: aggressive, amoral, approval seeking, avoiding, blaming, compliant, controlling, denial, dependent, dishonest, egocentric self-centered, faith/hope lacking, financial (problems), goals (vague or none), grief stricken, indifferent, irresponsible, intellectualizing, judgmental, legal (problems), manipulative, marital, family, medical, mistrusting, passive, pride, rationalizing, self-concept, social skills, sexuality, spirituality, vocational, withdrawal.

Upon examining this list, patients at Northern were told by their group counselors that there had been a mistake in the list and that three terms had been left off. These three terms were *guilt, anger,* and *resentment.* These are the emotions A.A. says are most likely to take the alcoholic back to drinking (A.A., 1976: 54-56; 1953: 44-45; 1967: 11, 48, 68, 83, 92, 99, 140, 311).

More important, perhaps, than taking the alcoholic back to drinking, is the fact that these emotions appear on those pages of A.A.'s texts that contain discussions of the Fourth and Fifth Steps. These, of course, are the two central steps (in addition to the First) Northern asks the alcoholic to take before leaving treatment. At this fundamental level of intertexuality (Kristeva, 1974), A.A. is woven directly and deeply into the treatment experiences of the recovering alcoholic.

Alcoholics Anonymous:
The Third Language of Treatment

I have identified two languages of treatment: the technical language of group therapy and chemical dependency, and the language of direct and indirect emotionality. The third language of treatment is the language of Alcoholics Anonymous. This language is contained in A.A.'s *Big Book*, in the Twelve Steps, and in the Twelve Traditions. It confronts patients immediately in the form of the Twelve Steps, as given on the first page of their patient workbook.

These Twelve Steps contain the following problematic terms and phrases: admitted, powerless, "lives had become unmanageable," "came to believe," "power greater than ourselves," restore, sanity, will, "lives," "care of God," "as we understood him," searching, fearless, "moral inventory," "admitted to God," "exact nature," "wrongs," "entirely ready," remove, "defects of character," "humbly," shortcomings, "persons we had harmed," "make amends," (direct amends), "injure," personal inventory, wrong, prayer, meditation, conscious contact, pray, "knowledge of his will for us," "power to carry that out," "spiritual awakening," carry this message, "practice these principles in all our affairs."

Informed that his treatment is based on the "Philosophy of Alcoholics Anonymous," the patient stares at this list of words and at these 12 steps and wonders what they mean. A sense of bewilderment and confusion is experienced. "What is a Step?" he asks. "How do I take a Step?" The following statement from a patient in Northern for five days evidences this confusion. A 32-year-old insurance salesman, he asks his group counselor:

What in the hell is a Step? How do I take these dammed things? How long does it take? When do I know I'm done? What if I don't take them?

His counselor replied:

> If you don't take them you'll drink and die or go insane. You've got no choice. You'll work these steps the rest of your life if you're serious about this business. I do. It works. I've been sober on these steps 8 years now. The only step you can take successfully and to perfection is the First Step. If you don't drink today you've taken that step. If you take that step back and drink again you'll go insane, just like you were when you got here. And your life will become even more unmanageable than it already is. Get the picture? These steps are here to help you get well [field observation, May 22, 1981].

Treatment at Northern was organized so as to give the patients a working familiarity with each of the Twelve Steps. Lectures were held every afternoon on one of the Steps. Patients were required to form small groups of three and four and hold group discussions on what each step meant to their group. They were then required to select a group spokesperson who would present the group's point of view to the entire patient community.

The third language and the third level of meaning that treatment relies upon is, then, the language of A.A. This language permeates, as a threatening presence, every interaction that occurs between patients and their counselors. Knowing that they will take a Fifth Step before they leave treatment, patients are constantly asking one another if they have started on this Step. But before they can take their Fifth Step, they must take the First Step. This is the business of the first week in treatment (see next section).

I turn next to the temporal structures of treatment that mediate and give interactional meaning to these languages of self and emotionality the patient has been presented with.

THE TEMPORAL STRUCTURES OF TREATMENT

Unlike the tuberculosis patient (Roth, 1963), the chronically ill (Fagerhaugh and Strauss, 1977), the mental patient (Goffman, 1961a), or the dying patient (Glaser and Strauss, 1964), who have lingering, indeterminate temporal treatment trajectories, the patient in an alcoholism treatment center has a treatment of specific temporal duration, usually defined in terms of three or four weeks, or one month. This 21-, 28- or 30-day treatment program is further subdivided into three or four one-week intervals. Specific treatment goals are set for each of these smaller time units.

Surrender and Treatment

Treatment is organized around a four-step model of surrender and recovery. Merryman (1984: 108-109) offers a convenient summary of these four steps, quoting a lecturer who is discussing the four stages of recovery:

> "The first," he said, "is the admission that you are an alcoholic. In our definition here, an alcoholic is somebody whose personal, social, or business life is being damaged by alcohol, and who will not or cannot do anything about it. The second stage of recovery is compliance, passively going along with treatment, while inwardly defying and denying. The third is acceptance, the realization that alcoholism is not a failure of moral fiber, but a chronic, fatal disease. The fourth is surrender, the visceral certainty that you are powerless against alcohol and cannot control your addiction by yourself, without help."

Each of the weekly intervals in treatment is built upon this four-step view of surrender and recovery; the ultimate goal of treatment being the alcoholic's complete surrender to alcoholism. Week one is focused on the alcoholic taking A.A.'s first step and completing what is called a "Step One Self-Assessment." This is called the "Recognition of Illness" phase of treatment. Week two is organized around compliance and the denial of alcoholism. It is often termed the "Acceptance of the Illness" phase. It focuses on A.A.'s Second and Third Steps. Week three is focused around the preparation of a Fourth and Fifth Step. That is, patients are required to prepare a "fearless and searching moral inventory of themselves" and to share this inventory with another human being. At Northern, patients shared this with a group and with a pastoral counselor. Week four involves a further push into surrender by the alcoholic and is typically termed "Family Week." Here the patient is confronted by his significant others who share with him the effects of his alcoholism on them. Weeks three and four are termed the "Action" phases of treatment.

In this phase the alcoholic is expected to have discovered her "real" inner self and to have shared this self with others. With this phase, treatment is terminated. Depending on the treatment center, the alcoholic, her family, employer, or insurance company will have paid between $3000 and $6000 for this final act of surrender.

Upon entering treatment the alcoholic is presented with a weekly timetable that will structure each of her days in treatment. A typical daily treatment schedule is as follows:

Organizing the Treatment Day

6:30- 7:00: wake-up (an alarm, or bell is rung)
7:00- 8:00: breakfast
8:00- 8:45: personal housekeeping and unit tasks
8:45- 9:30: community meeting, lecture
9:30-11:30: group therapy
11:30-12:15: lunch
12:15- 1:00: personal time
1:00- 2:00: Step group
2:00- 3:00: lecture
3:00- 5:00: personal fitness
5:00- 6:00: dinner
7:00- 8:00: personal time
8:00- 9:00: lecture (A.A.)
9:00-12:00: personal time (all patients in rooms by midnight)

For the first week of treatment no visitors are allowed. Phone calls typically are unrestricted, although at Eastern patients were allowed no phone calls in the first week, which was called "filter." After the first week visitors can be seen on Saturdays and Sundays, usually from 1-8 p.m. Patients are allowed to leave the treatment center and go on walks, if accompanied by another patient. The schedule does not apply to Saturdays and Sundays, the alcoholic's two hardest days in treatment (see below).

The Activities of Treatment

The focused activities of treatment, as suggested by the previous list, are group therapy, A.A. lectures, group meals, personal fitness, or recreational activities, small amounts of personal time, fulfilling unit tasks, and sleeping. If in the outside world the alcoholic lived by a timetable that was largely of his own, his family's, and his employer's making, in treatment he finds that temporal choices have been taken out of his hands.

Furthermore, if he was accustomed to doing what he wanted to do when he wanted to, he finds that his choice has also been removed. The assignment of unit tasks is intended to bring every alcoholic down to a common level. Hence, he will find that he may be given any of the following "tasks" to do on a daily basis: (1) clean ashtrays and pick up in the patient lounge; (2) set up and fold chairs after group lectures; (3) clear tables after each meal; (4) be responsible for the distribution of clean sheets and pillowcases on the unit; (5) ring the morning bell that wakes everyone up; and (6) keep the patient snackroom clean. These menial, largely janitorial, chores are rotated among patients during their three or four weeks in treatment. The forced performance of these assignments is intended to produce a sense of self-responsibility in the patient.

THE RESPONSIBILITIES OF TREATMENT

When she receives this timetable she also receives a list of responsibilities she is expected to fulfill. She will be expected to (1) be up daily by 7:00 a.m.; (2) attend meals three times a day; (3) attend all lectures; (4) attend all group and program activities; (5) go to group therapy daily; (6) go to all unit meetings and concerned persons groups and to one A.A. meeting a week; (7) refrain from smoking in bed, halls, and elevators; (8) wear her name tag at all times (which only gives first name and last initial); (9) be on her unit by 10:00 p.m., and let staff know when she is off the unit; (10) only leave the unit with another person and to sign in and out every 1½ hours; (11) report to the nurse's station at specified times; (12) read her books and complete all written assignments; (13) complete assigned unit tasks; (14) not be in cars with visitors; (15) clear all packages received in the mail through the nursing station; (16) be responsible for preparing a treatment program; and (17) understand that grounds for dismissal from treatment are (a) campus romancing, (b) chemical usage, (c) gambling, (d) leaving unit grounds, and (e) acting out in ways that are harmful to the center as a whole. This last point states that grounds for dismissal are determined by staff consensus and by patient irresponsibility. At Northern all patients "voluntarily" signed a patient agreement form upon admission stating that they understood these responsibilities, and that they had been informed of grievance procedures they could follow should they feel their patient rights had been violated.

THE INTERACTIONAL SETTINGS OF TREATMENT

Treatment is spatially organized into seven main interactional settings. Patients typically are assigned a bed in a double room; rooms having the appearance of being and not being at the same time motel rooms, army barracks, and hospital rooms. This semiprivate room is the only personal space the patient has while in treatment. Often a curtain can be drawn across the patient's half of the room. Northern, Westside, and Eastern each had television lounges and a patient snackroom where food, coffee, and fruit juices were always available. These two settings become the places where patients comingle, come to gossip, talk, and exchange views on how their treatment is going. Berryman offers this example:

> At half past ten he . . . went off to the Snack Room for coffee. Eddie was jittering by the freezer. Jeree looked softly up, Jasper and Mike were arguing. Eddie had come in about four o'clock, in frightful shape, and driven everybody crazy.
>
> Group therapy occurs in small rooms, usually having the capacity for no more than 12 patients. A.A. posters, including the 12 Steps of A.A., the Serenity Prayer, or prints depicting peaceful nature settings may hang on the walls. Group and community lectures often occur in the largest setting in the treatment center, which is the cafeteria.

In addition to these settings, the treatment center may have a recreational or personal fitness unit, including a swimming pool, volleyball or basketball courts, pool tables, weight rooms, and tables for playing cards, chess, or checkers. There may also be, as there was at Northern, nature trails to take walks along, lakes to walk beside, and woods to walk through.

Spatially and architecturally, the treatment center may give the sense of being a sanitarium or a unit in a large countryside hospital (Northern), an old family mansion (Westside), or a downtown residential hotel (Eastern). This sense of being something other than anything the alcoholic has ever been in before locates treatment in a setting that is clearly outside the normal world of affairs. Indeed, "outside" time may stop for the alcoholic. Daily newspapers may not be allowed. The evening news cannot be watched. The alcoholic finds that his time has become someone else's. He has stepped outside time in order to be treated for his disease of time.

LIFE ON THE TREATMENT UNIT

As the alcoholic fits herself to the temporal rhythms of the treatment center, her days come to take on a predictable shape. Berryman (1973:

81) observes: "Life on the ward became *really* existential only from ten to noon five days a week, and in Mini-Group three days."

A patient, Jack, at Northern made the following comments about Easter Sunday on the unit:

> Christ, its Easter. I'm depressed as hell. I got up at 6:00 and did my laundry. Jim and Charlie and I had breakfast together. I tried to take a nap and had bad dreams. The floor is overrun with families and children. Nobody has anyplace to go. They just keep walking up and down the floor, going to the lounge and then turning around and walking back. It's funny, you know. We all seem normal here. It's the families that seem strange and out of place. It's comfortable and nonthreatening here for us. We all have made-up things to do—Charlie has the bell to ring in the morning. Jim has the ashtrays to clean. I have the laundry. But we're all into our heads. This "head-work" is screwing us up. It's like we're all here, but nobody's here. Everybody stands around and waits for a phone call from a relative or a visit. We all get dressed up. For what? Christ, Marilyn wants to know what she should wear—her yellow suit or her blue one? She's not having any visitors. Who does she think she's dressing up for anyway? Ann from Seattle just said, "How can you get your shit together on Easter? You wonder what it's like on Christmas around here." Christ, these weekends are killers. No god damned thing to do! At least we have group during the week. Who wants to read the *Big Book* on Easter? I'm ___ sick and tired of standing in front of group and saying, "Hello, my name's Jack and I'm an alcoholic." I'm tired of smiling when I say that. Christ, Andy's been here six times. How can he say that and believe it? [Field observation, April 19, 1981].

Both Berryman and the patient Jack speak to the existential structure of daily life on the treatment unit. Living a collective life that must confront the hollow gaps of weekends, holidays, Easter Sundays, and family visits, patients in treatment produce for one another a shared sense of "anomie, frustration and despair." Meaningless "make-do" jobs (Goffman, 1961a: 261) do not give the alcoholic who is in treatment a deep sense of purpose. A structure of experience that is collective and shared and that alternates between long moments of emptiness and brief, high-pitched feelings of shared emotionality is thereby lived by each patient. Each patient carves out a mode of existence that is individual and unique, yet derives from this shared group perspective.

Saturday nights, after lecture, are often occasions when patients break out of the collective gloom that pervades daily life on the unit. Merryman (1984: 198) speaks to this point:

She came out of her room . . . and went into the large lounge. The furniture was pushed at random into one end of the space, as though painters would soon start work. There had been a record dance on Saturday night—a collection taken, pizza ordered in—Abby had gone, feeling like a teenager, relieved to detach herself in time and space.

The simple acts of ordering in pizza, of dancing and playing records can transform ward life into a temporal structure of shared emotionality that draws patients together, and out of—if only briefly—the mundane, yet troubling solitude they live on a daily basis.

Summary

I have discussed the central paradoxes of treatment, as well as the linguistic, interactional, and temporal structures that organize experience. I turn now to the First Step Inventory the alcoholic prepares during the first week of treatment.

WEEK ONE: FIRST STEP INVENTORY

Soon after entry into a treatment center the alcoholic is asked to fill out a "chemical assessment sheet." Often administered by an intake counselor, this assessment sheet asks the alcoholic questions such as the following:

(1) What chemicals have you used?
(2) How much and how often have you taken these chemicals?
(3) What is your drug of first choice? Second choice?
(4) How long have you used these chemicals?
(5) With whom do you use these chemicals?
(6) Describe how your behavior changes when you use these chemicals, compared to when you are straight.
(7) Have you ever hidden alcohol from yourself or from others?

The alcoholic is also asked to discuss the effects chemical use has had upon his relationships with others. He is asked:

(8) How do you get along with your family? Describe your relationship with each family member.
(9) Has your chemical use affected your family relationships?
(10) How does your family respond to your present situation?
(11) How has your chemical use affected your relationship with your friends?

(12) What do your friends say about your chemical use?
(13) Relate and explain any incidents or dangerous situations involving yourself or others due to your chemical use.

Questions concerning the alcoholic's self-concept are also raised:

(14) How do you feel about yourself?
(15) What are your goals and values?
(16) How have your goals and/or values changed due to your drug/alcohol use?

The alcoholic will be asked to repeat his answers to these questions in his third group day.

A consideration of these 16 questions reveals several points concerning how treatment conceptualizes the alcoholic and his "addiction." First, these questions make the alcoholic's relationship to the object alcohol and the social act of drinking problematic. By transforming alcohol into a chemical, questions 1-6 suggest to the alcoholic that he is a chemical dependent, not an alcoholic—that is, he is a drug dependent.

This transforms him into an addict, when he may have previously thought of himself as just an alcoholic. By placing him in the category of drug or chemical dependent, treatment widens the boundaries of deviance that now encircle the problem drinker. Treatment for chemical dependence places the alcoholic in the company of drug addicts, including heroin, cocaine, marijuana, PCP, and speed users. He will also find himself in the presence of prescription drug abusers, including persons addicted to Valium and other psychoactive mood-altering chemicals. The first six questions on the chemical assessment sheet tell the alcoholic that he has joined the world of chemical dependents, or drug addicts. Because his drug of choice was alcohol, he is as much of a chemical dependent as are drug addicts and persons dually addicted to alcohol and other drugs.

When the alcoholic is confronted with question 7, "Have you ever hidden alcohol from yourself or from others," he is forced to confront the fact that maybe he is not the first person who has attempted to protect his supply from others. If that is in fact the case, then perhaps he is not a normal drinker. He knows that normal drinkers do not hide their alcohol.

An alcoholic in his third day of treatment at Northern asked a fellow patient:

Did you really hide the stuff from your wife? I kept mine behind the dictionary in the bookcase.

His friend replied:

> Hell, yes. I had it behind the tool box in the truck. The boys at work were
> always kidding me about my "secret supply." We all used it. The wife
> never knew tho' [field observation, April 20, 1982, Eastern].

By sharing this information about themselves, these two patients solidify a personal relationship. They also confirm their lack of uniqueness
concerning the hiding of alcohol.

Questions 2 and 4 locate the alcoholic's drug use in personal history.
The intent is to create a personal identity of the alcoholic as a user who
has a particular history, or biographical relationship, with alcohol. By
asking how much and how often the alcoholic takes these chemicals, the
assessment sheet attempts to reveal to the alcoholic how much she in fact
uses on a daily or weekly basis. Question 6 asks the alcoholic to estimate
how her drug of choice affects her behavior when with others. This
question is developed in questions 9, 10, 11 and 12. Question 13 locates
chemical use with dangerous situations in the alcoholic's life.

The personal identity themes of this chemical assessment sheet are
elaborated in the three questions on self-concept, goals, and values.
Here the alcoholic is asked to assess the effects of her drinking on her
goals, values, and views of herself.

These 16 questions transform *facticities*, or lived experiences, into
facts. They become objective indicators of lived experiences with
alcohol and with drinking. As such they shift treatment immediately up
to the level of shared, social experience, for each patient is expected to
share this "factual" information about herself with Group. Once shared,
this information becomes part of the group's collective conscience
(Durkheim, 1897/1951) regarding alcohol use and its abuse. A shared
group identity of "chemical dependent," "alcoholic," "dual addict," or
"user" is thus forged out of the answers to this simple chemical assessment sheet.

Those 16 questions deal with both specific instances of lived experience and with generalities, or abstractions concerning the patient's life
goals and values. A two-edged reflective stance toward alcohol's
presence and effects on the drinker's life is produced. That is, by
reflecting on how much he drinks, how often, with whom, and by
examining the effects his alcohol use has on his friends and his family,
the alcoholic is forced to see that alcohol has permeated every sector of
his life.

Second, because questions 15 and 16 speak to the generalities of goals
and values, the drinker is forced to ask himself if he in fact has any goals

or values left in life. The intent of the assessment sheet is to set in motion a chain of inner thought that reveals to the alcoholic how *unmanageable* his life has become and how *powerless* he in fact is over alcohol. These, of course, are the two key terms in A.A.'s First Step.

The first several days of treatment are meant, then, to make the alcoholic acutely aware of his powerlessness over alcoholic. However, prior to talking in Group, this self-awareness is kept inside the alcoholic's inner stream of consciousness. He has yet to admit and share this powerlessness with others. He is forced to do this in his First Step Group, which will be discussed in the next chapter.

THE GROUP LOCUS OF EMOTIONALITY

Durkheim (1893/1964; cited in Bellah, 1973) has observed that emotions and emotional experience find their location in a society that has a reality that comes before the person. He states that feelings and emotional attitudes are "ways of acting, thinking, and feeling that present the noteworthy property of existing outside the individual consciousness" (Durkheim, 1893/1964: 2). These social facts exist as pressures against the person; they are collective manifestations. They are not the sole property of individuals, although persons create the illusion that they have created the emotions that they feel. Many of the emotions that are felt in the modern world have become solidified into rituals. When followed, these emotional rituals produce sacred, moral selves.

With little difficulty it is possible to translate Durkheim's arguments into the experiences of alcoholics who undergo treatment for their emotional illness of self. Indeed, the five paradoxes of treatment and the three languages of treatment represent collective manifestations of society entering into the inner emotional life of the person. Told that she is not unique, the alcoholic is taught how to interpret emotional experiences within a structure that is outside her. She is directed to a group where she will find the kind of self-treatment it is organized to treat. The languages of treatment become ritual extensions of the alcoholic self. As these languages are learned a new form of selfhood is experienced. The Steps of A.A.—especially Steps Four and Five— ritually embed the self in a social performance that produces a new, sacred self. Yet, treatment contributes to the illusion that the alcoholic is creating these experiences of emotionality. This is done in the directives that charge alcoholics to level and confront one another. Hence, a myth of individuality is sustained within a collective structure of experience that in fact treats every individual the same.

A Durkheimian conception of emotion and treatment suggests that a phenomenology of this process will be lacking to the extent that it does not locate emotion, feeling, meaning, and selves in a collective structure of experience. A purely dramaturgical and interactional analysis of this process is also deficient. This is so because treatment presumes a theory of self and selfhood that lies beneath the surface levels of polite, everyday interaction. A structural and behavioral accounting of emotion (Collins, 1975; Kemper, 1978) will also not explain the emotional experiences alcoholics confront in treatment. Ritual interaction chains (Collins, 1981), theories of emotional arousal, and a picture of emotional interaction being governed by exchange processes will not shed sufficient light on the inner transformations of self that accompany the treatment experience.

A psychoanalytic framework, whether taken from Freud (1954), Lacan (1977), or Kohut (1984) also has limited utility in explaining the emotionality of treatment. Although such frameworks are certainly compatible with treatment's theory of self, they cannot address the collective, Durkheimian nature of emotional feelings that are lodged in a structure outside the individual.

It is apparent that a theory of meaning, language, and feeling in the alcoholism treatment center must be one that is simultaneously collective, interactional, and phenomenological. As the alcoholic learns to internalize and verbalize the disease conception of alcoholism, he or she comes to take on the deviant label of "alcoholic." Yet this label is neutralized by the medical and disease conception of his or her illness (Trice and Roman, 1970). Thus, in a collective fashion, alcoholics learn how to (1) identify the emotions that lie at the core of their illness while (2) they teach one another how to talk the language that makes such understandings and self-identification possible. Their emotions and the meanings they apply to themselves lie in the group interactions they are forced into, and they lie in the collective representations of alcoholism their society has located in the treatment center.

CONCLUSIONS

Prior to the 1972 federal act that decriminalized public intoxication and mandated the establishment of treatment centers for the treatment of alcoholism, the alcoholic in American society was commonly seen as suffering from a lack of willpower and self-control (Beauchamp, 1980; Denzin, 1986a: chap. 1). The institutionalization of this act ushered in a new conception of alcoholism as an emotional disease of self. A new set of collective representations was brought into place and put into practice in the substance abuse treatment center. In such places persons defined as alcoholic now learn how to identify the emotional sickness that lies at the core of their inner selves. The languages of emotion that treatment teaches are transmitted through group interaction processes. Collectively, alcoholics come to assume the situational identity of alcoholic. This new identity can be seen as a situational adjustment to a problematic that is collectively confronted (Becker et al., 1961).

At the core of this identity is a new emotional understanding of self. These new emotions that come to be attached to the self find their origin in a reality that comes before the alcoholic. They reside in the new culture of alcoholism that has emerged within American society since the early 1970s. A new social world of emotionality thus exists in our society. I have shown how that social world is transmitted in and through the treatment process. In so doing I have suggested that a Durkheimian conception of emotionality, when combined with a phenomenological interpretation of emotional experience, offers the fullest interpretation of this social process, which turns on the reconstruction of meaning, language, and feeling in everyday life. Alcoholism, which begins as an individual act embedded in the outer fringes of drinking groups, becomes through treatment a collective phenomenon—a phenomenon that is recreated and redefined within the organizational and institutional structures our society provides for the alcoholic deviant. By grasping the structures of this process we come to better see how the individual's inner emotional life derives its fundamental locus from society itself.

3

EXPERIENCING TREATMENT

Today something happened. I talked with my wife. I didn't want to get drunk. I think my counselor has helped. I actually have hope today. I think I like these drunks and their meetings. I don't know what's happened. I actually want to live. Of course I'm sober today. I'm going to change my schedule this fall so I can come to those noon meetings [field conversation with Fritz, 23 days into treatment, same individual as quoted at the outset of Chapter 2].

Fritz, the alcoholic who speaks the above lines, evidences the kinds of transformations in self that may occur in treatment. Depressed and suicidal on his first day in a treatment center (see Chapter 2), he is now full of hope and promise 23 days later. In this chapter I examine the group and interactional experiences that structure these transformations in self. They begin and end in group interactions, all of which are organized around A.A.'s first five Steps.

ENCOUNTERING THE GROUP

The recovering alcoholic will encounter two distinctly different structures of group experience while in treatment. The first group she becomes a member of will number anywhere from 10 to 20 patients. This size will vary, however, depending on the treatment center's patient census at time of entry. This is her First Step Group. Her second group will be smaller, usually no more than 10 members. This is her Treatment (or Therapy) Group. Although she will spend no more than a week in her First Step Group, the remainder of her time in treatment will be in the company of her Treatment Group. The members of this group will, in all likelihood, be drawn from her First Step Group.

Both of these groups are short-lived, natural groups, formed out of the treatment encounters forged between patients and counselors. These groups are situationally bound to the treatment center, for the patient is unlikely to ever see any of his fellow group members after treatment ends. They are multiply bonded groups, based on the common identity of "alcoholic." Intense primary relationships, of a short-term duration, are thus formed; these relationships having the capacity (especially in the Treatment Group) of absorbing the patient as a total person. (On these dimensions, see Goffman, 1961b: 7-14.) That is, by the time the patient has taken his Fourth and Fifth Step in his Treatment Group, his fellow group members know more about him than he is likely to have ever shared with any other human being.

His First Step Group will be a non-sex, non-age stratified group. It will be constructed on the basis of who has come into treatment during the weekend, for group therapy presumes a five-day treatment week. Patients are cycled, then, if at all possible, through a five-day First Step Group and a three-week, 15-day, Treatment Group structure. If the First Step Group is non-age and non-sex stratified, the Treatment Group is likely to be formed along same-sex and approximately same-age lines. Intensive treatment replicates the age- and sex-stratified society the alcoholic has stepped out of. It is assumed that matters of sexuality, and deviance—although all alcoholically connected—are best handled within same-sex groups. (Some treatment centers do not follow this pattern, believing that alcoholics must learn how to deal with members of the opposite sex when sober.)

The importance of sexuality and age for the alcoholic's treatment experience is twofold. Perhaps for the first time in his adult life he is thrown into the company of males and females and asked to share his experiences in ways that he had never learned or experienced before. Second, he is likely to form friendships with individuals he would never have met in his everyday interactions in the outside world. In this way treatment exposes the protective shells the alcoholic has built around himself, opening him up to interactional experiences that are assumed to be therapeutic.

An Unexpected Community of Alcoholics:
Forms and Varieties of Relationships

Same- and cross-sex relationships and friendships thus form in treatment. These relationships form out of the patient's experiences in First Step Group. In this group (and in treatment more generally, that is, community, group lectures, recreation time), the alcoholic discovers an "unexpected community" (Hochschild, 1973). This unexpected community is based on the shared identity of being an alcoholic in treatment. Out of this shared identity emerges intense social bonds that are complementary, reciprocal, primary, and secondary. Some of the bonds have the characteristic of the parent-child relationship the alcoholic may have experienced, either as a parent or as a child. It is not uncommon, for example, to see an alcoholic in treatment taking a young alcoholic adolescent under her wing and caring for her.

Like the sibling bonds Hochschild (1973: 63-69) discovered in an old-age retirement community, alcoholics form sibling bonds of brotherhood and sisterhood with one another. These bonds involve mutual helping, the sharing of past experiences, the giving of hints regarding how to fill out a Fourth Step Inventory, how to talk in Group, and so on. Rivalry and hostility may emerge within these sibling bonds.

Alongside parent-child and sibling bonds exists the deeper bond of "being alcoholic" together. The alcoholic bond, or the alcoholic relationship, is one based on the common wreckage alcoholism has brought to the lives of the individuals who form the bond. This bond is deep and emotional, admitting of a love, or a caring intimacy that the alcoholic may never have experienced before. The alcoholic bond crosscuts sexual, sibling, and adult-child relationships. It forges the ground of commonality out of which all other relationships in treatment are formed. This bond appears in First Step Group.

There is a fifth relational form the alcoholic may enter in treatment. This is the Leader-Follower relationship that forms between the patient and his or her group counselor. Through a process of identification and surrender (which may be altruistic), the alcoholic may merge her ego and her self in the experiences and the identity of her counselor. The group leader, in Freud's terms (1921/1960: 59), is the group ego ideal, for he or she is a successful recovering alcoholic.

The alcoholic as patient may surrender his identity to the identity of the counselor, perhaps experiencing a transference of emotion that is both emotional and sexual. An emotional bond is thus formed with the group counselor and this may incorporate the polarized feelings of love and hate, for the counselor may be perceived as an other who is making the alcoholic undergo pain. A patient at Northern, in his third week of treatment, expressed these ambivalent feelings toward his counselor as follows:

> You know, I kind of like that old man Walt. He's a lot like my father, but he's sober and he cares and he seems to love us. But the sonofabitch makes me want to hate him. Who in the Hell does he think he is coming off like the High and Mighty, making us eat _____ and all that! Christ, I could kill him. Did you see the way he looked at me yesterday? But you know I think I'm getting better [field conversation, 39-year-old male, June 1, 1982].

Because every alcoholic forms and experiences an individual relationship with and to his counselor, group psychology in treatment is transformed into individual psychology (see Freud, 1921/1960: 56). That is, in each case the original relationship of patient to counselor must be created and reenacted within the context of group interactions. This interactional phenomenon must be woven through the personal history of each alcoholic who comes to treatment. He must learn how to reenact the parent-child, authoritarian, subordinate relationship he he has previously experienced in the other areas of his life. And, he must do this within a structure of shared experience; that is, every other alcoholic confronts this same situation. Every alcoholic in treatment experiences, then, a shattering of previous emotional understandings concerning what a relationship with another human being is like.

These five relational forms the alcoholic experiences in treatment—cross-sex and same-sex friendships, adult-child relations, sibling bonds, the alcoholic bond, and the counselor-patient relationship—set the context from which a group solidarity is formed.

Group Solidarity in Treatment

Treatment groups are pledged groups, in Sartre's (1960/1976: 829) terms, fused around the common goal of being in treatment together. Group members create an idea of themselves as being in group together. In order to act as a group they must form themselves into something they cannot be as individuals—that is, a group. Their Group Counselor becomes a third party who compels them to act as if they were a group. They are brought together as individuals in a room sharing the identity of alcoholics and are then asked to act as a group. They do this by individually internalizing the perspective of the group counselor, and the languages of A.A. and treatment. Bringing these points of view to bear upon their individual conduct they are serially transformed from their individual states of isolation into a shared group consciousness. They learn that their alcoholism is a disease whose meanings and pains can be socially shared.

A triadic process that draws each alcoholic out of her seriality into a common group point of view operates within the treatment group. This process is structured as follows: (1) alcoholic, (2) group, and (3) counselor. The alcoholic's individuality is enveloped within a group structure that is coordinated and held together through the actions of the counselor. A collective group consciousness emerges that aligns each individual within a structure that is larger than she is. This structure is externalized and symbolizes the focus of the alcoholic's daily existence in treatment. That is, five days a week she goes to treatment in group.

In this fashion the group is both outside and inside each individual at the same time. As a collectivity the group is externalized as a process that stands ready to be mobilized each time the group comes together. Yet the group is only what its members bring to it; the counselor will not do the work of the group. That is the assignment of each individual. The counselor is, then, the symbol of what the members must do for themselves. But more important, he or she is the means by which they may individually do only what they can do in group.

Out of this process emerges a solidarity and sense of "we-ness." This solidarity is fused through the sharing of the destructive experiences the identity of alcoholic has brought to the patient who is now in treatment and in group. By revealing himself to the group and by sharing in the experience of other members doing the same thing, the alcoholic discovers a new view of himself that could only have been given by becoming a member of the treatment group. A primary group, in Cooley's (1902/1956) sense, appears. The alcoholic feels as if he has come "home" to a group he has never before belonged to. He begins, in Schutz's (1964) terms, as a "stranger" to treatment and ends up a "homecomer," for he has found a place for himself, no matter how transitory, in his "Treatment Group." If his recovery is to continue after treatment, he will have to repeat this process in the A.A. groups he will find in his "home" community. If he fails to do so, he will lose what treatment has given him. He will lose his identity of "recovering alcoholic," and become once again a "stranger" in his "home."

FIRST STEP GROUP

These preliminaries discussed, I turn now to First Step Group. I shall offer a brief narrative account of how First Step Group works in the alcoholic's first week in treatment.

It is 9:30 on a Monday morning. In a large room that looks out over rolling hills and a lake are 16 men and women seated on folding chairs in a circle. They are in Hill House, the group therapy building at Northern. Alice, their First Step Counselor, introduces herself: "My name is Alice and I'm an alcoholic. Welcome to First Step Group. Let's go around the room and introduce ourselves. Mary, you go first."

> "My name's Mary Jones." Alice cuts in. "No, your name is Mary and you are an alcoholic. We don't want to know your last name. Look at your name tag. We don't use last names here." Mary corrects herself. "My name's Mary and I'm an alcoholic." Mary starts to cry, turning away from the group, trembling. The group looks away. Alice turns to Mary and says: "That's O.K. We all had to say it for the first time."

Informed, if they had not learned this earlier, that they are to introduce themselves by their first names only, followed by the word "alcoholic," the members of the group proceed to follow Alice's instructions, each member introducing himself or herself as instructed. Alice continues:

> We're here for one purpose. To find out if you're alcoholics. That's why you have your First Step Inventories and your First Step Assessments. We are going to go through your answers to these questions. Each of you is going to talk. Who can tell me what the First Step says?

Speaking to the First Step

Although each of these speakers in this First Step group will take a different stance toward the First Step, their speech acts collectively to create a conversational context in which alcoholism is openly discussed. This is the importance of this first session in group. Each alcoholic in the room knows that he or she will have to speak and answer Alice's questions. First Step Group, then, produces a context in which the alcoholic discovers, through her own talk, how it is that she is an alcoholic. If she does not speak, she does not make that discovery. According to treatment she makes that discovery by applying the First Step to herself. She must come to see that she is powerless over alcohol.

She must understand that her life is unmanageable. First Step Group conversations are about powerlessness and unmanageability. The alcoholic speaker is forced to illustrate, from lived experiences, how alcohol has taken control of her life.

Transforming Experience

In First Step Group the alcoholic learns, then, that the unique features of his life are of no particular interest to those who are managing his treatment. He is just an alcoholic who has finally found his way into a treatment center.

This movement back and forth from the unique to the general, from the lived experiences of the alcoholic to the interpretive structures of A.A. and treatment, becomes the overriding theme of the alcoholic's experiences while in treatment. He must return again and again to the unique features of his life as an active alcoholic. From those experiences he must find the general patterns that make him an alcoholic.

In lecture the alcoholic is informed that he belongs to a selfish program. He is told that by helping others he helps himself. He is also told that in order to keep what he has, he has to give it away. If he does not have sobriety he can't help anyone else. Therefore, he must return to the presence of other alcoholics in order to remain sober and to continue recovery. He is told that nonalcoholics can neither understand his illness nor talk his language. Hence, his treatment can only be accomplished in the company of other alcoholics who are also recovering.

Returning to Group

First Step Group continues for a week. Each alcoholic repeats the answers she has given on her Step One Assessment. She witnesses other alcoholics doing as she does. She hears her story in the stories others tell about their attempts to control their use of alcohol. She learns that the problems she has confronted have also been confronted by others. In fact the litany of problems becomes familiar and repetitive: divorces, losses of jobs, bankruptcy, DUIs, hospitalizations for alcohol-related illnesses, estrangement from children, loneliness, being drunk at the wrong time, hiding alcohol, violating one's morals in order to drink, black-outs, trips to psychiatrists, psychologists, and ministers, and even previous trips to treatment centers.

At the end of week one the alcoholic is expected to have recognized his powerlessness over alcohol. The unmanageability of his life is also expected to have been recognized and accepted. He will be evaluated at the end of this time in terms of his progress: more than expected or less than expected. If he has made less than expected progress he will be held back for another week in Step One group.

The following reasons may be given for holding the alcoholic back: denial, refusal to talk, overinvolvement in the world of family or work, not taking the program seriously, or debating with counselors. This discretionary decision to hold the alcoholic back may provoke an early termination of treatment on the part of the patient. Consider the following account. The speaker had been through treatment 10 years earlier. He had recently entered Eastern. In detox for 7 days, he had completed one week of treatment when he was told he would have to repeat that week.

> Hell, they told me I was too cocky. They tried to tell me why I drank. They said it was 'cause my old man beat me when I was a kid. I said, "You ain't got it right. I drank 'cause I wanted to. Me and the old man got along just fine." Then they said you're not taking this seriously. You're too worried about setting your business straight and you got too many calls from your kids and your ex-wife. What could I say? Hell, everything's coming in on top of me. I ain't been sober for 18 months and now I got a chance to get it turned around. Why shouldn't I be trying to get back on my feet? [field observation, October 15, 1984].

Three days after he was told he had to repeat the first week of group and could have no contact with his family or his work, he left treatment.

Treatment requires that the alcoholic make treatment his first priority. Treatment places the alcoholic under the power and the control of the treatment center. Although this is voluntary, it is a mandated condition of continued voluntary treatment. This premise was rejected by the above-described alcoholic.

First Step Presentation and
the Self-Fulfilling Prophecy

In the second half of the first week in treatment the alcoholics in Step One Group are expected to make a presentation to the group concerning what the First Step means to them. This sharing of a part of their autobiography to the group is intended to further the process of conversion and surrender to the alcoholic treatment point of view. Robert Lifton (1961) has documented the workings of this method in the indoctrination methods employed by the Chinese Communists after the

1949 Revolution in China. The Chinese methods were compulsory; those in the alcoholic treatment center are semivoluntary.

Treatment works through a process of *self-fulfilling prophecies* (Denzin, 1968: 349-358; Merton, 1957). That is, if the alcoholic patient publicly accepts her alcoholism, and develops a view of self that is in accord with the staff's view of a recovering alcoholic, then she will be seen as making progress in treatment. The alcoholic must come to see the treatment center as a legitimate source of help for her illness. She must view herself as being in need of treatment, and must learn to speak the languages of treatment. If she does so her treatment trajectory will be smooth and orderly and the prognosis for recovery will be judged by the staff as being good. Of course, the alcoholic may set in motion a series of self-defeating prophecies that will lead the staff to ask her to repeat one or more phases of treatment. The alcoholic who left treatment three days after he was told he had to repeat the first week of group in fact produced such a self-defeating situation for himself.

WEEK TWO: STEPS TWO AND THREE

If the alcoholic has successfully convinced his First Step Counselor that he has recognized his powerlessness over alcohol and the unmanageability of his life, he is moved into his Treatment, Therapy, or Peer Group. In this smaller group the primary alcoholic bonds that were beginning to form in First Step Group become stronger. By this time he is on a first-name, friendly basis with the alcoholics he will spend the remainder of his treatment time with. He will have spent a considerable amount of time with these alcoholics outside of group during the first week. He will have eaten three meals a day with them, attended daily lectures and community with them. He will have had talks with them, learned the names of their children and their wives, and he may have shared drinking stories with them. He probably knows where they live, what their occupation is, and he may have played gin rummy with them late at night after evening lectures.

Three males in their mid-40s are walking back from evening dinner. They are waiting for the elevator to take them up to the second floor of the treatment center. They have been discussing Bill, a 52-year-old alcoholic who had just been transferred to the psychiatric ward at Northern. Jim, a recently divorced auto mechanic and a Vietnam veteran, speaks:

It's not fair, what his wife's done to him. Serving them divorce papers on him three days after he's here and trying to do something about the booze. Christ he's just coming off the stuff, making headway, really talking, trying to get better and now she throws this shit up in his face.

Walt, an advertising executive, speaks:

I know. Maybe we should go over and see him. Call him. Do something to show him we love him and want to help. You know he stayed up till 3:00 this morning listening to me. He understands. He's a great guy. Its not fair. I agree.

Mike, a dentist, responds:

He's got himself all fucked up over this divorce deal. He's just depressed as hell. Let's go and see him. Hell, all they can do is tell us we can't see him. Let's go [field observation, May 13, 1982].

The three men then walked to the psychiatric unit at Northern and were allowed to see their friend Bill. Three days later Bill attempted suicide. He did not return to the treatment unit during the time these three men were at Northern. He left the psychiatric unit after six days, started drinking again and was killed while attempting to pass a motorcycle on a country road. This death, which was reported on the unit, was deeply grieved and became a topic of discussion in the treatment group the three men belonged to.

Their counselor, Walt, stated:

No alcoholic dies in vain. Bill's death helps me stay sober and it helps the three of you stay sober, too. His death tells me and you what can happen if we go back to drinking. Bill was sick. He had a disease called alcoholism. When he drank he got insane. Alcohol and alcoholism killed him. If one of you stays sober because of Bill's death he will not have died in vain [field observation, May 27, 1983].

Step Two

The second week of treatment examines the meaning of A.A.'s second and third steps. Step Two states: "Came to believe that a Power greater than ourselves could restore us to sanity." Step Three states: "Made a decision to turn our will and our lives to the care of God *as we understood him.*" This examination, as indicated above, occurs within the small group confines of the Therapy Group.

At Northern, alcoholics were asked five questions concerning Step Two:

STEP TWO SELF-ASSESSMENT

(1) What do you understand Step Two to mean?
(2) What does a "power greater than ourselves" mean to you? Are you aware of this power and how?
(3) What specific manifestations do you think your insanity took?
(4) What do you consider sanity?
(5) How did you come to believe?

Five questions were also asked concerning Step Three:

(1) What is your definition of decision?
(2) What is your definition of "will"—"Life"?
(3) How do you decide to turn your will over to the care of your higher power?
(4) How do you decide to turn your life over to the care of your higher power?
(5) What is the difference between turning your will over and turning your life over?

There are clearly more than semantic issues involved in these 10 questions. That is, the alcoholic is being asked to do more than produce a list of definitions of such words as power, insanity, sanity, decision, will, life, and turning over. He is being asked to bring the meanings of these words into his life and to reflect on how they have relevance for him as an alcoholic. Each word is intended to reference an instance of lived experience in the alcoholic's life that might in fact be a reflection of power, insanity, sanity, decision, will, or life. By coupling the word with lived experience the questions become more than semantic exercises. They are meant to anchor the alcoholic in an interpretive structure that will give new meaning to the experiences he has lived prior to entering treatment.

In Week Two of treatment alcoholics receive lectures on A.A.'s Twelve Steps, with primary emphasis on the Second and Third Steps. A lecturer at Northern is speaking on these two Steps:

> Any of you can see that there might be a power greater than yourself in your life. It might be money, it might be your boss, it might be your mother, or your wife. Some of you might believe in a God, or a tree, or in

electricity. This power is outside you. You can't control it. It is stronger than you are. Alcohol is a power greater than you are. You've admitted you're powerless over alcohol. Now you must find any other power, greater than you are, that won't kill you or drive you crazy. That's what these two steps are all about. When Step Three says a "power greater than ourselves can restore us to sanity" it means that you have been sane before in your life, but you're not when you are drinking. There is hope for you if you believe in this power. But you're got to see how you were insane when you drank. The Big Book and the Twelve and Twelve talk about alcoholism as an emotional illness. You are all emotionally sick people.

When you drank you may have been violent, you may have hit your wives and children, you may have driven your cars when you were intoxicated. You may have written bad checks, hidden your brooze, lied, and cheated. You did anything to drink and when you drank you were crazy. If you can't believe in a power greater than yourself you'll go back to drinking because the alcoholic by himself or herself can't stay sober. It's your choice. What are you going to do about it? [field observation, June 22, 1983].

This lecturer is interpreting Steps Two and Three. She is presenting the alcoholic with the dilemmas of self-control and will power that are contained in the fifth and sixth theses of alcoholism. She is returning the alcoholic to a new consideration of surrender.

The alcoholic will be asked to share the meanings these two steps have for him in Group. At Northern at the end of the second week of treatment each alcoholic was asked to stand in front of the entire community of recovering alcoholics and speak on the meaning of the first three Steps. The following is the statement given by Jack.

Step One. I know I'm powerless over alcohol. I take one drink and I can't stop. My life must be unmanageable. I have bills up to the ceiling and the family is about to leave and I've been put on notice at work. Step Two. I want to believe in God. I used to but I got away from the Church. But this isn't the God of my church. It's different. I want a God of love and caring. I know I was crazy when I drank. The last time I went out I ended up in a motel room across town under a different name. Now that's not sane!

Step Three. I want somebody else to run my life. A.A. and treatment seem to be doing a pretty good job right now. I hope I can stay with it [field observation, June 24, 1982].

Jack has internalized the central terms of Steps Two and Three. He speaks the language of treatment and A.A. By nervously presenting his interpretation of these two steps to the entire patient community he has publicly committed himself to the identity of recovering alcoholic. Whether he means the feelings his words and gestures convey is another matter.

Feeling the Language that is Spoken

The crucial test for every alcoholic in treatment is the test of feeling. Are the words that are spoken felt in the inner self?" This is the question that is raised over and over. Language emerges as a problematic in the expression and understanding of feeling. As the alcoholic learns A.A.'s steps she acquires an interpretive structure that stands one level above lived experience. Words such as sanity, insanity, powerlessness, unmanageability, will, and life are abstractions. They are "glosses" (Garfinkel, 1967) for lived experience. The alcoholic is asked to attach a level of feeling to these abstractions; that is to ground these feelings in her biography.

Evaluating Week Two

At the end of the second week the alcoholic is expected to have confronted at a deeper level the meaning of surrender to alcoholism. If her or she is in compliance and or denial, more confrontation will be required. Consider the following exchange between a counselor at Westside and an alcoholic woman in her tenth day of treatment. The counselor, Nancy, speaks:

> Jean, who do you think you are kidding? You think you can go home and drink again don't you? Do you want a divorce? Do you want to lose your daughter? Who are you playing games with? You talk good, but you don't mean it. Tomorrow you will have a chance to talk again to Group. If you don't want to stay here, just say so. There are 10 people outside waiting to get in here and take your place. There are plenty of people who are working and trying to get better. You're playing games with all of us.

Jean replies:

> I don't know. I don't think I'm like the rest of you. A lot of this stuff never happened to me that you all talk about. Sure I want to drink again. Who doesn't? If you say you're never going to drink again you're lying. Last night I dreamed of a tall cold Mint Julep. I love 'em. This stuff may be all right for you people, but not me. I'm leaving [field observation, July 30, 1983].

Jean left treatment the next day.

By the end of the second week a judgment is made concerning whether or not the alcoholic has accepted alcoholism. If, in week one they had been asked to come to a recognition of their illness, in week two they must evidence a commitment to change their lives.

WEEK THREE: STEPS FOUR AND FIVE

In a sense, all of treatment points to the taking of the Fifth Step. Step Four is preparatory to Step Five. Step Four asks the alcoholic to "make a searching and fearless moral inventory of ourselves." Step Five suggests that the alcoholic "admit to God, to ourselves, and to another human being the exact nature of our wrongs." When the Fifth Step is taken the alcoholic reaches the final phase of treatment, which at Northern and Westside was Family Week.

Rumors abound in treatment concerning good and bad Fifth Steps. Stories are told of patients who were made to do the step over. Accounts are also told of how the person who the patient told his Fifth Step to fell asleep. Outlines for the steps are passed around. Patients can be observed working late at night on their Fourth and Fifth Steps. Depressions set in; patients become moody and withdrawn. A general fearfulness appears on the treatment unit as the time for a group to individually take these two steps is scheduled.

As the anxiety level increases patients are drawn closer together. A general caring attitude emerges. If confrontation was a recurring theme of the second week of treatment, mutual and reciprocal self-support is the theme of the third week. In part this is the case because each patient must rely upon the other members of the group for feedback when he takes his Fifth Step.

At Northern the Fourth and Fifth Steps were structured as follows. At the end of the second week of group each patient was told when he or she would be giving his Fourth and Fifth Step to group. At this time each patient was also told to make an appointment with one of the pastoral counselors. It would be with that person that the alcoholic would individually share the Fifth Step. In effect, then, patients took two Fourth and Fifth steps—the first with their group, the second with the pastoral counselor of their choice.

In their patient workbooks patients received a guide for the Fourth Step. They were told to make a list of their good qualities, and to list their resentments, anger, and fear. They were also told to write a brief history of their lives up to the time of treatment (see Denzin, 1986a:

chap. 7 for a discussion of these two steps). They were also told to read those sections of the *Big Book* and the *Twelve and Twelve* that deal with these steps (A.A., 1953: chaps. 4-5; 1976: 64-67).

Unraveling a Life

In these guides to the Fourth Step the alcoholic is presented with a method for unraveling the patterns that make up life. Couched in the languages of A.A. and treatment, the guides suggest that the problematic areas of the alcoholic's life are those focused around the emotions of resentment, anger, and fear. Social relationships are the focus of each guide. These relationships are grounded in the alcoholic's worlds of work, family, sexuality, and self. Family history is emphasized in each guide, as are the emotions of self, including self-pride, fear, and self-esteem.

The alcoholic is asked to be a participant observer of his own life. He is asked to uncover the hidden themes in his life that have influenced his relations with others. The underlying rationalizations, delusions, and self-deceptions that he has employed are also addressed. The alcoholic is asked to put all of this down on paper, in black and white. This act, in effect, transforms the alcoholic into the position of the detached observer who might be writing a life story. In writing and speaking to his life as an alcoholic, the "alcoholic-as-narrator" becomes, like Leon Edel's (1984) literary biographer, the author of an "oral text" that has meaning only within his or her lifetime.

This, then, is lay therapy, involving the alcoholic in the dual identities of therapist and patient. In treatment this lay therapeutic model is located within the context of the therapy group. It becomes, in this sense, lay psychotherapy, which is guided and directed by a counselor. The alcoholic counselor will, of course, draw on a wide variety of treatment theories. Depending on his or her background in the field of human relations, any of the following psychotherapy models may be drawn upon: client directed, psychoanalytic, Adlerian, Jungian, problem solving, behavioral, cognitive, humanistic-existential, Gestalt, rational emotive, transactional, aesthetic realism, direct decision therapy, interpersonal process recall, or intensive journal therapy (see Corsini, 1984: 223-225).

Finding the Cause of Alcoholism

Treatment presumes that the underlying cause of the patient's alcoholism can be discovered. The Fourth and Fifth Steps are the key to this attempt to find the cause of alcoholism. Berryman (1973: 78-81) located the cause of his alcoholism in his relationship to his mother. Merryman's alcoholic (1984: 125, 159-160, 174-175, 277) discovered four central events in her life that were defined as the causes of her alcoholism. These were (1) a rape when she was six years of age; (2) her anger at her mother for controlling her alcoholic father; (3) her hidden fear of her husband because he represented her controlling mother; and (4) the hysterectomy she had after the birth of her last child.

At Northern the causes of alcoholism were located in the hidden and unknown cells of the Johari Window. The following causal agents are representative of those found by therapists and patients at Northern: homosexuality, bisexuality, rape, child abuse, spousal violence, alcoholic parents, and failures at work and in education. These factors were seen as being hidden within the self-structures of the alcoholic. It was assumed that the exposure of these factors would, in part, help the alcoholic stop drinking. Similar factors were discovered in the biographies of patients at Westside and Eastern.

TAKING THE FIFTH STEP

In taking the Fifth Step, the alcoholic shares a view of life she has heretofore kept hidden from herself and from others. With the taking of this step the alcoholic comes full circle in her alcoholic understanding of self. No longer completely bewildered by her compulsive drinking, no longer existing in an alcoholic haze, she sees the pattern of her life. She sees the destructive powers of alcohol and she understands that she is powerless over alcohol.

The Fifth Step clarifies for the alcoholic the meanings of the previous four steps. By laying her life out in front of her she presumably reveals to herself how powerless she has been over alcohol. She sees how unmanageable her life has been. She confronts the moments of insanity her drinking has produced. She sees the need for a power greater than herself in her life. She sees how destructive and chaotic a life run on her will power and on alcohol has been. She sees also that she has been restored to a sense of sanity and sound thinking that she had not previously experienced. Finally, she discovers that the life that has gone astray is her own. That is, the Fifth Step turns the responsibility for alcoholic drinking and alcoholic existence back on the drinker. In so doing it isolates the alcoholic at the center of her illness, forcing her to address what she did as an individual while she drank alcoholically.

A counselor at Northern is speaking to a group of patients about to take their Fifth Step:

> You must learn to ask for forgiveness and you must learn how to forgive. You must give up the feelings of resentment towards the past that you feel. If you do not you will drink again. You have a choice today. Only you can do this. If you have taken your first three steps and believed them, then you are on the road to recovery. You have all the power on your side now [field observation, May 16, 1982].

At Northern Steps Four and Five were termed the "Action Steps." As the alcoholic takes these steps he is evaluated on two dimensions. The first dimension is "Self Inventory." His counselor makes a judgment concerning whether or not he has discovered "the real self" through his inventory. The second dimension asks if he has "shared" this self with his group and with his counselor. These two evaluations are communicated to the alcoholic after he has given his Fourth Step Inventory to his Therapy Group.

At Northern, Eastern, and Westside the alcoholic read this inventory to his or her group. After the alcoholic presents this inventory he or she is asked to leave the room. The group counselor then asks the members of the group to produce a list of words describing the "assets" and "liabilities" of the alcoholic who has just made a presentation. At Northern the following terms were frequently employed, and applied, with slight variation to each alcoholic who gave a Fourth Step Inventory:

> *Assets*: sober, honest, clean, intelligent, articulate, responsible, likeable, friendly, reserved, open, sharing, caring, sensitive, willing, sincere, polite, respectful, loving, good mother (or father).
>
> *Liabilities*: shame, guilt, hurt, anger, resentful, self-pity, hatred, mistrust, blaming, rationalizing, defiance, minimalizing, justifying, inadequate, lonely, anxiety, low self-worth, fear, dishonest to self, analytic, stuff feelings, intellectualizing.

These words are written on the blackboard in the Group Therapy room. The alcoholic is asked to read them out loud when he reenters the room. The counselor then interprets these words, applying them to the biography of the alcoholic. This process is filled with anxiety and tension. The aicoholic has just shared his life with the group. Now he is being evaluated in terms of that life and the presentation he has made. His group is likely to draw close to him. Members nod in approval as he comes into the room. Coffee is poured for him. Cigarettes are extended to him. A space is made for him at the table. As he sinks into his chair his counselor speaks reassuringly to him, telling him that he made a good presentation, perhaps informing him that "he knows he will be able to make *it* and handle *it* when he leaves."

As he fits the words his group has given him to his life, the alcoholic breathes a sense of relief; relieved that the step is over, relieved that his life is not that bad after all. He wonders too, how he will live the meaning of those words into his life. That is, how will he stop mistrusting, being analytic, lonely, or inadequate?

An alcoholic is speaking to a fellow patient after his Fourth and Fifth Step Inventory:

> How was I? What in the Hell am I supposed to do now? I've still got the guilt. I still feel bad about what I've done. Maybe it is self-pity and rationalizing. I don't know. Hell it's hard to show feelings. Maybe I do stuff the shit. I do feel a Hell of a lot better about myself. I saw things I'd never seen before about myself. You know I'm not all that bad. To Hell with all those big words. I feel better [field observation, Westside, April 25, 1983].

Wrestling with the meaning of words as they apply to his life, this alcoholic speaks to his personal inadequacies as his group has presented these to him. He feels pain in the face of this self that has been reflected back to him. The looking glass the group has given him (Cooley, 1902/1956) has reflected a self he is not entirely comfortable with. Yet it is the self he has presented, as it has been defined by his group.

As the alcoholic witnesses fellow members of his group going through the same process he has gone through, the pieces of his self begin to fall into place. He begins to see that he is like every other member of his group. He begins to understand how the same list of words can be applied to all alcoholics, not just him. He begins to see that the pain he feels and felt is the same kind of pain his fellow group members are experiencing. This shared pain solidifies the Therapy Group. What is experienced and what is revealed about self begins to lose significance. Each alcoholic comes to understand that his alcoholism is but an instance of the universal destructiveness of this disease he shares with all alcoholics.

WEEK FOUR: FAMILY WEEK

The last week of the alcoholic's treatment brings his or her family into the treatment process. Having learned that alcoholism is a family disease (illness), the alcoholic must now confront the members of his or her family. Three processes are involved. First, the family members present the alcoholic with instances of how his or her conduct has affected them. This is a painful process involving leveling and confrontation. Second, the alcoholic presents to his or her family the new found "self of recovery." This self is grounded in the languages of treatment and A.A. It is also based on a set of experiences in Therapy Group that have not been accessible to the alcoholic's family. Hence he or she is literally a "stranger" to the family when the "homecoming" that characterizes Family Week occurs. They may not know who this new person is, nor will they know how to speak to this person—who is, after all, their father, husband, wife, mother, son, or daughter. A clash of perspectives, the old one (the family's point of view) and the other new, the recovering alcoholic's new self of treatment, thus takes place in family week. Whether these two views will be joined is problematic, both during family week, and after, when the alcoholic returns home.

The third process that is involved during Family Week is the presentation of an interpretive theory of alcoholic family interactions. This theory is often an eclectic mix of several theoretical points of view: Al-Anon, Social Work, Psychotherapy, Role Theory, and Communications Theory. These points of view are all applied to alcoholism as a family disease. The alcoholic and his or her family are located within this interpretive theory. They are asked to look at themselves as participants in an interactional system that is sick, or has been distorted by the disease of alcoholism. Family Week thus addresses the Second and Third Theses of Alcoholism and Recovery; viewing alcoholism as a relational and emotional dis-ease of self and other. A principal aim of Family Week involves an attempt on the part of the treatment center to convince the alcoholic's family members that they are also sick. This is difficult to accomplish because they share the alcoholic's belief that he or she is sick—not them. Although as Kellerman (1969) notes, many family members may feel that they—not the alcoholic—are sick, if not insane.

I shall take these three processes up in reverse order.

Treatment's Theory of the Alcoholic Family

In a quaint sociological fashion, alcoholics and their families at Northern were presented with a "role theory" of the alcoholic family. This theory contains six roles: the chemical dependent, the chief enabler, the family hero, the scapegoat, the lost child, and the mascot. It assumes a six-person family, with four children playing out the respective roles of hero, scapegoat, lost child, and mascot. The wife is, of course, the enabler and the husband is the chemical dependent.

Inner and outer selves are portrayed, with distorted, negative emotionality located at the core of each inner self. Family members are told that they have become trapped within a communication system that hides anger and resentment. They are told that they have withdrawn from one another into interaction patterns that are full of fear, pain, guilt, shame, confusion, insecurity, loneliness, and rejection. They are also told that each of their adaptive patterns (enabling, being the family hero, the scapegoat, the lost child, and the mascot) displays unhealthy, maladaptive adjustments to the alcoholic situation. Because they have refused to confront the alcoholic husband and parent in his alcoholism, they have become victims of his disease. In short they are as sick as he is.

An idealized picture of a healthy American family is presented to the alcoholic's family members. This picture stresses the fact that families are nourishing of all their members, are full of love, sharing, a haven of rest, a sanctuary of peace, a harbor of love, a place where holidays are celebrated with feasting, birthdays acknowledged with gifts, and thoughts of days gone by kept alive with fond remembrances.

If the alcoholic's family is anything, it is not a haven of rest, a harbor of love, a place where holidays are celebrated with feasting and days gone by remembered with fondness. The alcoholic's family is a nightmare of confusion, terror, pain, guilt, anger, and ugliness. There may have been good days in the past, but that past has long since been forgotten.

As the family members are presented with these two pictures of the human family, they are given a chart depicting the progression of alcoholism within the alcoholic family (Jackson, 1962). They are taken through the phases of denial, the attempts to eliminate the problem, the process of disorganization, the searching for outside help, the increase in violence and financial problems, and the efforts to escape the situation, including divorce and separation. Each of their adaptive strategies are located within this progressive evolution of the illness.

They are then brought up against the fact that the alcoholic is in treatment, as are they. Their task now becomes one of confronting the alcoholic situation they have all produced. This can only be done, they are told, through communication. Communication must involve confrontation and leveling. The alcoholic's family must confront the Five Paradoxes of Treatment. They are at a disadvantage, however, because they have less than five days to do this. Further, they may have only one group session with the alcoholic during Family Week. In this session everything that has built up over the years and months of the alcoholic's alcoholism must be addressed. High drama is played out in this moment.

Confrontation and Self-Presentation

Because the presentation of old and new selves is involved in the confrontation that occurs between the alcoholic and his or her family, I will combine these two processes in the discussion that follows. In preparation for the confrontation that will occur, each individual is given a "Family Week Participation Worksheet." This sheet consists of three major questions:

(1) Prepare a list of behaviors and incidents that have been hurtful and uncomfortable for you. Do not be judgmental. Describe behaviors and/or incidents (what you have seen and heard). (A full page is given for this question.)
(2) List behaviors, incidents, and features you like about each family member (half page).
(3) List your goals, needs, and expectations in each relationship (half page).

In the moment of confrontation the alcoholic is presented by each family member with answers to these three questions. In turn, each family member (if there is time) is presented with the alcoholic's views of them.

This confrontation, as indicated above, is accomplished through a mix of languages: family therapy, role theory, A.A., treatment philosophy, and the special languages of each family member. Tension radiates through the bodies of each family member as they confront one another. Young children may be fearful of confronting their alcoholic mother or father with episodes of alcoholic violence or alcoholic misconduct. Husbands may be bitterly angry at their wives for forcing them to come to Family Week, as may children. Indeed, complex negotiations and coercions may have been required in order to secure the physical presence of the family members during Family Week.

Merryman (1984: 197-198) describes this process by which family members are brought into this phase of treatment. Abby is speaking to her daughter Judy:

Abby said ... "This is a very hard call for me to make. I have to ask you to come to Family Week".... "Mom, that's a whole week out of school. You

want me to get good grades don't you? . . . "Stop pressuring me, Mom,"
Judy answered . . . "I can't take it. I don't want to come there and have all
those people dig into me and analyze me." . . . Now Abby's voice was
steely. "Okay, here's the word. I'm *telling* you to come to Family Week.
They say it's important for my recovery and there are things you need to
say to me. . . . I want us to be mother and daughter again."

The coercive structure of this conversation pits mother against
daughter, while it places the mother in the demeaning position of having
to ask her daughter for help. The help that is requested is not ordinary
help. It is the help that comes from confrontation. The mother cannot
make her daughter come and say the things she needs to say. Yet she falls
back on the full authority of her parental identity as she tells her
daughter to come. This is the presentation of a new self in a relationship
that had previously not contained such motherly self-assertion. In order
to avoid her mother's request her daughter relies upon the need to get
good grades. In previous interactions this ploy by her daughter would
have worked, for it would have permitted both interactants to stay out
of one another's respective fields of experience. By drawing her daughter
into this painful situation, the mother asserts a new self that has been
learned in treatment. This new self provokes anger and resentment on
the part of her daughter. This resentment adds to the earlier resentments
the daughter has felt toward her mother. Accordingly, in order for the
mother's treatment to move forward, the very emotions that have kept
them apart must be experienced anew. That is, they must confront the
emotionality that has driven them apart. In order to do this, new
resentments must be produced. That resentment, in turn, is laden with
fear and anger. Not only does her daughter resent having to come to
Family Week, she also resents and is angry over the fact that she is the
daughter of a mother who is an alcoholic. She is fearful of what this may
mean for her.

The fearfulness that characterizes the alcoholic's other who does not
want to participate in Family Week is elaborated in more detail in the
following comments of the mother of a 35-year-old female alcoholic in
her last week of treatment at Westside:

I can't come. I can't get somebody to drive me up there [she lives 35 miles
away], and it costs too much to be calling you all the time. Besides, I ain't
got nothin' to do with this stuff. So what if your Old Man was one, I ain't
goin' to be part of it. It scares me that you'd think I'd come. Don't you
love me? [field conversation as reported, October 22, 1984].

Faced with such a situation the alcoholic is left to the doing of Family Week without a family member present.

The following situation describes a family member who is anxious to take part in Family Week. Two parents of Norwegian ancestry and in their 60s want to help their son, Ricky, who is 24 years old and recently fired from his job as a high school janitor. He was drinking on the job. The father speaks:

> We want to help Ricky, he's our only son. We are here because we love him. I don't know why he didn't want us to come. His psychiatrist said he told him he hated us. He said Rick drank because he couldn't stand the fact that I never showed him any emotion. Now how could he believe that? [As he speaks these words Ricky's mother is sitting beside him, nodding her head, with a tightly drawn smile across her lips, hands crossed in her lap. Ricky's face is turned away, he is fighting to keep from crying. His hands are clenched, arms folded across his chest.] Ricky screams: "You never told me you loved me! YOU NEVER TOLD ME THAT! How am I supposed to know that? You just keep turning your back on me, sitting there in your chair, smoking your fucking pipe, reading your paper. We never did anything together. Nothing. Never! [field observation, Northern, April 20, 1984].

Here the alcoholic does not want the family member to participate in treatment. The frozen, angry emotion that is present in the situation speaks to the wall that exists between the father and son. The inability of the father and the mother to involve themselves emotionally in the situation suggests a gap between the words they speak and the feelings they communicate to their son.

Forms of Family Participation

The foregoing situations describe two variations on the relationship between the alcoholic and the family during Family Week. The alcoholic may desire his or her family to be present but members of the family do not want to participate (the case of Abby, the woman at Westside). The alcoholic's family may desire to be present, but he or she does not want them to come (the case of Ricky). The third variation is the situation where no part of the family wants to be present, including the alcoholic who is in treatment. At Northern this situation was frequent. The following interaction is indicative of this shared interpretation. The patient is 45 years old. His only family is his 80-year-old mother. He has been in four treatment centers. She has paid for his treatment each time in the past, but not this time. He blames her for his drinking. She blames him for all the money he has spent on "his alcoholism." She speaks:

> I don't know why Charles's counselor thought I should come here. We've tried this before. I don't want to be here. They told me I should come. I guess I had nothing better to do. Oh well, maybe it will work this time. I'll just be glad when I'm dead and I won't have to deal with this anymore.

Her son replies:

> I will be glad when you're dead, too. You old BITCH. You never loved me. You thought you could buy me off. You never let me go to college and be what I wanted to be. You made me stay home and take care of you. You get what you deserve. I wish you hadn't come either. I'll drink a case of Jack Daniels the day you die! I'll praise the Lord [field conversation, May 13, 1981].

Finally, there is the situation where the patient and his or her family all agree that Family Week will be mutually beneficial. They regard themselves as all being part of the same family illness. This orientation is most typically expressed by those families where the spouse and children have attended Al-Anon meetings and have come to adopt the A.A. and Al-Anon point of view regarding alcoholism as a family disease.

The following situation speaks to this variation on the family's attitude toward treatment.

An alcoholic's teenage daughter is speaking:

> I wish Mom could have come, but she just couldn't get off work and I believe her. I really want to be here to help Daddy and myself. I know I'm sick from this illness, too. I'm really proud of Daddy for coming into treatment. When I started going to Alateen and Daddy would take me it was like we were starting our family all over again. Mom would go to Al-Anon and we'd all go home together, maybe stop for cokes and pizza [field observation, as reported, Northern, May 16, 1981].

A process of socialization into the A.A. and treatment point of view has occurred in this family. The father reported his feelings after Family Week was over and he was about to be discharged from Northern:

> I think this has really been good for all of us. In Family Emily [his daughter] showed me how I had hurt her and how she had tried to cover it

up. She took care of me when I was sick 'cause Mom had to be at work at nights. I was scared as Hell going into this thing. I think it was worth it. We all feel closer. If we just keep up what we are doing now we have a chance to be happy as a family again [field conversation, Northern, 39-year-old male, manager of a franchise auto dealership, May 17, 1981].

Four interpretive stances underlie the family and the alcoholic's participation in treatment. Both parties may be willing and commited to participation. Both parties may be uncommitted to participation and have no desire to participate. The patient may desire to participate and the family does not. The family may want to participate and the patient does not want to confront them. Each of these variations produce, as would be expected, drastically different experiences for patients and their families as they take part in Family Week. Clearly, all agree that the first mode of participation carries the greatest promise for recovery, as recovery is conceptualized by treatment centers.

The Promise of Family Week

In the few brief hours the alcoholic and her family spend together, in and during confrontation, the bare, skeletal, ugly underside of their family is laid bare. In order for this to occur, the promise of something better is held in front of them. In lectures during Family Week they are told that families can recover from alcoholism if they all work together and if they continue to seek treatment, in the form of Aftercare, A.A., Al-Anon, and Alateen.

They are told that if they do not learn how to communicate openly and honestly with one another the destructive side of alcoholism will return to their family, even if the alcoholic does not start drinking again. They are also told they will have to change the behavior patterns they have adopted in the face of alcoholism. They are told that the alcoholic will be changing and that they will have to change as well. If they do not, the hollow marriage and family they had before treatment will return. No small undertaking, this challenge is the promise Family Week sets before the alcoholic and the family.

At Northern patients and their families were given checklists for hidden anger; anger and fight rules; lists of the risks involved in expressing anger; descriptions of destructive fight styles; 15 rules for fair intimate fighting; discussions of how silence is the real torture to direct toward a mate when angry; lists of characteristics describing nonassertive, assertive, and aggressive problem solving; a discussion of the rights of a person in an intimate relationship; a discussion of how to listen and how to focus; a discussion of the "if onlys"; an anatomy of a working relationship; a credo for having a relationship with another human being; a discussion of risks and risk-taking in an intimate relationship; a credo for an accepting community; an analysis of "letting go"; a poem celebrating "YOU"; and a statement regarding "goals for me."

Armed with this information family members were sent home after five days to attempt to repair and rebuild their family life. The family members faced many problems as they returned home. What to make of these "credos," how to put them into practice, when to use them, when not to use them, and how to give meaning to them without falling back into their old relationships together or living a life of cliches. Perhaps, most of all, they felt relief that Family Week was over. They would take the alcoholic's treatment as the promise they would build upon. For many it would be up to the alcoholic to put back together a life they had jointly allowed to deterioriate because of all of them had denied that they had an alcoholic in their midst.

ENDING TREATMENT

With the conclusion of Family Week comes the end of the alcoholic's treatment. His four weeks now over, he, along with his family, will go home to begin the process of recovery that treatment has set in motion. Treatment ends with two significant closing rituals: the giving of medallions for 30 days of continuous sobriety (or for having completed treatment), and the signing of *Big Books* and the exchange of names, telephone numbers, and addresses.

Medallions and Graduation

Graduation ceremonies were held at Northern and Westside every Friday afternoon from 3-5 p.m. This was a momemt of celebration for alcoholics, their families, fellow patients still in treatment, and staff. Cookies and fruit juices were served. Chaired by the senior counselor in residence, who typically made a short speech regarding the progress of recovery achieved by each alcoholic who was graduating, the ceremony opened with the saying of the "Serenity Prayer." Graduating alcoholics were then introduced to the group and asked to speak a few words, which typically involved mumbled thanks for what the treatment center had done for them.

Upon the conclusion of these brief speeches, round medallions—slightly larger than half dollars, gold plated, with the name of the treatment center inscribed on one side and the Serenity Prayer, or the phrase "today is the first day of the rest of my life, A.A." and "I am Responsible" inscribed on the other—were given out. On the bottom of the medallion was also inscribed Northern or Westside Alumnus. The alcoholic was told to hold onto this medallion and to exchange it at his "home A.A." group when 60 days of continuous sobriety had been achieved. Alcoholics were told that they should carry the medallion in their pocket and if they thought of buying a drink they should put the medallion in their mouth and wait until it melted before they bought the first drink.

The giving of the medallion signified four processes. First, it was a mark of accomplishment. The alcoholic had in fact completed treatment. Second, the taking of the medallion signified a commitment, probably not understood, that the alcoholic would now be living a life dedicated to recovery and to participation in A.A. Third, by connecting this first medallion with a second one that would be received after 60 days of sobriety, treatment reestablished its link to A.A. The medallion was a token that would give the alcoholic concrete entry into an A.A. group in his or her home community. The medallion also signified a new concept for the alcoholic: continuous sobriety. It would no longer be sufficient for him or her to drink only occasionally. Recovery presumes continuous sobriety. Fourth, the token was an advertisement for the treatment center. By inscribing its name on the medallion, the treatment center paved the way for its name and its program to be passed along by word of mouth through the A.A. "grapevine" the alcoholic would now be entering.

Signing Big Books

Upon the conclusion of the graduation ceremony alcoholics were free to leave the treatment center. Departure from treatment involved a related ceremony, which was the signing of the *Big Book*. Reminiscent of a high school graduation ritual, alcoholics wrote in one another's *Big Book*. Phrases such as the following are inscribed:

2 good
<u>2 be</u>
4 gotten
    [Name, telephone number]

Thanks for sharing, thanks for caring, the best of luck to you, a super guy. It's been great knowing you. I know that you will make it.
[Name, telephone number]

To a Great Gal and a Great Friend who made this stay much more pleasant. [Name, telephone number]

With all the love you have and A.A. I know you'll make it. [Name, telephone number]

A mixture of concern, affection, and superlative is contained in these phrases. Each statement speaks to making it, to being forgotten, and to the fear and pain that was experienced while in treatment. These phrases lift the author and the recipient above the turmoil of treatment, with all its agony and fear, into a realm of platitude. It is as if all is well now that treatment has been accomplished, yet each author masks a reference to the fact that "not making it" is a possibility. Not making it, of course, is the tragedy each wishes to avoid. Each alcoholic author has lived his or her own version of hell and has, if for only 30 days, escaped that hell, only to have experienced hell in another version in treatment. Yet they are free of alcohol now. Their medallions signifying the promise treatment has given them. The alcoholics leave treatment fearful and hopeful—afraid that they will drink again, afraid that Family Week will not work when they get home, afraid that they will return to the life of hell they have escaped from.

CONCLUSIONS

Treatment takes seriously (without noting) Bateson's (1972a: 310-311) argument that the alcoholic's pretreatment style of sobriety somehow drove him to drink. By restructuring the alcoholic's interpretive theory of self, emotionality, temporality, others, alcoholism, and alcohol, and by bringing the family into treatment, the treatment center changes the alcoholic's previous style of sobriety. It does so by changing his entire relational outlook on the world. Treatment attempts to locate the alcoholic within an interpretive system that is larger than he is. By grafting itself into A.A.'s philosophy, treatment gives the alcoholic the sense of a higher power. It gives him a sense of freedom from his past. It locates him, if only for 30 days, within a safe interpersonal environment wherein the depths of his hidden self can be explored. Treatment has also given the alcoholic a new language of self and it has exposed him to the Steps and the tools of A.A.

Hence, although the alcoholic may well return to the same setting he left in alcoholic despair and disarray, it is in fact a new situation he reenters. It is new because he is, if only for a brief period of time, a new person. He must learn how to live that new self into the old situations he inhabited as an active alcoholic.

Treatment as a Collective Accomplishment

The tendency to interpret treatment solely from the point of view of the recovering alcoholic must be avoided. That is, treatment is a collective, group phenomenon. This is evidenced by the central place the alcoholic's therapy group plays at every stage in the process she has experienced. From the identity of recovering alcoholic—which finds its locus in the interactions that occur in First Step Group—to the Fourth and Fifth Steps that are taken in the therapy group, the alcoholic's recovery is, in every instance, a collective, group accomplishment. Even Family Week turns on self-presentations that involve interactions with fellow group members.

The "paradoxes of treatment," as outlined in the previous chapter, thus define the culture of treatment. These paradoxes, fitted to A.A.'s first four steps, are collectively defined by each cohort of alcoholics who enter treatment together. The only constants in this system of cultural reproduction are the paradoxes, the treatment center (and its employees), and the disease called alcoholism.

Recovering alcoholics share in common with other classes of individuals who undergo group socialization experience (such as mental patients, medical students, prisoners, military recruits, college students) the following characteristics (see Becker et al., 1961; Goffman, 1961a).

First, they socialize one another. Second, they collectively develop adaptative strategies for handling problematic situations (the Fourth and Fifth Steps). Third, they develop their own meanings of the cultural problematics they are presented with (that is, the languages of treatment, alcoholism as a disease, and so on). Fourth, like prisoners who undergo a process of prisonization, or adaptation to an institutional point of view, alcoholics experience a medicalization of their illness that may be termed "treatmentization." They come to act like self-treating patients (Beauchamp, 1980; Szasz, 1975; Trice and Roman, 1970).

But more than a medicalization process occurs. Recovering alcoholics experience what may be termed a *reverse stigmatization of self*. They are taught to accept their alcoholism, to be proud of their recovery, and to carry the message of recovery to others. This experience with self, which involves radical self-transformations of a reverse stigmatizing nature, sets the alcoholic off from other classes of individuals who are also processed by and pass through socializing institutions. And of equal importance, while other institutional selves may find their progress in the outside world monitored by others (such as parole agents, military officers, senior physicians, and so forth), alcoholics do not experience this kind of supervision. That is, they are able to slip back into the world they left with their new identity hidden. As long as they do not become actively alcoholic, few people will care about their recovery career. In this respect, treatment has taught them how to be "normal" again.

If she has surrendered, then, to her alcoholism, if she has in fact worked A.A.'s first Five Steps, and if she takes up a life that makes A.A. centrally important, then her chances of recovery are excellent. If she does not, she runs the risk, as did Berryman, of returning at some later date—if she is still alive—to another treatment center to start the recovery process all over again. The following words often spoken at the end of the alcoholic graduation ceremony echo in her mind as she leaves treatment: "*Treatment is only three percent of the solution. A.A. is the other 97 percent. Treatment is discovery, A.A. is recovery.*" As she hears these words she is also told, as patients at one center were told, that "eight out of ten of you will drink again, and if you are lucky you may get back here to start all over again." I turn in the next chapter to the structures of experience that the alcoholic will confront in A.A. when she returns to her home community.

Part II

A.A. AND THE SOCIAL WORLDS
OF RECOVERY

4

THE A.A. GROUP

> Find a home group. Get a sponsor. Work the steps. Go to at least five meetings a week. Get involved. You'll get better [counselor, advice given patients leaving Northern after four weeks, June 1, 1984].

In this chapter I will examine the structures of interpretation the recovering alcoholic finds in Alcoholics Anonymous. With Maxwell (1984: 38-39) I assume that the alcoholic who enters A.A. finds a new social world. This world is structured around A.A.'s Twelve Steps, the Twelve Traditions, and around a fellowship in which "being an alcoholic" is the primary identity that is shared (Denzin, 1986a: chap. 7; Rudy, 1986).

A.A. offers the alcoholic an interpretive theory of alcoholism. That theory, which he will have confronted in treatment, must now be mastered, if only partially, if he is to remain sober and recover. Now that he is out of treatment the place he will go to learn about A.A. is A.A. meetings. It is there that he will find the answers to the directives he has received when he left treatment. That is, only in A.A. will he find a "home group," a sponsor, and five or more meetings a week to go to.

The alcoholic who leaves treatment confronts a void of experience. The close relationships with fellow alcoholics he has experienced in treatment are severed. The family context he reenters is a mixed blessing. It contains all the structures of the experience he previously drank to escape. Although "Family Week" may have set the conditions for hope and promise, he returns to his family, his job and his other interactional settings with apprehension and fear. Uncertain as to how he will present himself to others, he is caught between revealing his new identity of "recovering alcoholic" or hiding it. The desire to drink may return and he may not know how to deal with it.

His head filled with a new language, familiar with A.A.'s Twelve Steps, he may feel that he has no one with whom he can share his new-found sense of self. Yet A.A. is there, waiting for him, just as it was before he went into treatment. A.A. may, in fact, become a new family for him, if he chooses. But in order to find an outlet for the new self he has experienced in treatment, he must make the first step toward finding A.A. in his home community. The telephone listing for Alcoholics Anonymous is given in every telephone book in nearly all medium-sized communities of 5000 and over.

I will discuss, in order, the following problematics, as they reveal the underlying historical, structural, and interactional features of A.A. that the new member will confront. First, I will investigate the phenomenon of "alcoholic understanding" as this phenomenon is experienced in A.A. meetings. I will trace the meaning of "alcoholic understanding" back to the original A.A. meeting between Bill W. (William Wilson, 1895-1971) and Dr. Bob (Robert Holbrook Smith, M.D., 1879-1950). I will speak, in this context, to the issues of emotionality, self, interaction, and "types" of alcoholic understanding.

Second, I will offer an interpretation of the A.A. group, extending my analysis of the treatment group as given in the previous chapter to the A.A. group. Third, I will analyze the structure of A.A. meetings and the A.A. group, discussing the place of the Twelve Traditions, ritual, format, and temporality in the organization of A.A. meetings.

I will suggest that in A.A. meetings the alcoholic subject is transformed from a "suffering" alcoholic into a "recovering" alcoholic. How this transformation in subjectivity is accomplished is the central problem of this chapter. I will show how A.A. transforms the alcoholic into a "talking subject" who learns how to speak about his or her lived experiences within the language A.A. provides.

My intentions are to bring the structures of A.A. before the reader, as these structures are given to the new member. By offering a combination of historical, structural, textual, and interactional analyses of the "A.A. experience," I hope to reveal how the recovering alcoholic can in fact become a part of a structure of experience that is larger than he is. I will show how A.A. requires his presence and that of other newcomers for its continued existence. In so doing I will examine once again how the recovering alcoholic realizes his or her "universal singularity" in the company of fellow alcoholics who are also universal singulars in their recovery experiences. By drawing upon this universal singularity of each of its members, A.A. solves its own organizational problematic of membership replacement (and recruitment), while giving each of its members a context of interaction wherein recovery from alcoholism can occur. How this oneness of experience and purpose generates a structure of common experience that is mutually beneficial to all parties—A.A. and alcoholic alike—is my topic. Central to this process is the cultural and personal history A.A. rests upon—most important, the history of the first A.A. group. I briefly turn to this history as it is made available to the new member.

THE FIRST A.A. GROUP
AND LIVED HISTORY

A.A. tradition states: "Two or more alcoholics meeting together for the purpose of sobriety may consider themselves as an A.A. group." Consider the following conversation between two A.A. members. M, 48 years old, has been sober for over three years. He has arrived early at the meeting site of an A.A. group for its usual Thursday night 8:00 p.m. meeting. D, a 21-year-old college student, has recently received a medallion for six months of continuous sobriety. It is 8:05 and they are the only two A.A. members present. M states:

> Do you want a meeting? You know two alcoholics can have a meeting if they want to. Remember Bill W. and Dr. Bob? That first meeting was just the two of them.

D nods his head and speaks:

> Yes, I do. I remember that story. I heard it in Chicago. I need a meeting. I've only had two this week. I'll chair, if you'll read "How It Works" and "The Thought for the Day" [field conversation, as reported, October 2, 1983].

The meeting began. A third A.A. member joined the group at 8:10 and the meeting that had started between M and D continued until 9:00, with each of the members speaking in turn.

This account instances the reenactment of A.A.'s original two-member group. M and D drew upon their knowledge of the first meeting between Bill Wilson and Dr. Robert Smith. They used that pivotal moment in A.A. history as justification for their two-person A.A. meeting. That D had heard this story in a meeting in Chicago reveals how this key moment in A.A. history is kept alive and passed on to the new member. This story is a part of A.A.'s lived history (see A.A., 1976, 1980, 1984; Kurtz, 1979).

A.A. dates its *inception* to the first meeting that occurred between Bill W. and Dr. Bob. That meeting occurred at 5:00 p.m. and ended at 11:15 p.m. on Sunday, May 12, 1935 in the home of Henrietta Seiberling and her husband in Akron, Ohio. The *founding* date of A.A. is given as June 10, 1935, the day Dr. Bob had his last drink. The first meeting between Dr. Bob and Bill W. has subsequently been redefined, within A.A. folklore, as the first A.A. group.

The importance of the foregoing is elaborated in the following statements made by A.A. members in meetings. The first speaker has just returned from a Young People's Convention in Chicago. Sober slightly more than one year, he states:

It was great. The keynote speaker was sponsored by Bill W. He talked of the first groups in Cleveland and Akron. He told us to work the steps and follow the traditions. He talked about the fights they had in the early days in Detroit over the membership requirement of six months sobriety before you could come to a meeting. It was great! I'm really glad I went [field conversation, September 20, 1984].

This speaker conveys the importance of having heard an A.A. member sponsored by Bill Wilson. By listening to this man he is taken back into the early days of A.A. He is given the essential message of Wilson and Smith in 1935. He was a witness to an instance of lived history within A.A.

The next speaker is 76 years old. He has been in A.A. for 35 years. He knew Sam Shoemaker, the minister who worked with Wilson in 1934 when Wilson was trying to sober up men in Shoemaker's church in New York:

Old Sam Shoemaker used to say, "Keep it simple. Listen to what is inside you, practice the spiritual principles but don't come down on this God thing too hard with newcomers" [field conversation, July 4 , 1983].

This A.A. member keeps A.A. history alive by mention of Sam Shoemaker, one of the early advisers of Wilson and a person listed by

Wilson as having been central to the early beginnings of A.A.

The third speaker is a female, sober seven years. She states, in regard to self and ego:

> His majesty the baby. That's me. I'm a spoiled brat. I want things my way and I want it now. I keep getting in my own way. The *Big Book* and the *Twelve and Twelve* talk about me—I prefer Her majesty the baby! [field conversation, November 25, 1982].

The phrase "his majesty the baby" is attributed to Freud by Tiebout (1954: 612), who used it to describe the narcissism of alcoholics. Tiebout also employed the phrase in a letter to Bill Wilson, suggesting that Wilson was trying to live out infantile grandiose demands (Kurtz, 1979: 127). Alcoholics often apply this phrase to themselves. The speaker, perhaps not knowing the source of her phrase, was, as she spoke, connecting herself to a moment in A.A. history when Tiebout was chastising Wilson for his own self-centeredness.

These three statements by A.A. members, and the earlier account of a three-person A.A. meeting, reveal how A.A.'s history, its key figures, its mythology, its folklore, and its key phrases are kept alive in meetings and in A.A.'s oral tradition. As an instance of a social movement—which began as a small group, then became institutionalized as it routinized charisma—A.A. has developed a body of customs, a social organization, a set of traditions, an established leadership, and an enduring division of labor with social rules, in "short a culture, a social organization, and a new scheme of life" (Blumer, 1946: 199). The problems of goal displacement and factionalization of membership that often follow the routinization of charisma within social movements have not been observed in A.A. (see Marx and Wood, 1975: 396-397; Maxwell, 1984; Zald and Ash, 1966; Zurcher and Snow, 1981; but also Kurtz, 1979).

The oral tradition that underlies the A.A. social structure keeps the culture alive. It is conveyed through the stories and the voices of A.A. members. The sources and the details of the stories are authenticated in the printed texts Wilson took pains to create (see A.A., 1984; Kurtz, 1979).

ALCOHOLIC UNDERSTANDING

Consider the following interaction as reported. The scene is a hotel room in Minneapolis. Three men in their early forties are seated around a table. They have known one another for seven years. J has been in A.A. for three years. M has been recently hospitalized several times because of drinking-related illnesses. He has a bottle of Jack Daniels in front of him on the table. D, a friend of J and M, is a moderate drinker. He listens as J and M speak to one another.

M to J: You're not drinking. Can I get you something?

J to M: No, I've stopped. Go to A.A. now, been three years. Been hard. 'Specially after the break-up with Mona. Christ, before that I'd get up at 2:00 in the morning and drink. Walk into the closet to go the bathroom. Get lost in the apartment. Drive the back alleys home so the police wouldn't stop me. Hid the stuff all over the place. Couldn't stop.

M to J: I guess I'd like to. Try to, can't. Don't know what's goin' on. Get drunk when I don't want to. 'Fraid to go to class anymore, start to shake and lose my train of thought. They told me I might need to go into treatment. I'm afraid to.

J to M: I wish I had. I know what you're talking about. I was afraid too. But you know, this old drunk told me, he was an elevator operator downtown. He saw me shaking one night, he said, "It doesn't have to be this way anymore." I said, "What do you mean?" He said, "It doesn't have to be this way anymore. It isn't for me anymore, and I used to shake more than you do. I go to A.A. now." You know, those words stayed with me. Couldn't get them out of my mind. For months. I'd be at Curley's drinking. His voice would come back, "it doesn't have to be this way anymore." One night I said ___ it. I called up A.A. and went to a meeting in the neighborhood. Still kept drinking, but after three months I stopped. You know, M, it doesn't have to be this way for you. Do you want to do something about it?

M to J: Yeh, I guess so. What are your meetings like? Can I go to one?

J to M: Sure, there's one at 8:00 tonight. I'll take you.

M to J: O.K., I'll go. What do you think about treatment?

J to M: I know somebody to call. We'll look into it.

M to J: You know, you're the first person I've talked to who understands what in the hell I've been going through. The doctor told me I had to get out of town for treatment if I couldn't stop by myself. Christ, I can't stop by myself. My family doesn't understand. I want to stop, but I can't. I keep going back to it, even when I don't want to.

J to M: They told me that will power had nothing to do with it. They said it was a disease, like diabetes. I go to A.A. meetings for my treatment. Maybe it'll work for you. It does for me. Let's go [field conversation, as reported, April 9, 1981].

Three days later M entered treatment, after attending two A.A. meetings with J.

This account may be interpreted in light of Robert Smith's description of his conversation with Bill Wilson on May 12, 1935: "He was the first . . . human being . . . who knew what he was talking about in regard to alcoholism from actual experience" (A.A., 1976: 180). M makes nearly the same statement in his comment to J: "You're the first person I've talked to who understands what in the hell I've been going through."

This interaction between M, J, and D instances a moment of shared "alcoholic understanding." (It is also an example of a Twelfth Step call in A.A..) M and J had an A.A. meeting. J carried the message of recovery to M. He did so in a language that was based on his lived experiences with alcoholism. However, the conversation between the two men made no mention of alcoholism or of alcoholics, except when A.A. was brought up. There was no need to speak to these terms because M knew he was an alcoholic and J knew that he was, just as M knew that J was a recovering alcoholic. J put the phrase "it doesn't have to be this way anymore" in front of M. He recounted his own experiences with the phrase, in terms of his interactions with the man on the elevator. He conveyed to M the point that it could in fact be different for him, too. How it would be different was the problematic, for the fact that M wanted it to be different was not at issue. J offers three lines of action for M: staying as he is, A.A. meetings, and treatment.

J reenacts the original A.A. meeting between Wilson and Smith. He communicates the disease theory of alcoholism. He shares with M his own failed attempts to stop by himself, and he relates moments of humiliation when he acted under the influence of alcohol. In a few words he secures M's attention and shares his experience with active alcoholism in the process. Of critical importance was the fact that J shared his experiences before he obtained M's understanding of how recovery might begin. That is, M understood that J understood him on the basis of the experiences J shared with him. Authentic emotional understanding was produced between these two men. They came to share a common field of experience and a common understanding concerning their respective locations within that field, which was active alcoholism, or uncontrolled drinking.

Emotional Understanding

Elsewhere (Denzin, 1984a: 145) I have argued the following:

In order for true, or authentic, emotional understanding to occur, two or more individuals must experience a common field of shared experience

that they can enter into, each drawing, if necessary on his own
visualizations of the other's feelings, his own productions and repro-
ductions within himself of a common feeling, and the common partici-
pation in this publicly accessible field of experience. Experience . . .
precedes emotional understanding [italics in original].

I also argued that shared emotionality lies at the basis of authentic, deep understanding. In shared emotionality selves are joined in a common field of experience. The interaction between Wilson and Smith, and the interaction between M and J, rested on shared, authentic, alcoholic understanding. I will now unravel the meanings behind this assertion.

In shared emotional understanding a past set of experiences is shared, even if they have been unique to the two individuals in question. By drawing on that common but unique past, they are able to form a new, shareable field of experience. In so doing they appropriate the other's perspective and apply it to their own situation. A merger of shared emotional feelings is thus produced. In that emotional field the selves of the two interactants are lodged. A merger of biographies, of common pasts and a discourse in a common language that draws upon that shared past, emerges. "Feelings-in-common" about that past are felt and shared (Scheler, 1913/1970: 12-13). A sense of "fellow-feeling" (Scheler, 1913/1970: 14) occurs as each individual identifies with the feelings and the past experiences of the other. A reciprocal sense of "emotional infection" and "emotional contagion" appears. The heightened emotionality of each individual passes over to the other. Each, in a sense, becomes emotional because the other is emotional. Out of this process emerges a sense of emotional identification. Each individual identifies with and through the emotional feelings of the other. "Emotional embracement" ensues. The two individuals are drawn together into an emotional situation where relational bonding occurs. There is a merger of the two selves in the emotional situation they have produced together. A sense of warmth, fellowship, relief, togetherness, oneness, solidarity, perhaps even love and caring, appears. Embodied feelings are sensed and felt and ratify this sense of shared oneness. Tears, smiles, hugs, handshakes, and shared laughter may be experienced by both individuals (see Denzin, 1984a: 146-153, for a discussion of these forms of emotionality).

These forms of emotional intersubjectivity (feelings-in-common, fellow-feeling, emotional infection, emotional contagion, emotional embracement) are to be contrasted to "spurious emotionality." "Spurious emotionality," or "spurious emotional understanding," reflects those interactional moments when individuals mistake their own feelings and understandings for the feelings of the other. They interpret their feelings as the feelings of the other. Spurious emotionality arises in those situations where interactants refuse or are unable to enter into the other's field of experience. In such moments mistaken emotional memory may occur; that is, the subject thinks she has had an experience like the experience the other is presenting, but she is mistaken. She has not had parallel experiences.

In spurious emotionality the individual thinks she can understand and feel the pain and suffering of the other, but she cannot. As a consequence, she applies the wrong interpretive framework to the experience of the other, perhaps feeling sympathy for him when he does not want or desire sympathy. In this incorrect interpretive move the individual assumes that the feelings toward self she would apply to herself are the same feelings the other feels. She assumes that if she had had the experiences the other has had, she would feel the way he feels now, that is, prideful, hurt, guilty, angry, embarrassed. Thus, in spurious emotionality the individual views the other's experiences not from the other's point of view, but from her own. Mistaken, flawed, self-centered emotional sharing occurs. This leaves the other feeling that his experiences have in fact *not been understood.* Anger and resentment toward the "interpretive other" may be produced. The good intentions of the other are rejected. The other fails to understand how or why it is they have been misunderstood. In fact, they have not been misunderstood. They have misunderstood the experiences of the other toward whom they have spuriously (and perhaps unintentionally) directed misunderstandings and misplaced feelings.

In order for deep, authentic, shared emotional understanding to be produced and understood, a common field of shared and shareable experience must be created. This allows each individual to locate himself or herself in the experiential framework of the other. Without this condition being met, spurious emotionality or misplaced understanding is produced. Consequently, as argued previously, experience precedes emotional understanding. That is, understanding cannot be entered into a field of experience until a commonality of experience has first been shared and felt.

These conditions and forms of emotional understanding are central for the interpretation of alcoholic understanding. I turn now to the forms of alcoholic understanding.

Four Types of Alcoholic Understanding

Understanding, as the above discussion suggests, refers to "the process of interpreting, knowing and comprehending the meaning intended, felt and expressed by another" (Denzin, 1984a: 284). *Alcoholic understanding* refers to the process whereby two alcoholics interpret, know, and comprehend the meanings intended by the other in terms of previously experienced interactions with the active and recovering phases of alcoholism. Four forms of alcoholic understanding may be distinguished. The first form is the understanding that is conveyed between a recovering alcoholic and an alcoholic who is still drinking, but wishes to stop, or seeks help. The interaction between J and M in the previous account displays this form of alcoholic understanding, which may be termed *authentic alcoholic understanding.*" The second form of alcoholic understanding is that which is conveyed between two or more alcoholics who are recovering and are in, or have been in, Alcoholics Anonymous. The three statements given by alcoholics in the discussion of "lived history" display this form of alcoholic understanding, which may be termed "A.A. understanding." Each member who listened to those accounts knew who Bill W. was, had perhaps heard of Sam Shoemaker, and could relate to the phrase "his Majesty the baby."

The third form of alcoholic understanding transpires between drinkers who are active alcoholics and who may or may not have had experience with Alcoholics Anonymous. I term this *insincere alcoholic understanding*. In this mode both alcoholics justify their active alcoholism through recourse to the term *alcoholic*, or its equivalent—"lush," "drunk," "alkie."

These three modes of alcoholic understanding have all been experienced by alcoholics who regularly participate in Alcoholics Anonymous. Each member has moved from the understandings of alcoholic justification to an interaction with a recovering alcoholic who extended the understandings of alcoholic help that A.A. is based upon. Furthermore, as a recovering alcoholic, each member regularly participates in A.A. meetings where the discourse revolves around the languages and understandings of recovery.

The fourth form of alcoholic understanding is, as the foregoing might suggest, *spurious alcoholic understanding*. The alcoholic who wishes to recover, or who has recovered, has experienced this form of understanding many times in the past. His network of significant others—including his enablers—and his victims have bombarded him with the spurious understandings a nonalcoholic brings to bear upon the experiences and the relationships she has with a practicing and a recovering alcoholic. Although this other may feel sympathy and compassion for the alcoholic who is still drinking, she has not the experiences of the active alcoholic. She has not felt the pains of withdrawal. She has never hidden a supply. She has never felt the fear of a police car stopping her for drunk driving. She has not been hospitalized for alcoholic-related illnesses. She has not felt the embarrassment of seeing the word "alcoholic" on a medical record. She does not know what it means to try to stop drinking and not be able to. She has never attempted to work while under the addictive influence of alcohol or drugs.

In the absence of these and related experiences, the alcoholic's other stands as an "outsider" to the inner, lived experiences of the alcoholic's who is attempting to control and manage his alcoholism. All of the good intentions of the other produce misplaced, spurious alcoholic understandings. The following words by an alcoholic married for 45 years to the same woman address this point:

> I've lived with that woman for 45 years. For 30 of those years I was an alcoholic, drunk every day. And after those 45 years she'll never come within a hair on a gnat's ass in understanding me. She can't. She's not an alcoholic. I don't care how many of those Al-Anon meetings she goes to. She'll never understand me! Never [field observation, February 24, 1984].

This fourth form of alcoholic understanding draws the recovering alcoholic back to Alcoholics Anonymous, for in A.A. he or she finds a community of others who are understanding in ways that are not spurious. In the fields of experience that A.A. offers, the recovering alcoholic experiences, over and over again, authentic emotional understanding. And, as important, this form of understanding is experienced alongside alcoholically grounded feelings-in-common, and shared alcoholic fellow-feelings, including emotional infection, emotional contagion, and emotional embracement. In short, in the presence of recovering alcoholics the alcoholic first discovers, and then rediscovers, a sense of self that was long since lost—if ever possessed—to alcoholism.

Every alcoholic who recovers has experienced this process of having "received" the message of recovery from another alcoholic. If the alcoholic has gone through treatment this process of coming to understand alcoholic understanding will have been repeatedly experienced. As the alcoholic learns to attend A.A. meetings and becomes a regular A.A. member of the A.A. social world in his or her community, the word "understanding" will be one of the most frequently repeated terms he or she hears. Alcoholic understanding, in all its forms, and the meanings and terms that flow from that phrase, constitute the frame of reference or universe of discourse from which all other A.A. discourse flows.

I turn next to the topics of the A.A. group and the A.A. meeting. It is in the context of these two phenomena that the recovering alcoholic learns to achieve and experience the kind of self-understanding of alcoholism that was first promised when "the message" was carried to him. My intentions are to offer a view of the A.A. group that is consistent with Sartre's (1960/1976) dialectical theory of groups. It will be necessary in this discussion to define such terms as *group, fused group, pledge,* and *"Third Party."*

THE A.A. GROUP

An A.A. group is a historical structure of dyadic and triadic relationships that coheres within a shared universe of discourse. That universe of meanings (Mead, 1934) turns on the omnipresence of five unifying forces: alcohol, alcoholics, recovery (or not drinking), A.A. history, and A.A.'s conception of a "higher power." These processes give the A.A. group its reasons for being. The A.A. group is pledged, in Sartre's sense (1960/1976: 419-420) to the primary purpose of "staying sober and helping other alcoholics to achieve sobriety." As such, this purpose externalizes the group in the form of a pledge. That pledge fuses or joins the members in the pursuit of this common goal, which is both individual and collective. The group, then, mediates between the individual and active and recovering alcoholism. It provides an arena of interaction wherein recovery from alcoholism on a daily basis may be accomplished. Individual action is realized only through group action. Similarly, the group is individual action; that is, the group inserts itself into each individual. Each A.A. member embodies the A.A. group. The group extends itself through and into each group member. Conversely, the group embodies each member as a part of itself. The group, then, has a reality that is both individual and collective.

The A.A. group is opposed to seriality, or separateness. Indeed, it is a premise of such groups that the loneliness of alcoholism requires interactional and interpersonal treatment in a group context. The first A.A. group between Wilson and Smith was a "fused group." A fused group (Sartre, 1960/1976: 828) is "a newly formed group, directly opposed to seriality." Such groups are initially unstructured. The members are drawn together because of the need to not be alone. They share a common perspective and a common desire to be joined, or fused, in a common purpose. Out of fused groups emerge "pledged groups"

(Sartre, 1960/1976: 829). Pledged groups are organized around an agreed-upon distribution of rights and duties enforced by a pledge. Such groups are structured by a "Third Party" (see following discussion). The A.A. group is a pledged group organized around the Twelve Steps and the Twelve Traditions.

Institutional structures may emerge out of pledged groups, and indeed this has been the case with A.A. That is, an overall institutional structure, bound together through the "Twelve Concepts for World Service" written by Wilson, and the A.A. Service Manual (A.A., 1983-1984) organizes the workings of A.A. groups internationally.

The pledge is a historical act that connects each member to A.A.'s collective history, while it secures a biographical commitment on the part of the member. It is a pledge that works against group divisiveness, for it unifies all members against taking a stand on politics, organizations, religious sects, denominations, or institutions and causes. It becomes, as Sartre (1960/1976: 419) argues, both a mediated reciprocity and a practical device that directs members to concrete action within the group and within their individual lives. It forges group membership on the part of each individual while constituting the grounds upon which collective group membership is based.

As mediated reciprocity, the pledge seals a bond between all group members. It makes all of them equally accessible to the demands and commitments the pledge entails. A.A.'s "Slogan of Responsibility"—which reads, "I am responsible when anyone, anywhere, reaches out for help. I want the hand of A.A. always to be there. And for that I am responsible"—speaks directly to this mediated reciprocity that each member assumes when the pledge is taken. The pledge confirms a commitment to the A.A. community. It makes every member available to any other A.A. member for purposes of interaction regarding A.A.'s stated purpose.

When the member walks through the doors of an A.A. meeting, he or she also embodies the Third Tradition, which is an extension of A.A.'s basic purpose. That tradition reads, as noted previously, "The only requirement for A.A. membership is a desire to stop drinking." By entering an A.A. meeting the member announces the fact that she does not want to drink today and that is why she is present at the meeting. It is irrelevant to the A.A. members present that she may not know that this is what her actions mean, for they know what it means to them. Her presence announces a commitment, if only transitory and even inauthentic and insincere, to the identity of alcoholic and to A.A.'s pledge (see Stone, 1962, on identity and placement).

The A.A. group is unified through a duality of third parties. A third party is understood as an individual (or concept) who (or that) "unifies a group by observing or commanding it" (Sartre, 1960/1976: 830). The collective history of A.A., including the Steps and the Traditions, becomes a third party that guides and directs group conduct. This history is also realized most concretely through the lives of recovery experienced by the cofounders, Wilson and Smith. Because every A.A. group has old-timers, or their versions of Wilson and Smith, the history of how recovery may be accomplished is present in every group. But above Wilson and Smith stands the "higher power" they directed every member to find. This "higher power," or "God as we understand Him," is the most powerful missing Third Party that organizes and commands A.A. group interaction. But that missing third is present in every member. Hence, this absence is a presence (Derrida, 1973) that is realized interactionally as each member invokes his or her under- standing of the "higher power." This absence, whose presence makes a *difference* (Derrida, 1973: 145), simultaneously externalizes the group while it is internalized in the lives, actions, and words of each member.

The "Third," in the form of the generalized pledge (to sobriety, A.A., and the higher power), moves at three levels within the A.A. group. First, it joins members to one another in the form of dyadic and triadic social relationships. Second, it permits each individual to have a relationship between self and the higher power, or the "Third" as the "Third" is understood. Finally, it operates at the level of the group as a momentary collectivity that exists through its "group conscience."

The pledge, then, in the form of the "Third" is inserted directly into the lives of each group member. Yet the group as a concept, embodied in the traditions, transcends the life or action of any given member. Therefore, the group resists *envelopment* (Sartre, 1960/1976) and embodiment in the cult of a single personality or charismatic leader.

At the same time, the daily or regular A.A. group works against seriality, or separateness, which would draw the individual member away from the group. For in order to maintain and sustain the pledge to sobriety and to the group, the individual must return to the group. For there, in the group, the individual can announce himself or herself as an alcoholic, and in so doing, become a part of the group once again. The daily meeting of the group reproduces for the individual and the group this experience. This solidifies the member's commitment to the pledge, to the group, and to himself or herself.

The pledge, then, mediates interactions between group members. It forms the line of action along which reciprocated group interaction flows. The A.A. group thus becomes a lever for group and individual history. Because the reality of the group lies in individual action, the group must be reconstituted as a collectivity each time its members come together. This is accomplished, as I shall show below, through the A.A. readings that structure the beginning of every A.A. meeting. The group must recreate an idea of itself each time its members assemble for a meeting. It does this by forming itself out of what it is not, and what it is not is a seriality of unrelated individuals. The group, then, externalizes itself as a "thing in itself," with separate status in the world. In so doing, it becomes an externalized-internalized force in the life of each member. At the same time it assumes its own history, and becomes a structure in its own right.

A.A. Tradition

In this dialectical duality of third parties (The "higher power," A.A. history, the pledge, the presence and absence of alcohol) the A.A. group fuses individual and joint action into a shared field of experience that becomes an "A.A. group having a meeting." This interrelationship between group and individual action and purpose is succinctly stated in A.A.'s First and Fifth Traditions, which respectively state: "Our common welfare should come first; personal recovery depends upon A.A. unity;" and "Each group has but one primary purpose—to carry its message to the alcoholic who still suffers." These two traditions are mediated by the Second Tradition, which states: "For our group purpose there is but one ultimate authority—a loving God as He may express Himself in our group conscience. Our leaders are but trusted servants; they do not govern."

The Second Tradition thus positions God, or the higher power, above and within every group. Group conscience, or the will of the group membership, is seen as embodying the ultimate authority of God. Because personal recovery depends on A.A. unity (Tradition One), each individual becomes an embodiment of the group. Each member's conception of God is thus mediated through the common welfare of the group, which in turn becomes a collective sense of God and group purpose, which is also individual purpose.

Group Conscience

Group conscience is a key to the working of the group. It is evidenced in the following interactions. The setting is as follows. A member with two years sobriety from a western city has assumed the chairmanship of one of the oldest A.A. meetings in the community. This meeting has a core of members with the longest sobriety in the community (average of 14 years). The chair makes the following motions:

> I would like to have a group conscience on changing this meeting into two groups on Wednesday. We're too big for one group. I would like to also move that we not read from the *24 Hour a Day* book because that's not A.A. I also propose that we just read "How It Works" and not the Traditions. Do I have a second?

A silence of five minutes followed in which no member (25 present) spoke. Then an old-timer of 16 years spoke:

> I helped start this meeting. As long as I come here I want everything read. That's part of how I got and how I stay sober. I vote no.

A second old-timer spoke:

> I'm with B, but I've only been here five years. But in Ohio we read everything. I don't think we should change. I like tradition.

A third old-timer spoke:

> I'm with G. I vote no. We can set here all night and have a group conscience. But I came here to have a meeting and stay sober. Let's have a meeting [field conversation, as reported, December 27, 1982].

A group conscience was taken and no one seconded the Chair's motion. His motion failed for a lack of a second. The meeting was held. Three weeks later the "Chair" made an amend to the group, speaking of his attempt to govern the group and asking for the group's forgiveness.

In this extended example, group conscience was at work. It worked through the silence of the group and through the talk of the three old-timers. In a collective sense the group—through the old-timers—asserted its collective history and took a stand on change. When the third speaker announced his primary purpose, which was to stay sober and have a meeting, he spoke to A.A.'s Fifth Tradition, and thereby joined the group conscience around a tradition that all members were committed to. In short, he announced for the group what A.A.'s primary purpose was.

THE A.A. GROUP AT WORK: THE MEETING

The "group conscience" is, as just indicated, a key to the working of the A.A. group. Infrequently invoked in an explicit fashion, the group conscience reveals how the group is simultaneously greater than its members, while being only what its members give to it.

It is now necessary to indicate how an A.A. group works. This requires an analysis of the A.A. meeting, which will involve a discussion of group names, meeting times, types of meetings, and A.A. ritual. There are two types of A.A. meetings: open and closed (see Denzin, 1986a: chap. 1). The *open meeting* is open to any individual who has an interest in alcoholism. A *closed A.A. meeting* is attended only by individuals who call themselves alcoholics and have a desire to stop drinking. In a closed meeting last names may be revealed and topics that would not be discussed in the presence of nonalcoholics may be talked about (see Maxwell, 1984: 9-10). *Speaker meetings* involve an A.A. member telling his or her story. *Lead meetings* involve a speaker talking for about 15 minutes on a topic, which is then turned over to the group.

Groups exist in and through their meetings; hence, to study an A.A. meeting is to study the A.A. group. However, groups exist over and above the meetings that they hold, for group members have interactions that occur outside the boundaries of meetings. (See Goffman, 1961: 9-11, for a distinction between groups and encounters or gatherings. In this context an A.A. meeting is a multifocused encounter, organized in terms of the sequential speaking of each member.) Groups are registered in the Annual A.A. Directory of Groups. This recording of the group's existence lists its name, and the names and telephone numbers of two A.A. members who may be contacted concerning the meetings of the group. The two A.A. members whose names are listed are typically the Group's Service Representative (GSR) and its secretary-treasurer, or alternative GSR. These two representatives of the group are nominated and elected through the group conscience. They typically represent members who have displayed a commitment to the group and its meetings. (See A.A., 1983-1984: 34-37, for a discussion of the functions of the GSR.)

Group names may take any form, drawing, for example, on A.A. slogans such as the "Day at a Time Group," the "Serenity Group," or the "Goodwill Open Discussion Group." On the other hand, the group may take its name from the address where it meets, calling itself, for example, "The Oak Street Group," the "Downtown Group," or the "Campus Group." The group may use the name of the day that it meets as its name, for example, "The Tuesday Night Group." Local A.A. knowledge within a community may connect the name of a group with its meeting place, for example, the "Tuesday Night Group at the Treatment Center." Special interest groups (women, gay, nonsmokers, Latino) may take their name from this special interest (such as the Tuesday Night Women's Group).

By assuming a special name the group identifies itself and its membership and locates itself within the universe of A.A. meetings that exist within the local A.A. community. Each group is, then, an autonomous structure within the A.A. social structure. Each group is financially independent and financially self-supporting, depending for its existence on the contributions its members make at its meetings. A contribution of one dollar or less is an expectation within the A.A. meeting structure. In order to secure this contribution a basket is passed during each meeting. These contributions go to pay the group's rent— which is often to a church—to buy the group's literature, and to pay for the purchase of coffee the group serves at every meeting. The presence of coffee and a coffee pot, along with a multitude of ashtrays for cigarette smokers, a table with chairs, A.A. slogans, and an address of a church, tell any A.A. member that he or she has found the site of an A.A. meeting. These are the universal symbols of an A.A. meeting.

Annually, semiannually, or quarterly, each group makes payments to the New York offices of A.A., to its district office, and to the local intergroup that it may belong to. A suggested ratio of 60%-30%-10% operates. After the group has paid all of its local expenses, if group conscience agrees, 30% of its funds are sent to New York, 10% are sent to its district, and 60% to its intergroup.

Although groups may have meetings at any time of the day or night, the universal starting time of all evening A.A. meetings is 8:00 p.m. The expected duration of an A.A. meeting is one hour, although meetings may extend beyond one hour. In some cities of the United States meetings may last two hours as a normal expectation. The size of an A.A. meeting may range from two members to over 50, although meetings of over 50 typically break up into smaller groups of 10 or fewer members. Members typically sit so that they are in face-to-face contact with one another, although in large meetings this may not be possible.

Within A.A. the terms *meeting* and *group* are used nearly interchangeably. Thus, members speak of "The Monday Night Group," or "The Monday Night Meeting," and in such usage convey the same information—that is, there was a meeting of the Monday Night Group. However, the above-mentioned differences between a group and its meetings must be kept in mind. Moreover, when a group dies it is because it stops having meetings. A group stops having meetings because members stop coming. Hence, the three key elements in a group's life are members, meetings, and the group name. No one of these terms can stand alone.

The Structures of an A.A. Meeting

I turn now to the actual structure of an A.A. meeting. The following is the format used for closed meetings by a group named the "Church Street Group." This group has daily noon meetings (12:00-1:00). The average size of its meetings is 15 members. This group has been in existence for two years, although its members are drawn from an earlier group that had existed for four years. Although the membership at any meeting changes, a core of five members is regularly present. Hence, the group draws from the entire A.A. community for any one of its daily meetings. The format the group uses borrows from the Al-Anon Program for its closing. The original outline for the meeting was brought to this community by a member who had acquired it in Ohio in 1979. It had previously been used as the format for another group and its meetings.

It contains the following elements: (1) salutation by chairperson, announcing himself or herself as an alcoholic and welcoming all members to the meeting; (2) a moment of silence followed by the "Serenity Prayer"; (3) a reading of A.A.'s "preamble" (see Glossary); (4) a reading of "How It Works" from A.A.'s *Big Book*, which contains A.A.'s Twelve Steps; (5) a reading of the Twelve Traditions of A.A.; (6) a reading of the "Thought for the Day" (Hazelden Foundation, 1956); (7) a short greeting to all new members; (8) a call for anniversaries and A.A. birthdays; (9) a call for announcements concerning group and A.A. business; (10) a call for a topic; (11) discussion, during which time each member of the group speaks, if he or she desires to; (12) closing remarks, including a call for seconds, asking if members wish to speak again; and (13) closing with the Lord's Prayer.

As can be seen there are 13 moments in the A.A. meeting, which range from the chairperson's introduction to reading of the Twelve Traditions and the "Thought for the Day," which is taken from a Hazelden publication, and which contains a reading for each day of the year. New members are asked to introduce themselves by their first name only, if they choose. If a member has a birthday of one year or more, a medallion will be given and often a birthday cake, with the number of candles representing years of sobriety, will be presented and eaten by the group after the meeing. Sobriety days of 30- and 90-day intervals are also marked by the giving of medallions, as are six months, nine months, and then one year.

If a newcomer to A.A. is present at the meeting, and if it is that person's first A.A. meeting, the group will by tradition discuss the First Step (see Denzin, 1986a: chap. 7). This will involve each member briefly telling the story of how he or she got to A.A. in the first place. These brief life stories (Thune, 1977: 79-88) recreate a shared past that the new member can enter into.

If the First Step is not the topic of discussion, the Chair may suggest the thought for the day. Or a member may come forth with a topic, such as depression, loneliness, resentment, anger, fear, the desire to drink, overconfidence, family, work, anonymity, gratitude, or the holidays and staying sober. Once a topic is selected, the Chair may say: "O.K., let's talk about resentment. Who would like to start?" The Chair then either calls on someone or a person volunteers to begin speaking. Each member at the meeting speaks in turn, usually for one to three minutes, depending on the size of the meeting and the member.

The following is an account of a closed meeting in which the topic of discussion was the Twelfth Step. The Chair of the meeting was Cl. I offer the interaction of that meeting as an instance of an A.A. group in action.

Members

Cl	Chair; 36-year-old male graduate student, 9½ years sobriety; divorced, one child.
N	42-year-old male professor, 1½ years sobriety; married.
Ws	72-year-old male, retired, 8 years sobriety; married.
Dk	61 years old, architect, 1 year sobriety; married.
Dn	27-year-old college senior, 3 years sobriety; single.
Je	37 years old, electronics technician, 2 years sobriety; married.
Khy	graduate student of education, 1½ years sobriety; divorced, one child.
Dr	33 years old, secretary, 2 months sobriety, in program 12 years; single.
Sh	45 years old, grocery-store clerk, 3 months sobriety, in program 5 months; married, four children.
Jn	48 years old, sales clerk, 6 months sobriety; married, children.
Jl	37 years old, gift shop clerk, 7½ years sobriety; divorced, two children.
Tn	41 years old, master craftsman, 2 years sobriety, in program 5 years; married, two children.

Dv   33 years old, supervisor, 6 months sobriety, slip last week; married.

Topic: Twelve Stepping

Cl: Does anyone have any problems or topics for discussion?

Tn: I do. Twelve Stepping. I have a problem. I got a neighbor who is fighting this thing. I've talked to him several times. Yesterday I went over and I gave it to him straight. I said he couldn't fight this by himself. He needed help. Either a treatment center, a psychiatrist, a minister and religion, or A.A. I got overinvolved. I know in my guts that I let my emotional self get too far involved. I'd like to hear your thoughts on this.

Ws: I'm Ws. I'm an alcoholic. I wasn't going to speak today. Eight years ago today they took me to the fifth floor. Not the second, not the third, but straight to the fifth. The floor for the crazies. I was Twelve Stepped while I was there. You had a successful Twelve Step, Tn. You came back sober. You carried the message.

Dk: I'm Dk. I'm an alcoholic. I wasn't going to say anything today. I'm glad to be here. It's a good environment. I think you should be complimented, Tn. You're carrying out the program. You're practicing all the steps. I hope I can do that someday.

Khy: I'm Khy. I'm an alcoholic. I don't know what got me sober. It was many different things. It had to be a sum that was greater than its parts. It was 10% this part, 20% this part. It was things I did and didn't do. I know that it finally worked and it worked when I was ready. I don't know how it worked. I don't think it is any specific thing we do.

Cl: I'm Cl. I'm an alcoholic. Two-and-a-half months ago my father killed himself. The day of the night before he killed himself I felt that something was wrong. I was at the club (city) and I called the man who got me into A.A. I said, do you need a meeting tonight? He said that he did. He came over and he told me, "I don't know if I should tell you this but 10 years ago I took your father to some A.A. meetings." That made me feel good because I knew there was nothing I could do for my Dad.

Dv: I'm Dv. I'm an alcoholic. I don't know. I'm working with someone right now. He's sober, sober, then drunk, drunk, then sober, then drunk. I don't know what works. I know I was successfully Twelve Stepped. I hope to be able to do that someday. Thank you, I'm glad to be here today.

Je: I'm Je, I'm an alcoholic. I don't know either. I remember how it was— sober, sober, drunk, drunk, I'd tear everything all up and then just want to hide hoping that if I did nothing it would all go away. But then I'd get drunk again, and it would start all over. It was hell. There are a couple of old-timers with over 30 years. I learn from them. They just sit back and wait. But they'd go out at 3:00 in the morning to help somebody. I got too emotional. I want them to be helped now. To cut out this nonsense. I see one fellow. He came for a while. Now he and the wife go to church. I see him in the grocery store. He looks like hell. He's shaking, he turns his head the other way. He's probably afraid I'll say something to him. I never do 'cause I don't want to scare him off. Maybe he'll get it someday. Thank you, I'm glad to be here and to be sober today.

N: I'm N. I'm an alcoholic. I'm glad to be here today. I don't know. It's a mystery. There's a fellow in treatment right now. I Twelve Stepped him a year ago. I did it all wrong. You're s'posed to separate the wife and the husband. That's what the *Big Book* says. Hell, she was all over him. Interrupting, talking all the time. How he had such a problem. How he was an alcoholic. They'd call me. She'd get on the extension phone and they'd both talk. She wouldn't give him a chance. She's an alcoholic, too. I did it all wrong and today he's in treatment and thanked me for the Twelve Step call a year ago. I don't know. It's a mystery [laughter throughout group].

Dv: I'm Dv. I'm an alcoholic. I don't know. Last weekend I Twelve Stepped my mother. I had a bottle of Usher's Green Label this far from my mouth [holds hand in the shape of a cupped fist next to his mouth]. I finally went to a meeting, took a piece of every bit of literature they had, took them home and put them on the kitchen table and left. It'll just keep up until something happens. My mom's only happy when she's into her wine. Maybe my dad will go to Al-Anon. Thank you. I'm glad to be here and to be sober. I'm glad I didn't have to be Twelve Stepped today.

Jl: I'm Jl. I'm an alcoholic. I don't know. I'm not very good. I called A.A. the first time and went the next night. Nobody even came and got me. Then I complained for the next two years. Before I go on Twelve Step calls I read "How It Works" in the *Big Book*. I'm usually 45 minutes late! Where I work, the gal's boyfriend is a drunk. He's afraid to look at me. They know I'm a recovered alcoholic. The guys thinks I'll turn him in to the authorities, whoever they are! I know my best effort in life got me into A.A. I'm glad to be here and to be sober.

Jn: I'm Jn. I'm an alcoholic. My only advice to Tn is to be patient. It takes time. It may take several days for everything you said to sink in. Thank you.

Dt: I'm Dt. I'm an alcoholic. I'm just glad to be sober and be here today. Thank you, Cl.

Sh: I'm Sh. I'm an alcoholic. I'm like N. When I was Twelve Stepped the whole family was there. My son (I have three kids) sat so close to me. I don't think he had ever sat that close, since he was a little boy and could sit on my lap. I went for two months for my family. Then I slipped for five weeks and then I came back for myself. I'm glad to be here and to be sober today. I hope I can help somebody someday like I was helped.

Cl to Group: Are there any other comments? If not, we'll close [Group stands, holds hands, and says the Lord's Prayer in unison].

The meeting was over at 1:05. All members had spoken. It was a normal, ordinary A.A. meeting of the noon group.

The Prose of the Group

From this record of a group meeting I wish to extract the following points. First, it will be noted that each member speaks "on topic," addressing in every instance A.A.'s Twelfth Step. However, only a specific part of the Twelfth Step was discussed—carrying the message. Second, the discourse that is produced reflects back upon itself. Member after member turns to the original topic announced by Tn, and then adds their own experience of either being Twelve Stepped, or having done a Twelfth Step. Third, as each member personalizes the topic, a part of their biography is shared with the other group members, that is, reading the *Big Book*. Fourth, the "mystery" of sobriety and of A.A. is spoken to. No member claims to know how he or she got sober. Fifth, alcoholics who are still drinking are brought into the meeting. The presence of these absent others serves to remind each member of how it was when they were still drinking. Sixth, humor emerges as problems in speaking to alcoholics who are still drinking are discussed. Seventh, each member evidences gratitude for being sober, and conveys a sense of thanks to the others for being present at the meeting. Eighth, a successful Twelve Step is defined for the group. If you carry the message and return sober you have been successful. This point is critical, for when the A.A. member enters the "alcoholic situation" of a person who asks for help, alcohol is often present. If the member is uncertain of his or her sobriety, the desire to drink may return and the member may in fact drink on the Twelve Step call, in which case the group may lose a member to active alcoholism, when the intent of the Twelve Step call was to help another alcoholic.

These eight points must be positioned within what I call the "prose of the A.A. group." This prose is an individual and collective production that speaks the language of ordinary people woven through the understandings of A.A. and recovery. It is proselike in structure, coming forth in full sentences, and in logical and illogical sequences. Each utterance is framed within the shared interpretive structures of Alcoholics Anonymous. In each member's talk, thoughtful, meaningful, biographically specific information is produced and shared. Taken for granted (Garfinkel, 1967) meanings are glossed over (Twelve Stepping, crazies, message, treatment, alcoholic), as each member speaks to the topic at hand. A reaching back into the member's biography is evidenced as talk is produced.

These are not the utterances of the workplace, the home, the telephone, the letter, the hospital emergency room, the psychiatrist's office, or group therapy (see Grimshaw, 1981: 222-226; Schenkein, 1978;

for reviews of these other forms of talk, and Goffman, 1981). These utterances are embedded in the sequential talk of A.A. members doing an A.A. meeting. The sequentiality, the biographical detail, the hovering presence of alcohol as an organizing "Third Party," and the shared constraints of A.A. tradition and ritual serve to produce a structure of "understanding" discourse that is perhaps unique to A.A. meetings. The "talk" and the "prose" of A.A. is sober talk. It is poetic, poignant, nuanced by the dialects, twangs, accents, and speaking idiosyncracies of each member. It is a prose that is at once personal and collective; as each member speaks for herself, she speaks to the group as a collectivity. But because no member speaks for A.A., the talk that is shared is "self-talk" (Goffman, 1981). By offering her prose to the group, each member thus contributes to a group discourse that is greater than the sum of its spoken parts. The totality of these parts gives a poetic and narrative unity to the group's meeting. As such, a historical continuity in the group's life is produced. This continuity derives from the contributions of each member.

A.A. Talk

A social semantics (Grimshaw, 1981: 222) of A.A. talk, involving both conversational analysis (Cicourel, 1981; Schegloff et al., 1977; Schenkein, 1978) and discourse analysis (Labov and Fanshel, 1977) suggests that this form of talk occurs within both restricted and elaborated linguistic codes (Bernstein, 1971), in which the unit of meaning is the speech event (Hymes, 1974: 52-53), not the reciprocated speech act (Searle, 1970) of ordinary conversation. As each A.A. member obtains his or her turn in the speaking event that is the meeting, an emotional footing (Denzin, 1984a: 265; Goffman, 1981: 124) is established. This footing aligns the speaker with the topic at hand (in the previous account, the Twelfth Step) and permits a projection of self in terms of the speaker's own experiences with the topic. Code switching into an emotional vocabulary that is personal is immediately evident in each speaker's talk. As the speaker draws upon personal history in the elaboration of his or her talk, the et cetera clause (Cicourel, 1974; Garfinkel, 1967) is employed. That is, each speaker is permitted to elaborate on the topic at hand, to introduce new topics, to adumbrate a topic, and to bring seemingly unrelated topics under the rubric of the main topic (e.g., Cl's mention of his father's death).

The rule-governed structure of A.A. meeting talk does not admit of easy analysis within the format of conversational analysis (Schegloff et al., 1977). That is, speech does not occur within easily analyzable adjacency pairs, nor are there problematics concerning how conversations are begun, carried on, and ended. Rather, when a speaker's turn is given, he or she will always begin with the "My name is ___ and I'm an alcoholic" introduction to the group. Once launched into his or her turn, each speaker then proceeds to relate a story or semi-story regarding the topic at hand, or to simply acknowledge the topic and then give thanks to the group for being present. The ending of each speaker's talking turn is typically signalled by thanks being given to the chair and an utterance concerning gratitude for being sober today. Hence this talk, although having rule-governed openings and closings, is filled out by middles that are wholly at the speaker's discretion. Nothing in the preceding talk of another member need by keyed upon, elaborated, or spoken to, although it often is.

Member talk, then, is primarily dialogic. That is, it entails a dialogue with self and with the A.A. group. This dialogue, which can become a monologue when the speaker only speaks to himself or herself, is dialectical and emergent. It is governed by the string of associations the topic at hand triggers in the biographical memory (pre- and post-A.A.) of the speaker. If the member has related a story or an account before, he or she will make an apology for repeating the story. A justification for the repetition will, however, be given—that there are members present who have not heard it before.

The dialogic structure of the member's talk does not involve a reciprocated conversation with another member; rather, the member speaks to the group, as in a monologue. However, a monologue is not produced, for the collectivity is addressed. Hence, what is given is a one-way dialogue that dialectically turns back on itself. Self-referential in structure, the member's talk thus incorporates the attitude of the group as the member speaks to the topic at hand.

Face-Work and Emotion

Face-work and impression management (Goffman, 1967) are not integral to the member's talk. As with the talk of treatment, which stressed emotionality and the "exposure of self" in interaction, A.A. talk similarly places a value on, and incorporates into its discourse, talk that in ordinary conversation would be defined as displaying a "loss of face." Crying, the revelation of deviance while under the influence of alcohol, discussions of bouts of insanity, mentions of crippling fears or depressions, and talk of failures in marriages and social relationships are all sanctioned and accepted within the talk of A.A. meetings. Positive face-work and the maintenance of face, or self, through the usual means of interactional social control (Grimshaw, 1981: 225) are not problematics in an A.A. meeting, as they apparently are in other areas of everyday social life (Goffman, 1974). Indeed, shows of emotionality and the apparent loss of face are valued and treated with compassion and care within the A.A. meeting.

These features are most evident when a member reveals a "slip" to the group, for at one level a "slip" could be regarded as a loss of face. But within A.A., members are praised for speaking of their "slips," for to do so indicates that the member reaffirms his or her desire to be a member of A.A. Consider the following account. The speaker is 37 years old. He had been sober for three months and then drank for four days. As he speaks, his hands shake, his face is unshaven and alcohol can still be smelled on his breath. He is crying as he talks:

> I'm back here because this is where I need to be. Always before I would wait until I was healthy again. I didn't want anyone to know that I had been drinking. My false pride would keep me away, even after I drank. I let things pile up in my head. Resentments, fears, anxieties, little things and big things. Then I decided that a drink would be all right. I started with one, then I got a bottle and then another bottle, and then another. I was afraid to stop. I couldn't bear the D.T.s and the dreams. But I made it through last night. I want to get better (breaks down crying again). I don't know what's wrong with me. I need help, God I need help [field conversation, November 30, 1985].

Each member who spoke after this individual thanked him for coming back. A box of tissues was passed to him as he cried. Members offered him rides to other meetings. His show of emotion was not taken, then, as a sign of the loss of face.

The following account speaks to another instance when face is not lost when a member shows emotion. The speaker is a valued member of the group. He has been sober over 10 years. He too cries as he begins speaking:

> I don't know what to do. Decided I had to bring it to you people. My 15-year-old daughter told me and mom that she's pregnant. Told us last night. I ordered her to her room and didn't speak to her 'til this morning. I could kill her and him. Christ, I don't know what to do. Never expected this to happen. I sure as hell ain't goin to drink 'bout it. That's for damned sure. But what in the fuck are we s'posed to do? [field conversation, December 2, 1985]

Here the member breaks down over a family crisis. Each of the 16 A.A. members at the group thanked him for sharing his problem and each offered advice, based on personal experience. Two female members of the group, who were social workers, shared their telephone numbers with him and offered family planning assistance.

These self-accounts speak to the above argument that within A.A., as in treatment, shows of emotion are valued and not taken as losses of face. An additional point may be made. The speakers in these accounts are male. The masculine show of emotion in American male culture is a proscribed, not a prescribed social act (see Hochschild, 1983). To be emotional is to be weak and feminine. A.A. inverts this cultural proscription.

This brief analysis of A.A. talk suggests, with Hymes (1974), that the speech event, not the sequential speech act, is the primary unit of analysis. A detailed ethnography of A.A. communication would reveal how each member builds a biography out of the speech events he or she produces within a sequence or network of A.A. meetings. That is, the member produces a personal oral history of recovery that is told each time he or she takes a turn at speaking at an A.A. meeting.

Only when the member tells his or her story to an open meeting will all the details of this personal history be drawn together into a single narrative account. Up until that time—which may never occur—primarily all that other A.A. members will learn of the speaker will be what he or she chooses to disclose when a turn to talk comes at an A.A. meeting. The rules that govern these self-disclosures by the speaker may be unconscious, or deeply buried within the member's biography.

The A.A. group exists, then, in and through a shared oral tradition that is structured by the rituals of Alcoholics Anonymous. This oral tradition is, as just indicated, personal and collective, but always given meaning within the overall interpretive system of Alcoholics Anonymous. In order for the oral tradition to exist, groups must have meetings. In order for groups to have meetings, they must have members. But there can not be members without groups for members to belong to. Hence, a dialectic of the personal and the group is woven through every structure of A.A. The meeting, then, is the interactional site for A.A. in action.

It is in the meeting, as the above transcripts reveal, that the alcoholic subject is transformed into an A.A. member who is recovering from alcoholism. By announcing himself or herself as an alcoholic, each member makes his or her history of recovery available for others to draw upon. By sharing this history of recovery, each member becomes part of a group that is recovering together. This can only be accomplished in and through the talk of each member. Talk, then, is the means to recovery. That talk, proselike in structure, autobiographical in nature, anchors the personal history of each member in the collective and shared history of the A.A. group. In this way the member's personal life becomes a part of the shared, group consciousness. The A.A. group becomes a public structure of private lives. I turn now to A.A. ritual, beginning with a brief discussion of ritual and group life.

Ritual and Oral History

Rituals are conventionalized joint activities, given to ceremony, endowed with special emotion and often sacred meaning (see Denzin, 1984d: 246-247). Performed around a clearly defined set of social objects, or lines of action, rituals, when performed, confer upon their participants a special sense of the sacred. The settings in which rituals are performed are given special, interactional meaning, and may be termed *ritual settings*. Ritual performances legitimize the selves of the ritual performers, and give a sense of solidarity and community to the group members who witness or participate in their performance. Permitting of few variations, rituals are subject to the pressures of interactional normalization. When performed, the ritual dramatically recreates for the group its central and basic worldview. Within the "frame" of ritual, group members act ritualistically, thereby connecting themselves to their collective past. In the same motion, they make a purchase on the future, for the ritual act secures a movement into the future that will be guided by the ritual in question.

Durkheim (1912) and Goffman (1971) have suggested that rituals are positive and negative. Malinowski (1913/1962), Radcliffe-Brown (1922), and Warner (1962) have suggested that rituals may be performed for purely magical, mystical, or religious reasons. That is, when performed, rituals are believed to give group members some control over the future or over the uncontrollable. At this level rituals provide a symbolic bridge between the person and the group, for by entering into the ritual the person is joined to the group through the ritual acts that are performed. Emotionally and symbolically, rituals, as Shils (1976) has argued, embody the central, core values of the group.

Interactionally, rituals symbolize the problematics of the group. At the heart of any organized group exists a set of rituals that, when communicated to the newcomer, serve to draw him or her into the inner fabric of the group. Rituals, then, stand at the intersection of individuals, societies, and groups (see Denzin, 1984e: 246-247).

A.A. ritual, enacted through the meeting, yet permanently recorded in the texts and readings of A.A., may be analyzed in terms of these dimensions. I shall take up the key A.A. rituals in turn, beginning with the readings that structure an A.A. meeting.

The reading of the A.A. "Preamble," "How It Works," the Twelve Traditions, and the "Thought for the Day," brings into every A.A. meeting the collective history of Alcoholics Anonymous. Although many groups do not read "The Thought for the Day" or "The Traditions" or all of "How It Works," the A.A. Preamble is always read. These A.A. readings are endowed with solemn ceremony. Members listen quietly as they are read. Each reading references a problematic in the A.A. program and a problematic in the member's own program. When the meeting is called to order by the Chair the ritual self of being an A.A. member at the meeting is brought into existence. From this moment until the last words of the Lord's Prayer, the members are within the "frame" of an A.A. meeting. This becomes a sacred moment in their day, as attending Mass might be for another individual. The A.A. readings permit few variations. They are read in order, exactly as they were read at the last meeting. Wherever an A.A. member goes these readings will be presented in the same sequence, with the same words. In this sense A.A. ritual admits of no variations.

These readings embody the A.A. worldview. By listening to them being read the member becomes a part of A.A.'s oral history. Furthermore, by hearing these readings read out loud the member obtains some measure of protection against taking a drink today. In this way the A.A. rituals serve as mechanisms for ensuring sobriety in a world that is regarded as uncontrollable and unmanageable. Because they focus explicitly on the problematics of A.A.—sobriety and its maintenance—these ritual readings keep A.A.'s primary purpose constantly in front of the member.

These rituals are positive, joining rituals. They bring members into one another's presence, providing a bridge between the loneliness of alcoholism and the community of A.A. recovery. By allowing the newcomer to read, A.A. invites that member to move more deeply into the inner structures of the fellowship. In this way newcomers are incorporated into group life.

The "talking" rituals of the A.A. meeting are meant to ensure that each member has a chance to speak. Interruptions are infrequent. Each member is allowed to speak as long as he or she desires, and usually on any topic. The talk is structured by turn taking, and ritualistically each member knows that when it is his or her turn to speak, the floor will be granted. One's place in the speech event that is an A.A. meeting is determined in one of three ways, depending on the chair's choice of rules. From the Chair, a left-to-right or right-to-left order of seating arrangement can be employed. That is, the chair speaks, then turns to the person immediately to either his or her left or right, and asks that person if he or she would like to speak. After that person speaks, the person immediately next to them speaks, and so on, until everyone around the table has spoken. Each member knows, then, when they will be called upon to speak. It is during this time of waiting to talk that each member organizes the "speech" that will be made.

If the counterclockwise or clockwise method of speaker designation is not employed, the other mode of speaker selection—common in the community I studied—is to turn the meeting over to the group and have members select who will speak next. This method of member designation involves the Chair asking a person to begin the meeting, and then asking that member to call on someone when they are done. In turn, the member who is called upon is asked to call on someone. In this manner the meeting runs itself without a Chair. The meeting concludes (as do all meetings), when all members have spoken and the Lord's Prayer is said in unison.

The talk that the member produces will contain references to the A.A. rituals, including the Steps and the Traditions. It may also contain humor and profanity. As the member speaks, he or she is accorded the full ritual status of "A.A. membership." In this sense, no member's talk is any more important than the talk of any other member. There is no ritual hierarchy between A.A. speakers, only a distinction between the person who is at his or her first meeting, and all other members. That is, A.A. ritualistically accords the newcomer the status of being the most important person in the room. This is because they are at the first meeting. This status, however, will soon wear off if the member becomes a regular in the group.

The "anniversary rituals" of A.A. were already discussed. The giving of medallions for continuous sobriety signals status passage moments within A.A.'s social structure. Length of sobriety thus becomes a ritual marker of commitment to A.A. and to the A.A. way of life. As sobriety lengthens the member grows into becoming an "old-timer" or "regular" in the A.A. group.

The "closing ritual" of the A.A. meetings centers around the saying of the Lord's Prayer. This is done by the group members standing, holding hands, and saying this prayer in unison. When the prayer is completed members often add "Keep coming back." This phrase, coupled with the A.A. handshake, which is the universal greeting when members enter one another's presence at an A.A. meeting, signals the continuity of A.A. fellowship.

A.A.'s rituals, then, are kept alive through the oral tradition of the A.A. meeting. The meeting place of the group, which is also given sacred, ritual, meaning, comes to symbolize the meaning of the group to its members. These meetings and their places join members simultaneously to the meeting, to the group, and to the fellowship of A.A. more broadly conceived. They do not embody all that A.A. is, but without them, what else A.A. *is* would not be possible. These rituals, then, transform the member into a "talking subject" who is learning and has learned how to speak to his or her experiences of recovery within the ritual structure A.A. provides.

CONCLUSIONS

Beginning with the original A.A. meeting between Wilson and Smith, I have presented the historical, textual, and interactional structures that A.A. rests upon. The several levels of A.A., which range from its historical texts to the network of meetings that exist in a single community, and extend to the international community of A.A. and to the New York offices, find their immediate meaning in the biography of the individual A.A. member who comes to find himself or herself as a recovering alcoholic within the A.A. meeting. Each A.A. meeting, like the members who make it up, is an universal singular, epitomizing in its structures, its talk, and its rituals all A.A. meetings that have occurred in the past or will occur in the future. The single-mindedness of purpose that underlies all of the structures of A.A. permits this historical continuity that joins the past with the present. A.A., at all its levels and in all its forms—personal, group, in texts, in oral histories, in its bureaucratic structures, in its rules, as a social movement, its rituals, and its traditions—is a unique social structure. Although none of the units or forms that make up the A.A. structure are themselves unique, the overall structure is.

The key to this uniqueness is alcoholic understanding and the shared experiences that A.A. draws upon. These experiences permit A.A. members to form social groups among strangers, yet to do so within a historical structure of understanding that makes no alcoholic a stranger to a recovering alcoholic. How this is accomplished has been the topic of this chapter.

The A.A. group stands in stark contrast to the primary groups studied by Cooley (1902/1956) and Schutz (1964: 106-119). The A.A.

group is a group of strangers who create a fellowship of interaction that is based on shared, common experiences that the broader culture and alcoholism have produced for each individual. Yet this community of strangers is often interpreted by the member as being family:

> I lost everything. Family, home, wives, kids, job, everything. Even my parents turned against me. I fought like hell to get it all back and it didn't work. They went off to be who they were and left me to find myself. I think they hated me. Lot of self-pity on my part. I finally found you people. Now you're my family. Wherever I go, you're there. Wherever I go. But I got me a "home group" back in L.A. and that's where my new permanent family is. Gives me everything I ever wanted and ever looked for. I feel like I'm needed again [field observation, as reported September 2, 1982; 47-year-old male, salesman, over three years sobriety].

This family that is found within A.A. envelopes the member within a noncompetitive collective structure that is larger than the member (Bateson, 1972a). Largely male based, this A.A. culture, and the "families" that it spawns, permits the creation of shared pasts, feelings of solidarity, and the sharing of common futures (Couch et al., 1986). These processes are, of course, at the center of all long-standing social groups, including families. In this sense A.A. universalizes the desire for "groupness" that lies within our culture (see Bellah et al., 1985).

In the next chapter I turn to "slips" and relapses. How the alcoholic produces and manages these events determines, in large measure, the shape and form recovery will take.

5

SLIPS AND RELAPSES

Why did I slip? I guess it's because I never surrendered fully to myself and accepted that I was an alcoholic. Oh, I knew I was an alcoholic, but I thought I could control alcohol. Finally somebody said to me, "Why can't you stay sober?" and it hit me, "Why can't I stay sober?" And then I decided, "Why not?" [field conversation, September 13, 1984, male, 55 years old, account executive].

Slips, there's no such thing as a slip. All my drunks were planned. I just wanted to drink, period! [field conversation, December 4, 1985, 35-year-old male, carpenter].

Slips, relapses, or the return to controlled and uncontrolled drinking are commonplace occurrences for alcoholics. Baekeland (1977: 388) observes that even if the alcoholic has received treatment for alcoholism "he is notoriously prone to relapse." Relapse is mostly likely to occur within the first year of treatment, often within six months (Baekeland, 1977: 388-389; Pattison et al., 1968: 611). It can be estimated that 7 of 10 alcoholics who are treated for alcoholism will in fact relapse (see Baekeland, 1977; Baekeland and Lundwall, 1977; Blane, 1977; Pattison et al., 1977; Pendery et al., 1982; Rubington, 1977). Whether they return to normal, controlled drinking is problematic (Pendery et al., 1982). Of the alcoholics who come to A.A. it has been estimated that 37% relapse within the first year (Leach and Norris, 1977: 489; Maxwell, 1984: 3-4).

In this chapter I examine the phenomenon of relapse, drawing my primary materials from the A.A. community I studied (1980-1985), which numbered over 300 regular members. Within that group there were over 20 members who regularly slipped and returned to A.A. meetings. It is these members that I study in this chapter. I also observed over 100 other members who slipped, or relapsed, almost immediately after leaving treatment. These individuals did not become part of the A.A. community I studied, hence their accounts provide only a background to the more intensive analysis I will offer.

In *The Alcoholic Self* (Denzin, 1986a: chap. 7) I offered a brief outline of a "situational theory" of slips and relapses. In this chapter I develop and further elaborate that interpretive structure. It is grounded (Glaser and Strauss, 1967a) in the case materials just referenced. It is my contention that recovery cannot be understood until relapse is placed within proper perspective. Relapse stands on the opposite side of recovery; indeed, it may negate a recovering career. However, relapse may be a necessary part of any alcoholic's recovery (Royce, 1981: 268-270). Hence, to study relapse is to study a basic facet, perhaps the central facet, of recovery.

My argument will proceed as follows. First, I will briefly review prior studies and theories of relapse, including those offered by social scientists and A.A. In this context I will introduce A.A.'s distinction between being dry, "dry drunks," "white knuckle sobriety," and "sobriety." A typology of slips will be offered. Second, I will present my situational interpretation of slips and relapses. I will discuss selected slips that were reported by the relapsing alcoholics in my study, distinguishing types of alcoholic identities and the slips associated with those identities. Third, and closely related to slips, are alcoholic drinking dreams. I shall examine these dreams as they relate to the alcoholic's attempts to remain sober. Fourth, I will conclude with a fully stated, grounded interpretation of slips and relapses.

PRIOR STUDIES AND THEORIES OF RELAPSE

Studies and theories of relapse fall into two basic categories: A.A.'s surveys and theories of slips (see A.A., 1967, 1975, 1976; Leach and Norris, 1977; Maxwell, 1984) and social science studies of relapse following treatment. I shall take up these categories in reverse order.

Social Science Findings

Within the sociological and psychological literature on relapse two major lines of research stand out. The first are the studies of Sobell and Sobell (1978), Sobell et al. (1980), and Pattison et al. (1977). These investigations, building on the findings of Davies (1962), argue that (1) alcoholism is a multidimensional, not a unidimensional, phenomenon, and (2) social drinking of a controlled nature is possible, even desirable for some alcoholics. Perhaps reflective of the fact that treatment, of any variety, has only modest success in producing continuous sobriety for any type of alcoholic, this literature attempts to build a multidimensional theory of alcoholism that integrates drinking for some alcoholics into its understanding of recovery. This literature does not offer a theory of relapse. It attempts to incorporate or redefine relapse within a broadened conception of normal, controlled social drinking. (See Pendery et al., 1982 and Denzin, 1986a: chap. 2 for a criticism of this literature and the approach it proposes.)

Rubington's Theory

The second major line of research and theorizing within the area of relapse can be found in the work of Earl Rubington (1977) on abstinence after participation in halfway houses.

Rubington (1977: 363), reviewing research on abstinence after participation in halfway houses, reports that on the average only 20% of exresidents are sober six months after discharge. Rubington lays the foundations for a theory of rehabilitation (recovery) as it occurs within halfway houses. He suggests the following explanation. (1) Membership in a halfway house creates strains and tensions concerning an adherence to group norms that requires sobriety. (2) The alcoholic accordingly must learn how to manage this strain and tension while submitting to the authority structures of the halfway house. (3) Two social communities, staff and residents, thus coexist within the same cultural setting. The main interest of staff is in maintaining their authority, whereas the main interest of residents is in reducing that authority. (4) Three social situations thus exist: those in which residents are in the company of one another, those that place residents in the company of staff only, and those that combine residents and staff. (5) Four social types emerge in the halfway house: mixers, who mediate between staff and residents, company men who take the staff point of view, regular guys who side with residents, and loners who give no sign of aligning with either staff or other residents. Four exresident social roles or types also emerge: alcoholism professionals who graduate from being residents in halfway houses to working in the field of rehabilitation, reformed drunks who lack membership in a group, abstainers who rejoin conventional society, and drunks who were intoxicated when they entered treatment and return to a drinking life after the halfway house. Rubington (1977: 374) predicts that mixers are likely to end up as alcoholism professionals, whereas company men will become reformed drunks, "regular guys" drunks, and loners abstainers.

Rubington's theory suggests that relapses are greatest for regular guys. This is so for several reasons. First there are always more regular guys in any halfway house. Second, regulars establish friendship with other regulars. Third, when relapses occur, they take two forms: paired and sequential. Paired-relapse occurs when two residents leave together and get drunk. In sequential relapse, one person relapses and then another "feels compelled to follow his example" (Rubington, 1977: 377).

Staff, Rubington (1977: 378) says, may seek to intervene and stop these relapse chains. They may counsel residents to take preventive action. However, Rubington argues that regular guys, by virtue of how they have adapted to the halfway house culture, are reluctant to talk about their desires to return to drinking; indeed, they may have little practice in doing so. They may also feel that it is out of character to speak of such matters. Thus, a wall is built upon between regular guys and staff, resignation sets in, and the alcoholic gives in to the inevitable, which is to drink.

Rubington's formulations have three important implications. First, they suggest that recovery and relapse are group phenomena that are embedded in social contexts. These contexts may produce relapse when recovery is intended. Second, they may be applied to treatment centers. Although the short-term nature of treatment works against a well-developed structure of social identities that Rubington finds in halfway houses, mixers, company men, regular guys, and loners also emerge within treatment facilities. Similarly, the division between staff and residents that Rubington finds in halfway houses also appears in treatment centers. However, the intensive nature of the treatment experience works against a strong countercultural point of view that seems to be evident in halfway houses. To the extent that patients in treatment form friendships with fellow patients, and if these friendships extend after treatment, then the paired and sequential patterns of relapse that Rubington observes also seem to hold (see following discussion).

The third implication of Rubington's formulations applies to A.A. That is, within A.A., mixers, regular guys, loners, and company men also emerge. Company men, also called "*Big Book* Thumpers," take the official, organizational view of Alcoholics Anonymous. Loners attend meetings, but form few friendships or A.A. attachments. Regular guys form friendships within the A.A. fellowship. Mixers attach themselves to long-term A.A. members and attempt to bridge the gap between newcomers, themselves, and old-timers. Across these four social identities must be arrayed newcomers (or pigeons), old-timers, regulars, and "slippers," or persons who regularly attend A.A. and relapse. Consistent with Rubington's predictions, newcomers who were regular guys in treatment and who maintain friendships with other regular guys (who are also newcomers) tend to slip, or relapse more than loners, company men, and mixers. They tend to relapse in the paired and sequential fashion outlined by Rubington.

Rubington's work indicates how the institutions that are created to produce abstinence may in fact lay the conditions for relapse. I turn now to those studies and theories that deal with relapse within Alcoholics Anonymous.

Relapse in A.A.: Leach and Norris

Leach and Norris (1977) and Maxwell (1984) review the results of the 1968, 1971, and 1981 A.A. "sobriety surveys." Several critical findings emerge from these and other data. First, as previously indicated, 37% of A.A. members relapse within the first year. This is of course an important finding. It suggests that the socialization experiences that occur in treatment lack the power to keep the alcoholic sober for any length of time. Because 7 of 10 alcoholics who undergo treatment appear to return to drinking—whereas 7 to 10 alcoholics who go to A.A. regularly stay sober—the interactions that occur within A.A. appear to hold the key to sustained sobriety. Second, those members who relapse tend to (1) attend fewer A.A. meetings, as well as other A.A. functions; (2) be referred by sources other than self (such as family, employer, physician, courts, attorneys); and (3) keep returning to A.A. out of a desire for fellowship and long-term sobriety. Third, the longer a member is in A.A. and does not relapse, the greater the likelihood that he will remain sober for two years or more. Fourth, in order for the sobriety career to build and extend beyond three years, the member will maintain regular A.A. meeting attendance (three or more meetings a week) at least up to and beyond five years of sobriety. Fifth, after five years this attendance pattern at meetings will decline, but not stop. In short, sustained sobriety within A.A. requires lengthy and continuous involvement in the A.A. social structure. In the absence of that participation and involvement slips and relapses will occur, and they are most likely to occur within the first year of sobriety.

The Leach and Norris and Rudy Models

Leach and Norris (1977: 483-484) offer a nine-step model for becoming an abstinent A.A. member. These steps are (1) learning of the existence of A.A.; (2) perceiving A.A. as relevant to one's needs; (3) being referred to A.A.; (4) making personal contact with A.A.; (5) attending a closed A.A. meeting; (6) participating in other A.A. activities and internalizing the A.A. norms; (7) taking the last drink; (8) making a Twelve Step call; and (9) speaking at an A.A. meeting. Noting that not every abstinent member passes through these nine stages, and that "hitting bottom" should be added as a stage, Leach and Norris suggest that members who relapse after passing through these stages must go through the stages again, at least in some fashion.

Rudy (1986) has proposed a modification of the Leach and Norris work, inserting "hitting bottom" as the first stage in his six-stage model. His other five stages are (1) going to the first meeting; (2) making a commitment to A.A.; (3) accepting one's problem; (4) telling one's story, (5) and doing Twelve Step work. Rudy then distinguishes four types of alcoholic careers: (1) pure alcoholics, (2) convinced alcoholics, (3) converted alcoholics, and (4) tangential alcoholics. Pure alcoholics regard themselves as alcoholics before coming to A.A. Convinced alcoholics become convinced of their alcoholism after A.A. participation. Converted alcoholics come to A.A. believing they have a drinking problem and become converted to the A.A. point of view. Tangential alcoholics have alcoholic self-conceptions, but do not regard alcohol as being a major problem in their lives.

The Leach and Norris and Rudy models (see also Trice, 1966, 1957; Trice and Roman, 1970) have the benefits of specifying a stepwise, temporal projection of how one becomes an A.A. member and learns how to be abstinent. However, Rudy's model is primarily concerned with A.A. affiliation and not with becoming abstinent. The Leach and Norris model glosses over the problematic of "hitting bottom" and too quickly passes over the process by which the alcoholic comes to the self-understanding concerning the desire to no longer drink. Neither model addresses the range of problematic situations that can lead an alcoholic back to drinking. Nor do these models fully locate "becoming abstinent" and slipping within group or interactional contexts, as Rubington's framework does. Consistent with Leach and Norris and Rudy, it can be argued that relapsing alcoholics are those A.A. members who have not yet hit bottom and made self-commitments to having their last drink.

Conversion

Rudy's model does have the benefits, however, of speaking to the conversion process that occurs within Alcoholics Anonymous. Following Travisano (1981), Stark and Bainbridge (1980), Lofland and Stark (1965), Rudy (1986), Greil and Rudy (1984), and Snow and Phillips (1980), conversion to A.A. may be conceptualized as a process signalling a radical transformation in personal identity. Such a process leads the alcoholic to come to see the world from the point of view of new A.A. significant others. As an identity transforming organization, A.A. produces a massive restructuring of the alcoholic's identity and meaning systems. Critical to the process of conversion that transpires for the alcoholic are the formation of affective bonds and the production of intensive interactions within the A.A. social structure. Ideologically and emotionally, A.A. encapsulates—to use Greil and Rudy's and Lofland's terms—the new alcoholic member. (See Chapter 6 for a further elaboration of these points.) I turn now to A.A.'s theory of relapse.

A.A.'S THEORY OF RELAPSE

Drinking in A.A., of course, is regarded as a taboo self-act, one to be avoided at all costs. Yet, because the A.A. group is organized around the principle of carrying the message of sobriety to the alcoholic who still suffers, the member who drinks and returns to A.A. is typically welcomed back. In a Durkheimian sense (1897/1951; 1893/1964; 1912/1961; Erikson, 1966) drinking when in A.A. defines the outer boundaries of acceptable group conduct. The interaction at the A.A. meeting described in the previous chapter, where a member who had just drank returned to a meeting, instances the typical A.A. reaction to slips.

Within A.A. (1967: 11, 52, 68, 99, 154, 184, 197, 213-214, 251-291; 1975: 4-5, 63-74) the following reasons are given for slips: (1) the drinker has not yet hit bottom; (2) he or she is not working the spiritual program;

(3) they went into "slippery" (that is, drinking) places; (4) they have not changed their friends and playmates; (5) the drinker has tried to take control over his or her life; (6) the member has not surrendered to alcoholism; (7) the member has not been attending enough meetings; (8) he or she has not been working the program, including reading the *Big Book*, doing the Steps, and getting rid of negative thinking and resentments.

A.A. sums up this position, or theory of slips, by reinterpreting a slip as a "slip in thinking." It is argued that the member has slipped away from the A.A. program, and did not fully let go of the old ways of thinking. Hence, he or she did not want the program badly enough to go to any length to get it.

The following elder member of the A.A. group I studied summarizes the A.A. position on slips.

> Slips are in thinking. Slips are what my wife wears. Slips are when you slip on a banana peel. You don't slip in A.A.. Hell no! You go out and get drunk. That's what I did. I stopped going to meetings. I got back in the driver's seat and took control of my life. I held on to imaginary resentments, went back to my old drinking places, forgot my higher power, stopped calling my sponsor and forgot just how bad it was the last time before I stopped drinking. I had to hit a new bottom before I could accept in my gut the fact that I'm an alcoholic and will be one until the day I die [field conversation, April 1, 1985].

A.A.'s interpretive theory of slips conceptualizes the return to drinking as an attempt on the part of the alcoholic to once again take control over his or her life. Drinking thus becomes a symbol of being in control (A.A., 1967: 213; see Bateson, 1972a and Denzin, 1986a: chap. 2).

The Disease of Alcoholism

A.A.'s disease, or illness, conception of alcoholism (A.A., 1975: 63) leads to a threefold view of slips. First, it is assumed that drinking is the normal state of affairs for an alcoholic; being sober is abnormal. Second, when an alcoholic slips in the early stages of his recovery a slip is expected, for he has yet to learn how to be sober. His disease is still talking him into drinking. Third, once an alcoholic has recovered and maintained one year or more of sobriety, a slip is no longer explained solely in terms of the illness. Rather, it is interpreted as being a willful self-act. These are often called "planned" drunks, in contrast to the perhaps unplanned slip of the newcomer. Thus, alcoholics who drink after a long period of sobriety are seen as using their illness as an excuse for drinking. On the other hand, newcomers are seen as drinking because their illness causes them to drink. *This interpretive strategy locates alcoholism as the cause of slips at one point in the recovery career, while inverting its causal position in the later stages of recovery.* The following member speaks to this point:

> The fucker doesn't want to get sober. He's using alcoholism as an excuse. He just wants pussy. He don't want to give up control. He wants everything he had before without making any changes. He ain't got no excuse to be drunk 'cept himself. Christ, he was sober two years before he went out. You figure it out [field conversation, May 2, 1983; speaker has been sober for seven years].

Being Dry versus Being Sober

An additional feature of A.A.'s theory of slips must be noted. This is the distinction between being dry, being sober, and being in a "dry drunk" (see A.A., 1967). Being dry references an individual who has gone without drinking for a period of time but has not worked the A.A. program. All A.A. members can reference times in their lives when they went without drinking. They may have taken a pledge not to drink, or they went on "the wagon." After entering A.A. these periods of being dry are contrasted to "being sober." Being sober means working an A.A. program that produces sobriety and serenity, or peace of mind (Denzin, 1986a: chap. 7). "Being sober" is then contrasted to a "dry drunk." In a dry drunk the member displays all of the characteristics of a person who is staying dry, but has negative emotional feelings about herself and others. A dry drunk is seen as being a prelude to drinking.

No Excuses

Once the member has internalized the A.A. program and surrendered to alcoholism, there are no longer any excuses for drinking. If the member drinks again it is because he or she has retreated into denial in a search for an excuse to drink. In the A.A. groups that I studied the following "Thought for the Day" (Hazelden Foundation, 1956) was often quoted:

> I hope that nothing can happen to me now that would justify my taking a drink. No death of a dear one. No great calamity in any area of my life should justify me in drinking.

By stripping away the excuses that could be given for drinking, A.A. attempts to locate the member within a social structure in which excuses for drinking become causes for staying sober. This presupposes a radical change in the member's relationship to the world. He or she has been schooled in the belief that drinking is a way to solve life's problems (see Bateson, 1972a; Madsen, 1974; McAndrew and Edgerton, 1969).

Should the member drink after joining A.A., he or she is encouraged to share that experience with the A.A. group. The December 7 (Hazelden, 1956) "Thought for the Day" addresses this point:

> When people come back to A.A. after having a slip, the temptation is strong to say nothing about it. No other A.A. member should force them to declare themselves. It is entirely up to them. If they are well-grounded in A.A., they will realize that it is up to them to speak up at the next meeting and tell about their slip.

A member with seven years of sobriety when he had a slip discusses what he did:

> I don't know how it happened. I found myself at the end of a bar with a shot and a beer. I drank it and was overwhelmed with guilt. We was going to Pittsburgh for a family vacation the next day. I waited 'till we got there and then I went to an A.A. group and told about it. I had to get it off my chest. I didn't want to tell the people in my home group. Pride, I guess. But later I did [field conversation, June 25, 1982].

Time and Slips

A.A. folklore divides the first year of sobriety into three-month segments and associates problems with slips at the end of the first month, three months, and then six and nine months. A self-fulfilling prophecy is created (see Merton, 1957; Thomas and Thomas, 1928). Members begin to speak of problems concerning the desire to drink at each of these temporal intervals. The following member is coming up on nine months. She states:

> I want to drink. I wanted to drink at three months and six months, but this is the worst yet. I dream of drinking. I see Manhattans in front of me. I want to escape everything. Just run and hide in a bottle. This is harder than three months. Is this what you call white knuckle sobriety? I feel like I'm hanging on with my finger nails [field conversation, July 2, 1984, 35-year-old nurse].

White knuckle sobriety is using all of one's strength not to drink. Members speak of this, as this individual does, in problematic situations when they want to drink, but do not. By creating temporal expectations for drinking at specific sobriety intervals A.A. sets in motion self-fulfilling prophecies that may in fact lead members back to drinking. In this organizational sense A.A. may work against its primary purpose.

Types, Causes, and Meanings of Slips

The following understandings concerning slips must be stated. First, slips, or relapses, only make sense in terms of the length of time the individual has been sober. That is, a relapse can only occur after the alcoholic has made an effort to be sober for a period of time. Being dry three days and then drinking is not a relapse from sobriety but a return to drinking. A.A.'s distinction between dry and sober is critical for understanding this distinction. Second, slips within and outside A.A. constitute two different phenomena. Those that occur after the member joins A.A. are interpreted as "slips from A.A." by the member and other A.A. members. Slips that occur outside A.A. are not so interpreted. Thus, a slip by an A.A. member carries implications for a recovery group, whereas solitary slips outside the program do not.

Third, the length and frequency of the slip must be considered. Some are short term, as when an A.A. member has one or two drinks and then returns to A.A. Others are long term and start a chain of controlled and uncontrolled drinking. Still others are intermittent, spaced at regular and irregular intervals. Fourth, the consequence of the slip for the drinker must be considered. It may lead to alcoholic troubles (DUIs), or no troubles at all. It may serve to bring the member back to treatment and A.A., or the member may never again enter a recovery career. Fifth, the perceived causes of the slip must be considered. If an alcoholic in a halfway program slips because a friend slips, the cause is located in the actions of another. If an alcoholic drinks because his wife dies, this is a problematic situation of another order, even though the cause is still located in another person or an event. The range and types of problematic situations that are seen as causing slips must be interpreted before the slip can be understood. The planned or unplanned nature of the slip in relationship to the problematic situation must also be considered.

Sixth, slips must be understood in terms of group and interactional processes. That is, relapse is not just an individual act. It occurs within social settings. It involves the real and imagined presence of others. It becomes an emotional (and at times instrumental) social act in which the alcoholic attempts to return to a mode of self-understanding that alcohol was seen as once producing. To the degree that it occurs in the company of other alcoholics who are slipping, it is a group and interactional production. Even if the slip is solitary—that is, the alcoholic drinks by herself—it occurs against the frame of reference that A.A. and treatment have offered. The drinker sees herself as going against the normative and cultural structures that treatment and A.A. have given her. In this sense the slip is a social act that is enveloped in the social perspectives of others, even if they are not present as the drinker drinks. A recovering alcoholic, sober four years, describes this process.

> I looked into the bottom of the glass and saw W's face there. I looked in the mirror on the wall and saw the A.A. group behind me. I turned away and they were in front of me. I thought I was out of my mind. I'd only had one drink and here I was feeling guilty and seeing A.A.s everywhere [field conversation, November 2, 1984].

To summarize, slips are multidimensional phenomena, involving more than an alcoholic taking a drink. They are social in nature, having their origins in the organizational, institutional, group, family, and interactional experiences of the alcoholic. The following types of slips may thus be identified: (1) the slip of the A.A. newcomer; (2) the slip of the A.A. member who has established lengthy sobriety; (3) the paired and sequential slips that occur after treatment in treatment centers and in halfway houses; (4) solitary slips that occur outside A.A.; (5) solitary slips that occur within A.A.; (6) short-term slips; (7) intermittent slips; (8) long-term slips; (9) slips that lead the member back to A.A.; (10) slips that divert and bring a halt to a recovery career; (11) planned slips, or drunks; and (12) unplanned slips.

It will not be uncommon for individual A.A. members to have experienced some or all of these forms of the slip. Consequently, any A.A. group will be made up of members who have experienced each of these types. The presence of these forms of "slipping experience" within the A.A. group serves to highlight the adage that any member could slip at any time for any number of reasons and for any length of time, and perhaps not get back. These considerations in mind, I now turn to the situational interpretation of slips.

A SITUATIONAL INTERPRETATION
OF RELAPSE AND SLIPS

In *The Alcoholic Self* (1986a: chap. 7) I suggested the following reasons for an alcoholic's return to drinking: (1) the belief that he can once again control alcohol; (2) a desire to return to old drinking contexts where sociability was experienced; (3) a phenomenological craving for alcohol coupled with a high stress situation in which, in the past, drinking was used as a means of reducing anxiety and stress; and (4) a failure to fully commit to the A.A. program.

I next proposed that Becker's (1960, 1964) model of situational adjustments to problematic situations could be applied to the phenomenon of relapse. Stated succinctly, I argued that alcoholics slip when the transformations of self that have occurred in the early stages of recovery have not been complete. If recovery has produced an alternation, but not a transformation, in identity (Travisano, 1981), then when problematic situations arise the likelihood of the alcoholic drinking is high. This is so because the member has not committed himself to the identity of being a nondrinking, recovering alcoholic. In McCall and Simmons (1978) and Stryker's (1980) terms, the salience of the identity of recovering alcoholic is low, or not near the top of the hierarchy of identities the member holds about himself. The member has adopted a transitory identity of being a problem drinker who has overcome the problems that made him a problem drinker in the first place. Large classes of alcoholics who undergo treatment together are likely to develop this transient or uncommitted alcoholic identity. Hence, upon release from treatment, when they confront problematic situations their likelihood of drinking is high.

Problematic Situations

Three classes, or types, of problematic situations set the contexts for the return to drinking. These are (1) problems in the areas of work, money, and financial security; (2) problems in social relationships, including friendships and work relationships; (3) problems in the areas of intimate relationships, including family, lovers, parents, and children (see Adler, 1927).

Cross-cutting these problematic situations are the problematics of self, emotionality, and temporality. The Six Theses of Alcoholism (and Recovery) focus on these three processes (Denzin, 1986a: chaps. 1 and 5). Alcoholism is a dis-ease, or an uncomfortableness with self, time, and emotional feeling. The alcoholic used alcohol as a means of dealing with self-feeling, fear, anxiety, and time. He or she dwelled on the negative emotional experiences lived in the past. Fearful of the future, the alcoholic lived in the present with the aid of alcohol.

Self, emotionality, and temporality thus intersect with the three basic problematic situations the alcoholic confronts in recovery. The alcoholic may be unemployed, working marginally or financially insecure, or he may be overworked, and placed under high stress at work. Alcohol may then be used as a means of escaping the fears and anxieties that flow from these work- and money-related problems. Unemployed, he feels the crush of uncommitted time and drinks to escape time. Overworked, he feels the pressure of the future and drinks to reduce the fears of failure. In both instances, his self-definitions draw him to alcohol as a means of dealing with his emotions, the time he can't control, and the pressures he feels. The member who remains within a sociability network that still drinks may be drawn to alcohol (and friendship) out of a desire to still belong to a social group. He persists in lodging valued portions of self in alcohol-centered social settings. The individual who resides within an intimate social relationship that is still drinking centered feels the same pressures. If the relationship is in a state of emotional confusion, drinking may be turned to.

In each of these three contexts (work, friendships, and family), the alcoholic derives valued senses of self and emotional feeling. Still divided against herself, still caught in the self-centered narcissism that she experienced as an active alcoholic, the member falls and slips when these contexts and the problems they are seen as containing emerge in her life. She may create "imaginary" problems out of or in these situations and then justify drinking. A.A. (1976: 37) calls this finding some "insanely trivial excuse for taking the first drink." She will be more likely to drink if she has not become embedded in the A.A. social structure. If she attends only a few meetings a month and goes to no outside A.A. functions or gatherings, then she will drink when the situational opportunity to do so arises. Consider the followig account.

The first time I drank was almost three months to the day after I left treatment. I was getting married that day. My wife-to-be asked if it would bother me if we had wine at the reception. I lied and said no. There was wine everywhere. When I was in treatment my counselor had said that he thought I could handle "it" again. I thought he meant alcohol. He meant living. Anway, I was anxious and nervous as hell that day. I could smell and taste the wine. Late that night I had glass of wine when nobody was looking. That started me off on a four-month slip. At that time I was only going to the Monday night meeting. That was the only time I thought of myself as an alcoholic. Then I quit going to that meeting. I had no A.A. contact at all [field conversation, July 16, 1981].

Holidays

The social occasion is a recurring problematic for the recovering alcoholic. Such occasions often intersect with work and family relationships, as given in the office Christmas Party, the New Year's Eve Party, Halloween, St. Patrick's Day, and so on. Such ritual gatherings are drinking occasions in American society (see Goffman, 1963a). In the past the member probably drank to excess on such days. Now that he is sober he approaches them with fear. The following individuals speak of Christmas. The first two are in treatment at Eastern. The first is a 32-year-old male.

> I get out on Saturday. On the 21st there's an office party. I'm leaving it up to the wife whether we go or not. Last year I was drunk and made a fool of myself. I just ain't sure what to do.

A second speaker states:

> I was drunk on every holiday. Nothin' different about Christmas 'cept everybody else is drunk, too. I liked these days 'cus the cops didn't notice me when I stumbled down the street drunk.

A member with four years sobriety states:

> The holidays are like every other day. I can't get too far ahead of today or I get drunk. To me Christmas is a day to celebrate sobriety, the greatest gift of all. You people give me this gift every day, if I come here. You can't buy it, you can't give it away, you can't keep it unless you give it away. You are my family and I come here on Christmas to be with you.

A member with seven years sobriety said:

> At these deals I just get a glass of soda as soon as I get there. People think I'm drinking gin or vodka and nobody says anything. Helps me to remember how I used to make an ass of myself at these things. The *Big Book* says we can go to drinking occasions if our purpose is to stay sober and not vicariously take part in other people's drinking. We have something special to bring to these things because we are sober.

These four accounts juxtapose two positions on the holidays and on drinking occasions. Newcomers to A.A. and treatment approach these gatherings with fear, apprehension, and in terms of a background of experience that defines these moments in drinking terms. The two regulars in A.A. had redefined these problematic situations within A.A.'s framework. They have learned how to pass as drinkers.

Because the holidays are notable occasions for excessive drinking, the meetings in November and December in A.A. are often given over to those topics. Large numbers of individuals come into A.A. during these months, seeking situational help for these problematic situations.

The following member confirms Baekeland's (1977: 388) observation that of those alcoholics who relapse after discharge, 50% do so in one month. This member relapsed eight days after leaving treatment, which was just before Thanksgiving. He states:

> Fuck, I didn't know what to do. The old man and old lady [father and mother] wouldn't let me stay in their place. I couldn't stay in detox, my bike wouldn't run. The garage didn't have my car [a Porsche] fixed. The job on the farm didn't turn up. My daughter who I hadn't seen since she was born was comin' to see me two weeks before Christmas, and I didn't have no money. What would you do? I went to find my old drinkin' buddies. Least they'd understand and maybe they could give me some work to do so I could get back on my feet. I only had three beers. That's O.K., ain't it? I didn't call none of you people [A.A.] cause I didn't want to bother you. Hell, it was the holidays. Nothin' you could do anyway [field conversation, November 30, 1985].

Not only does he confirm Baekeland's observation, but he supports the above interpretation. This individual attended only one A.A. meeting in the week after he was discharged from treatment. He confronted problematic situations in the areas of work and family. He returned to old interactional settings as a means of dealing with his problem. He did not use his A.A. connections as a way of dealing with his situation. When he drank, he drank with old friends and two former A.A. members who were also having problems in their lives. This was, in Rubington's sense, a paired relapse. This member has yet to attend an A.A. meeting since his relapse.

Side-Bets, Self, and Redefining the Problematic

This situational theory presumes that in order for a committed A.A. identity to be built the member must make side-bets, or interactional commitments into the A.A. social structure. Within the A.A. groups I studied specific indicators of side-bets included: (1) writing one's sobriety date on the group's A.A. sobriety calendar (see Glossary); (2) agreeing to open up and chair a group's meetings for a month; (3) fixing coffee for a group; (4) coming early to meetings and staying late; (5) offering members rides to meetings; (6) putting one's telephone number on the group telephone list; (7) talking with newcomers and getting involved with them; (8) interacting socially with other members outside A.A. meetings, for instance, breakfasts, coffee, and so on; (9) announcing one's 3-, 6-, 9-, and twelve-month birthday dates to the group;

and (10) introducing A.A. members to family members and friends. These actions and others like them serve to integrate the members into the A.A. network. They lock the member, so to speak, into a recovering identity.

But the member must not only become a regular A.A. member. He must become socially involved in A.A. outside meetings. If this is not done, the identity of alcoholic is only anchored in those situations where the alcoholic confronts other alcoholics, which will be A.A. meetings. If he attends few meetings, the opportunity for announcing and hence acting on this identity is reduced. As Stone (1981: 188, 193-194) suggests, one's identity is established in part by how others place him in a social situation. If the A.A. member announces himself as an alcoholic at an A.A. meeting and if others place him in the identity of alcoholic at meetings, then he is given the identity of alcoholic in that situation. If he avoids such situations this identity placement will not occur. However, if he carries this A.A. identification over into situations that extend beyond A.A. meetings, the likelihood of adopting a transsituational identity of recovering alcoholic is increased.

On the other hand, if the member does not become an A.A. regular, the chance of becoming embedded in A.A. is reduced and the identity of alcoholic becomes primarily situational. If the member adopts the "loner" identity he is not likely to become fully committed to the A.A. self. This increases his likelihood of drinking when problematic situations arise.

In addition to making side-bets into A.A. members must learn how to redefine themselves in relation to the problematic situations that arise in their lives. They can only learn how to do this by attending meetings. At meetings they will listen to members who engage in this process of redefining self in relationship to problems. They will see members who confront problems and do not drink, and they will also learn how to bring their problems to the tables and talk about them. The Leach and Norris (1977) materials suggest that newcomers who attend three to seven meetings a week learn to do this. Such members are apparently successful in building uninterrupted sobriety careers that extend beyond the first problematic year.

Borrowing from Stone (1981: 194), what such members accomplish is the building of a recovering self that is a *"validated program which exercises regulatory function over other responses of the same organism, including the formulation of other programs"* (italics in original). That is, the recovering alcoholic constructs a validated program of identity placement that governs her conduct in any and all situations that are confronted. Central to that identity is the self-understanding that the person will not drink. This transsituational self is learned in

A.A. meetings. It leads to a self-validating program that prohibits drinking in any situation.

The following member illustrates these points. At the time of this writing she has over four years continuous sobriety. She went through three treatment centers and is a regular attender of A.A. meetings. She is speaking after four months in A.A.

> I don't believe what I've done. Since I got sober this time I've had four deaths in the family, one wedding, and a graduation. I haven't had to have a drink. Before I would have been sloshed, drunk out of my mind, gin bottles at my feet. Its only because I've been coming here every day and talking about it that I've made it through. Seeing people with seven and eight years helps too [field conversation, February 5, 1982].

Types of Recovering Identities

Two basic alcoholic identities, transient and enduring, or uncommitted and committed, are thus distinguished. A member with a committed alcoholic identity will (1) closely attach himself or herself to a sponsor; (2) work all of A.A.'s Steps; (3) become an A.A. regular; and (4) carry A.A. over into the other pivotal areas of his or her life. Such a member will maintain regular contact with a sponsor and call a sponsor, or go to meetings (or both) when problematic situations arise. He or she will learn how to talk about these problems without drinking. The A.A. member who brought the problem of his daughter's pregnancy to the tables who was discussed in the last chapter is an instance of how this works. The member who drank eight days after treatment is an instance of how it does not work. The member with the uncommitted alcoholic identity may attach himself or herself to a sponsor but will not use the sponsor. He or she is unlikely to become a regular A.A. member, and the Steps will not be worked on a consistent basis. The member will compartmentalize his or her alcoholic identity, or neutralize that identity when in the presence of persons outside A.A.

As the alcoholic builds a committed recovering identity, he or she becomes more deeply embedded in the A.A. social structure. They may become regular guys, mixers, or company men; although some who remain outsiders and loners maintain sobriety through meeting attendance.

The "Hopelessly Alcoholic" Identity

A member may be fully committed to an alcoholic identity, go through treatment several times, attend meetings on a regular basis, yet return to drinking. He or she will sink into a long period of intoxication in which they ask for help while they continue to drink. Their lives may collapse around them, yet they continue this line of action. The following member is representative. He is intoxicated as he speaks at an A.A. meeting:

> I'm an alcoholic. I know that. I just don't know how to stop. I been through detox four times in the last week. I had four months after my last treatment center. Then the old lady set me off again. Christ, that's an excuse. I just started drinking. Now she wants a divorce and I'm about to be livin' on the street. Don't do like me. Come to your meetings and stay off the stuff 'cause when you start up it ain't easy to stop. I think a part of me wants to die and kill me. I'm just all fucked up. Just a god dammed drunk. That's all I am [field conversation, December 3, 1985].

This member is still drinking. He has no doubt in his mind that he is an alcoholic. He is on the verge of being either a revolving-door drunk or an institutional alcoholic (Pittman and Gordon, 1958; Straus, 1974; Wiseman, 1970).

The next member died from alcoholism at the age of 47. She had been through two treatment centers and at one time was sober for over one year. Well liked within the A.A. community, she called herself a "crazy, grateful alcoholic." She states:

> I keep thinking I can control it. Just a few drinks to feel good again. A little vodka and orange juice. But I can never stop. I try to get sobered up by Friday night so I can go to my home group. I've got no excuse for drinking anymore. None. I just do it. I know I'm killing myself. I know I'm an alcoholic and things go good for me when I don't drink [field conversation, January 2, 1983. This woman died eight days later].

Slips and Identities

When committed alcoholics slip, their slips are more likely to be short-term and are brought to the A.A. tables for discussion. These members become committed to building long-term sobriety careers. They mobilize their self-pride behind the length of time they have been sober. They also work to interpret the conditions that produced their slip or slips. The following individual slipped eight days after she had three months of sobriety. She is attempting to interpret her slip.

> I hadn't gone to meetings for nine days. I kept everything at work bottled up inside. I wasn't talking to my friend. She knew something was wrong but I wouldn't talk to her. I got resentful. I got angry at my boss and at my

parents. Then I got mad at my friend 'cause she didn't understand me. I
got pissed at myself for being mad at everybody. Finally I said, "Fuck it,
go get drunk and show them." I only had enough money for a half-pint in
my pocket. I bought it and drank it. Then I called my friend and told her
what I was doing. Then I went out and got a fifth and went home and
waited for her to come. She got there and I bitched and screamed and
yelled and cried. She poured it out 'cause I asked her to. Then she took me
to detox and I stayed the weekend [field conversation, 29-year-old female,
September 2, 1985].

This member discussed her slip at an A.A. meeting the day she got out of
detox. She has been discussing her slip ever since. She has just obtained
three months of sobriety again. She has increased her meeting attendance. She discusses her problems at the tables. Her slip was short term
and indicative of the slip of a member committed to building a
recovering identity within A.A.

"The Neutralized" Alcoholic Identity

Alcoholics who build transient or less than fully committed alcoholic
identities will gravitate within the A.A. social structure to other
alcoholics who have similar identities. They will have continuously
interrupted sobriety careers. Such members may, however, maintain
interactional commitments to A.A. They will still attend meetings, talk
at meetings, and they may even discuss their slips on a regular basis.
These members confirm the Leach and Norris (1977) finding that
regular "slippers" return to A.A. because they seek the fellowship A.A.
offers. These members will neutralize their alcoholic identity, incorpo-
rating slips into their conceptions of themselves. They will not regard the
slip as a deeply deviant act that places them outside the A.A. cultural
order. They will legitimate the slip in terms of its failure to cause
problems in their life. Their techniques of neutralization (Sykes and
Matza, 1959) deny harm to themselves or others. Yet, as they neutralize
their slips they speak from a "double bind" position (see Bateson,
1972e). That is, to the degree that they are committed to A.A. and want
others to see them as being committed to A.A. they cannot justify their
slips. But to themselves they must justify the slip. Hence, these members
locate causes that account for the regularity of their slips. The following
member is representative.

First I thought it was the old lady and them horses she loves more than
me. Then I thought it was the job and the fact that other people was
getting more money than me. Then I thought it was 'cause my ma's an

alkie. Then I thought it was 'cause I got so dammed much free time on my hands with my job. Then I thought it was 'cause I don't get involved in A.A. and work with others. Now I think it's 'cause I never really hit bottom. You know I never lost everything. It wasn't as bad for me as it was for you other people. I just live this program one day at a time. I ain't had a drink today. But I did last Friday. Two Tequilla Sunrises with my brother and sister-in-law. No excuse. Just had 'em. That's all.

Sometimes I start to worry. First I had 11 months. Then 7 months, then 6 months, then 3 months three times. Now I ain't had 3 months in a year. Seems like it's gettin' worse. Maybe I ain't working this program the way I should [field conversation, October 17, 1985; 34-year-old male, middle management].

This individual attends three or fewer meetings a week and does not involve himself in A.A. social activities. His wife will not go to Al-Anon. He has moved through a sequence of causes for his slips and has ended with the one A.A. puts in front of every member; that is, hitting bottom.

Two Bottoms

There are two bottoms a member may hit (see Glossary, and Denzin, 1986a: chap. 6). There is the bottom that leads the member sincerely to seek help. The member in the last quote hit that bottom when he entered treatment over three years ago. Then there is the bottom that keeps the member from drinking. This may be the same bottom that brought him to A.A. the first time, or it may be the bottom that is hit when the member slips and relapses after coming to A.A. Some members call this "field research." This last member has not yet hit a bottom like the bottom that sent him into treatment. Until he does he will continue to relapse.

The following member speaks to the distinction between these two bottoms.

When I went into treatment everything had gone. Work, family, health, the whole dammed thing. My drinking was out of control. I couldn't stay stopped and once I started I couldn't control it. So I was sober three months and then I went on a four-month binge. It was O.K. at first. A drink or two and walk away from it. Then it was a bottle which would last two or three days. Then it was a bottle every day. Then I ended up in a motel and wanted to kill myself. I didn't, but I still drank. The last time I drove my family out of the house again. They were afraid to be around me. That next day I surrendered. I decided I just didn't want this life of hell anymore. It just wasn't worth it. I just couldn't take it anymore. Was I going to drink today or not? That day I surrendered and it's been over four years since I've had a drink. That last bottom did it for me [field conversation, November 22, 1985].

The "Situational" Alcoholic and Slips

The relationship between slips, bottoms, and alcoholic identities is further illuminated in the relapse of the "situational" alcoholic. A situational alcoholic is a member who adopts the A.A. identity for a specified period of time, in response to an alcohol-related problematic situation that has arisen in her life. Once that problem has been dealt with, the member then ceases to be a member of A.A., or she remains on A.A.'s margins and fringes. A common pattern is the following. An individual receives a DUI. She is then mandated to a DUI school where instructions on drinking and driving are given. Facing the loss of a driver's license, the member then seeks outpatient counseling from an alcoholism counselor, who refers the individual to A.A. She then makes contact with A.A., secures a sponsor, and becomes a regular attender of meetings. This pattern of involvement holds until the person's court date comes up. Then she asks A.A. members for letters of reference concerning her attempts to work the A.A. program. These materials are supplied. The individual has the court hearing. The judge revokes her license for one year, commends her for her recovery program, and suspends jail or prison time, although the individual is assigned a probation officer. The individual reports her success to the A.A. group and is never seen again. If the individual persists in having alcohol-related problems she may keep in touch with A.A. A member who conforms to this pattern is speaking to an A.A. member:

> The judge said fine things about me and A.A.. There were eight of us in court at the same time. He took everybody's license. He sent six people to prison for a year. He commended me for what I had done. I just want to thank A.A. for everything. Without A.A. I would have gone off for a year [field conversation, as reported, October 28, 1985; male, academic occupation. After three months of sobriety, he slips until his court date and has not been to an A.A. meeting since his court date].

This individual continues to maintain infrequent contact with A.A. members. He has returned to drinking and has indicated that he may need to go into treatment to deal with his problems.

From "Situational" to "Committed" Alcoholic

The following member came to A.A. because of a DUI. He went through the same sequence of experiences as did the last situational alcoholic. However, he made the transition from being a situational alcoholic to a committed alcoholic. He speaks:

> I came here because of the DUI and because the drinking had just gotten out of control. I just kept coming and I found something I've always wanted and tried to find in the bars. I guess it's fellowship and a feeling that you're liked and needed. Anyway, I keep coming back. I never want to go back to where I was before [field conversation, as reported, November 9, 1985, three days after the member's one-year birthday in A.A.].

This alcoholic was sober from his first meeting onward. He attended three or more meetings a week and became involved in chairing meetings and in outside A.A. affairs. Drawn to A.A. because of alcohol-related problems, he resolved those problems but became a converted, or committed, A.A. member in the process (see Rudy, 1985). The situational alcoholic has not made that transition. His relapses are thus slips away from Alcoholics Anonymous.

Slips of Old-Timers

Reviewing the previous argument, alcoholics slip when they have not fully committed themselves to the A.A. framework, and even then some may slip. A complete transformation in identity, including a commitment to the A.A. concept of a higher power, appears to secure the alcoholic's sobriety for that length of time that the commitment is sustained. If the alcoholic withdraws from A.A., drinking will be taken up again. Sobriety was just a situational adjustment to problematic situations in the alcoholic's life. Now that those problems are removed the alcoholic takes up drinking again. The return to drinking is increased if the time since the member's last drink is lengthy. The following alcoholic demonstrates these points. He had 22 years of sobriety when he slipped.

> I was Mr. A.A. in town. I worked with the courts, the hospitals, the treatment centers, with anyone who needed help in the alcoholism field. I went to meetings, sponsored scores of people. Then I retired two years ago. I got to thinking I was immune from the stuff. Stopped going to meetings, forgot the higher power, took control over my life. But I was still Mr. A.A. in my mind. Then I let go of that. Said to myself that I'd had enough with drunks. On December 15 I decided I could drink. I bought a half-pint and drank it. Then I bought a half-pint the next day and drank it. I started bringing it home in my briefcase. After my wife went to bed I'd

have the half-pint. This went on for a month until one night she came out
of the bathroom and caught me. I think I wanted to be caught. She said,
"What are you doing?" I felt like my pants were down around my knees,
like a little kid with his hand in the cookie jar, 'cept it was a bottle of booze
in my hand. She got mad and afraid. Asked me what I was going to do. I
said, "I guess I better call my sponsor and go to a meeting and tell them
what I've done." I called my sponsor and that's what he told me to do
[field observation, June 28, 1982, 73-year-old alcoholic].

This man sponsored his sponsor into A.A. He returned to meetings for
two weeks and discussed his slip. He now attends meetings on a regular
basis. At the time of this writing he has slightly over three years sobriety.

As this member told his story around the A.A. tables alarm, shock,
and gratitude were expressed. He was welcomed back and thanked for
telling his story. Soon members who had not discussed their slips began
to talk of slips that had been hidden from the group. This man's story
has become a point of reference in the A.A. community I studied, for it
solidifies the belief that no member is immune from a slip. He defined
the outer boundary of sobriety in the A.A. community. He provided a
point of reference for other members. His case served to highlight the
importance of meetings and the continual activation of the alcoholic self
in the meetings.

Interpretation

I have examined the following categories of slips that were contained
in the typology of slips offered previously: (1) slips of newcomers; (2)
slips of regulars; (3) slips of old-timers; (4) short-term slips; (5) regular
and intermittent slips; (6) slips that halt a recovery program; (7) slips
that bring a member back to A.A.; (8) slips that occur outside A.A.
(those are not brought to the tables); (9) paired relapses; (10) slips of a
solitary nature that occur within A.A.; (11) planned slips; and (12)
unplanned slips (the man who told his story in Pittsburgh).

An examination of these cases reveals that the 12 categories of slips
merge into one another. That is, a member who is building an A.A.
identity may have a planned, short-term slip that is immediately brought
back to A.A. A member who stays outside A.A. may have an unplanned
slip that is joined with the slip of another member and the slip may be
short term, or take on the contours of a long-term relapse. Similarly, a
member who adopts the "hopelessly" alcoholic identity will experience a
sequence of drinking episodes that are punctuated by only brief periods
of recovery. In this case, the member relapses into recovery, perhaps out
of exhaustion. In addition, the slip of an old-timer may be long term or

brief, but eventually it is likely to bring the member back to the tables. The following account speaks to this point.

> I had 17 years with you people. Then one day I decided I would take one drink and I did. It took me 10 years to get back to you people. I'm sure glad to be back. I got 10 days. Someday I'll tell you my story. Thank you for letting me talk [field conversation, October 1, 1985].

A typology of slips, then, only offers an initial point of departure into a phenomenological interpretation of the relapsing process. As a process, slips are always embedded within the situations and the biography of the individual. Any member, as indicated, may experience each form of the slip. Because A.A. groups are made up of members who have experienced each form, knowledge of them is thus passed on through the A.A. social structure. Members learn how to plan slips, how to ask for help when one occurs, how to talk about them at meetings, and how to plan against one when the desire to drink returns. In this manner slips become group phenomena, located as they are in the talk and culture of the A.A. group. A member with over four years of sobriety phrases this understanding as follows:

> You don't have a relapse in order to be an A.A. member, but if a relapse will convince you that you are an alcoholic it can be useful. But some people never make it back. I had to relapse. When I was early on in the program I heard A [a member with 15 years in A.A., but never more than 8 months of continuous sobriety] say he hadn't had his last drink. I knew then that I was going to drink again. And I did. I learned to be careful about what I said at the tables [field conversation, October 22, 1983].

I turn now to alcoholic dreams. In the discussion of their drinking dreams A.A. members socialize one another into sobriety.

ALCOHOLIC DREAMS

Alcoholics in and out of treatment report dreams of a "drinking" nature. Although these dreams may occur months and even years after the alcoholic has stopped drinking, their vivid occurrence is often cause for alarm. Their widespread discussion around the A.A. tables suggests that they are not isolated occurrences.

Recent research on the "alcoholic withdrawal syndrome" (Gross et al., 1974: 206-208, 230-236) reveals that there is little question that the alcoholic's sleep and dream patterns change in relationship to the effects of alcoholic intake and withdrawal. Sleep patterns change as a result, in part, of the effects of "alcohol upon the brain biogenic amines" (Gross et al., 1974: 208). Although alcoholic hallucinosis is common during the withdrawal process, the symbolic content of the alcoholic's dreams during and after withdrawal have not been analyzed in detail.

Interpreting the Alcoholic's Dreams

It is possible, of course, to analyze the dreams alcoholics report in any of a number of different ways (see Boss, 1958, 1963, 1977; Foulkes, 1978; Freud, 1900/1968; Hall, 1953/1966; Hall and Nordby, 1972; Hall and Van de Castle, 1966; Jung, 1961). In the main, I shall follow each of these authors in an attempt to offer an interpretive grammar of the dreams alcoholics discuss at the A.A. tables. That is, these dreams represent repressed wishes or desires to drink. Their manifest content focuses on the drinking act and on its consequences for the alcoholic. Like Jung's "little dreams" they represent continuations of waking preoccupations. When discussed at the tables they become part of the collective consciousness (and unconscious) of the A.A. group and its members. With Boss (1958) I assume that these dreams can be taken at face value. They do not necessarily have deep, hidden meanings, as Freud might propose. In any case, alcoholics take them at face value. A content analysis of them (see next section), following Hall (1953/1966), reveals that they focus on problematic events in the dreamer's life. These include problems in the areas of family, friends, sexuality, work, the pre-alcoholic past, drinking misfortunes, and guilt produced while in the active stages of alcoholism. A grammar of these dreams (Foulkes, 1978) suggest that they become reinterpreted with A.A.'s Twelve Steps. A central component of these dreams is the fear of drinking again, for in the dream the alcoholic is seen as drinking.

The following accounts are typical. A member with seven years sobriety is chairing the Wednesday Night meeting. He opens the meeting with the following topic.

> I'd like to talk about dreams. Alcoholic dreams. I've been sober seven years. Last night I dreamed I was drinking again. I had a cold martini. I was in the old lounge where I used to drink. Soft music was playing and I was with my wife. I had one martini, then another, and then we had a fight. I woke up in a cold chill. I've been nervous and anxious all day. I even called my old counselor. She said that these were typical and not to worry [field conversation, December 18, 1982].

Following this, 15 A.A. members, with varying degrees of sobriety (1 month to 15 years) proceeded to discuss their drinking dreams. A member with 1 month sobriety stated:

> I was sitting in front of a pitcher of beer. Three glasses, all mine, in front of me. I drank them real fast, then I woke up, shaking and crying. I haven't been able to get this dream out of my head. It happened last week.

Another member, with four years sobriety, stated:

> I was in my backyard, a bottle of Jack Daniels on the picnic table. I was drinking out of it. Christ, I never did that. It was getting dark and I could hear the birds chirping. I woke up with a start. I actually felt hung over. My head was foggy. I was thirsty like I used to be in the mornings after a heavy night of drinking. My hands were even shaking. I'd been sober one year and two months at the time.

Another member, with four years sobriety, stated:

> This happened last year around Christmas time. I dreamed I was drinking gin in front of the fireplace. Everybody had gone to bed. I was burning papers in the fire and suddenly the mantel caught on fire and the kids' stuffed animals started burning. I threw my drink on the fire and woke up in a cold sweat. Actually, this was pretty realistic because one Christmas I did start a fire that burned the mantel.

A member with five months sobriety reported a dream he had while in treatment.

> I had a dream that lasted two days when I was in treatment. It came to me even when I was laying on my bed in the afternoon with my eyes closed. It was like I was peering over the edge of a long tunnel that was looking down on a family dining room table in my grandmother's kitchen. It was Sunday dinner. My mother, my brother, my father, my grandfather, my grandmother, and myself. We're all fighting. My mother is pouting and crying. My grandmother is being cheerful. My brother is laughing at my mother. My grandfather is looking out the window. My father is silent because he never came to these dinners. I'm shouting at my mother. The table is filled with food and nobody is eating.
>
> In one version of this dream my two daughters are at the table, too, and their mother is sitting beside me. I'm drinking wine. Yet in the dream I'm 14 years old. It's very frightening. All of these people are alive and looking at me, but my grandparents are dead. As I look down on this situation it's

like I'm reliving my childhood and adulthood. I'm watching myself dream. These images won't leave me!

I told my counselor about this and he told me that he had had dreams like mine. He said he hated his parents and had used the booze to escape from them. He told me that I had to forgive myself and my parents and my grandparents.

The member with 15 years sobriety talked at the end of the meeting.

I'm an alcoholic. I'll be an alcoholic until the day I die. I'm powerless over alcohol, even in my dreams. Hell, I still have those dreams. Last year on vacation I dreamed I was back with a bottle of gin and the boys at work. These dreams are like dry drunks. They help keep me sober today. They remind me of how bad it was. They also tell me that my primary purpose is to stay sober. If I have to drink in my dreams in order to stay sober when I'm awake, that's O.K. Better there than in real life. These damned dreams also tell me that the desire to drink will return. That's what the *Big Book* says.

This elder member of the A.A. group offers a definitive interpretation of the drinking dream. He locates the dreams within A.A.'s primary purpose, indicates that he still has them, and suggests that they are valuable because they prevent the member from actually taking a drink. Such a reading accords with the arguments made by the theorists already cited. They represent continuations of preoccupations that occur in the alcoholic's waking life. To the degree that the member has internalized A.A.'s position on abstinence, the dreamer who drinks is experiencing a repressed desire to drink. The guilt that is felt aligns the dreamer with A.A.'s normative position. That the dream is reinterpreted within A.A.'s First Step suggests that members who have these dreams are still struggling, at the out-of-consciousness level, with surrender and with their powerlessness over alcohol.

The discussion of these dreams around the tables indicates how A.A. members bring their personal, private conscious experiences into the collective consciousness of the group (Durkheim, 1912/1961). That these dreams in fact constitute "slips" suggests that even as the member stays sober he or she dreams of drinking. These dreams underscore the position that alcoholics stay sober in A.A. by talking about drinking. By talking about the tabooed act they kept it at a safe distance from their daily lives. According to Boss (1977) it can be argued that these dreams are not (as Freud would argue) just symbolic and the product of dream-work acting on unconscious dream thoughts and repressed wishes. Nor are they just compensatory. Rather, the alcoholic's dreams illuminate the ways in which he views his sober existence. Their symbolic content is real.

In the dream, then, and in its discussion, members enact and reenact the troubling act that brought them to A.A. in the first place. These dramatic, often traumatic, experiences that are shared awaken the alcoholic to the fact that even his or her private, dreaming life has become a part of a larger social structure.

A GROUNDED INTERPRETATION
OF SLIPS AND RELAPSES

A summary of the foregoing analysis suggests the following statements concerning the alcoholic's slip. First, it cannot be predicted in advance, although a given alcoholic may know when she plans to take her next drink. Second, a slip for an A.A. member is a slip away from A.A. Third, it is a return to a mode of self-interaction in which the member attempts to escape from, or deal with, the problems of the present by placing alcohol between herself and the problem. Fourth, planned or unplanned; short-term, intermittent, or long-term; performed by a newcomer, a regular, or an old-timer; real or dreamed; the slip is a return to the self of the past. Fifth, the slip is an attempt by the alcoholic to take control over his life, to once again become the "captain of his own ship" (Bateson, 1972a). Sixth, the slip is a risk-taking act that denies the past failures and problems the alcoholic confronted when he drank alcoholically.

Seventh, the slip of the A.A. member is a group and interactional phenomenon, for until the member came to A.A. he did not conceptualize his returns to drinking as slips. Eighth, understood thus, the slip signals a failure in socialization as A.A. organizes such practices. Ninth, the member who embraces the A.A. program on a regular basis is the least likely candidate for a slip for she has internalized the A.A. position that there are no longer any excuses for drinking.

The situational view I have presented suggests, then, that alcoholics who slip do so only to the extent that they define themselves as "situational alcoholics." Such members come to A.A. out of an attempt to solve a particular problem in their life. When that problem is solved, they relinquish the identity of alcoholic and return to previous conceptions of themselves. If, however, on the way to solving the problem that got them into A.A. they fully surrender to their alcoholism and become committed A.A. members, their likelihood of slipping is minimized. Alcoholics thus pass through phases or stages as they become sober. For some, slipping is part of becoming sober. For others, slipping becomes a part of their A.A. identity.

Turning from the individual to society, it is possible now to understand how society, through its laws and its courts, enters into the production of situational and committed A.A. members. By remanding drunken drivers to DUI schools, to treatment centers, and to A.A., the courts place individuals in positions in which, through a process of surrender and conversion, they may become recovering alcoholics and committed A.A. members. This may happen in spite of the individual's true intentions or initial desires.

A.A.'s position on these matters is clear. The individual need not have an honest desire to stop drinking in order to be an A.A. member. All that is required is a desire. Hence, they welcome such individuals as society sees fit to send to them. On the other hand, A.A.'s position on abstinence is also clear. Once an A.A. member, one is expected to learn how not to drink. To hold any other position would be to open A.A. up to alternative theories of controlled drinking and problem solving. This would create factions within A.A. and produce large classes of situational alcoholics. Such a position would also undermine A.A.'s theory of alcoholism. Furthermore, it would destroy the basic, underlying premise of A.A., which is that all alcoholics are the same. No alcoholic, once recovery has started, has an excuse to drink. This fundamental principle obliterates the influence of class, status, and power within the A.A. social structure. It reduces every alcoholic to the same level. To do otherwise would be to lay the foundations for a theory of recovery that fitted reasons to drink to different classes of individuals and to different classes or types of problems. A.A. is effective organizationally because it refuses to waiver on this basic point.

CONCLUSIONS

I have offered a situational interpretation of slips and relapses. A typology of slips was offered, based on my interpretation of the experiences of alcoholics who slipped during the period of my fieldwork (1980-1985). Alternative views and theories of relapse were reviewed. I have incorporated portions of Rubington's, Leach and Norris's, and Maxwell and Rudy's formulations into my framework. Central to my understanding of the relapse is the identity the alcoholic forms about himself or herself as an alcoholic. Variations on the committed alcoholic identity were examined, including the situational, hopelessly alcoholic, and neutralized identities. The committed recovering alcoholic identity becomes a validated program of self-indications that prohibits the alcoholic from drinking in any situation.

In my analysis of slips I distinguished being dry from dry drunks, sobriety, and white knuckle sobriety. I also examined the dreams alcoholics report around the A.A. tables, suggesting that in those dreams lies a merger of personal and collective consciousness.

Slips and relapses are at the heart of the recovery process. This phenomenological and interactional analysis has attempted to reveal how this is so. In the next chapter I take up a more detailed analysis of the recovering self, showing how A.A. in fact gets inside the self-system of the A.A. member.

6

THE RECOVERY OF SELF

I can't seem to get it. I get one foot stuck in the shit of the past and one foot ahead of me in the future and I fall flat on my ass, drunk in the present [male alcoholic, second week of treatment, third treatment center, 35-year-old painter].

Those "normies" don't understand us [recovering alcoholic, sober three months, female, 48 years old].

You'll change. You'll be the last person to see it, but you'll change. I have [recovering alcoholic, 14 years sobriety, age 74, male, June 30, 1982].

The problematic that organizes my analysis centers on the relationship between A.A. and the self of the alcoholic. The question that must be answered is the following: "How does A.A. get inside the self of the individual so that he or she moves from the identity of a situational alcoholic to the identity and self-understanding of a committed, recovering alcoholic?" I assume that this transition in selfhood occurs around and outside the A.A. tables. In these contexts the member learns to talk about himself or herself within the language and framework A.A. offers. This study in A.A. and the self is an analysis of talking and storytelling.

The following topics or issues must be analyzed: (1) the old self of the alcoholic that remains after treatment, the remnants of which are brought into A.A.; (2) temporality and change; (3) humor and becoming an A.A. storyteller; (4) fear and guilt, as these emotions accompany the changes in self that are experienced; (5) laying the self of the past to rest; and (6) fully accepting the alcoholic identity and becoming integrated into the A.A. social world. As these problematics are mastered, the recovering alcoholic is learning how to talk in A.A. meetings. He or she is learning how to bring "sobriety" problems to the tables. A brief discussion of the self theories of James and Mead, as well as an excursion into gender and A.A., will be required under point one above.

Conceptualizing Recovery

Upon leaving treatment for alcoholism the alcoholic is likely to confront two structures of experience: slips and relapses and the A.A. group. (He or she will, of course, also confront work and family. These contexts must be absorbed into the alcoholic's A.A. experiences, as well as into his or her attempts at remaining sober. See next discussion.) These were the topics of the last two chapters.

As indicated in Chapter 4, the alcoholic who leaves treatment confronts a void or emptiness of experience. His friendships in treatment have been severed. His family is still in a state of disorganization. His work career must be taken up again. He must learn how to live sober, if he is going to recover from his disease of alcoholism, which treatment has told him he will have until he dies. Treatment has activated, or bought to the surface, the negative emotions of his past.

In this frame of mind it is not surprising that he drinks and relapses. He experiences his alcoholism as a dis-ease of time and self. He starts his recovery career still locked within the feelings of guilt and shame that his alcoholic past has produced. These feelings create a fearfulness and anxiety concerning the present and the future. In the past he drank to deaden these feelings of self. Now sober, he fights not to drink as he attempts to overcome these negative feelings. He does this by becoming a regular member of A.A. How this occurs is the topic of this chapter.

In Denzin (1986a: chap. 7) I outlined the three-act play that I called "Recovery." This play has three acts: (1) "Sobriety," (2) "Becoming an A.A. Member," and (3) "Two Lives." I suggested that each of these acts had stages or phases within themselves. It is necessary to review briefly each of these acts and their phases. "Sobriety" involves (1) hitting bottom; (2) reaching out for help; (3) making contact with A.A.; (4) announcing one's self as an alcoholic at an A.A meeting; (5) slipping and returning to A.A.; (6) maintaining contact with A.A. and learning how not to drink on a daily basis; (7) becoming a regular A.A. member; (8) learning A.A.'s Twelve Steps; and (9) becoming integrated into an A.A. network, getting a sponsor, and working Steps Four and Five.

Act Two incorporates phases 6, 7, and 8 as just discussed. Act Three has four distinct phases: (1) taking Steps Four and Five; (2) acquiring a "spiritual" program; (3) learning how to live sober; and (4) coming to see that one has led two lives: before A.A. and after A.A.

I suggested in that earlier analysis that the alcoholic who moves through these three acts and their phases will experience a radical transformation of self. He or she will become a committed, recovering alcoholic who builds a lengthy history of continuous sobriety within the A.A. community. Previously lived alcoholic-centered family relationships will undergo change as the alcoholic and his or her other learn the languages of recovery offered by A.A. and perhaps Al-Anon. New languages of self, new meanings of alcoholism, alcoholics, and drinking will be acquired. The alcoholic and his or her other will move through transformations and alternations of identity that will make them new kinds of individuals, to themselves and to others (see Travisano, 1981: 244; Denzin, 1986a: chap. 7) This earlier discussion provides the framework for this chapter.

The Six Theses of Recovery

As in Chapter 2, the Six Theses of Recovery structure my analysis. The alcoholic recovers the self that was lost to alcoholism by working through the central processes referenced by these theses. The Six Theses, stated here for purposes of summary only, are: (1) *The Thesis of the Temporality of Self*—the alcoholic recovers self through the temporal structures of experience that A.A., not alcohol, now offers; (2) *The Thesis of the Relational Structures of Self*—recovery occurs within a radical alternation in the relational structures of experience that A.A., not alcohol, now offers the alcoholic; (3) *The Thesis of the Emotionality* of *Self*—recovery involves a relinquishing of the prior emotional understandings of self the alcoholic clung to; (4) *The Thesis of Bad Faith*—recovery requires a rejection of the structures of bad faith that had previously supported the alcoholic's active alcoholism; (5) *The Thesis of Self-Control*—the alcoholic must come to believe that he or she can no longer control the people, places, or events that constitute his or her world; (6) *The Thesis of Self Surrender*—only through a continual surrendering to powerlessness over alcohol will the alcoholic maintain sobriety.

OLD AND NEW SELVES

A.A. presumes a transition between two selves: the old drinking self of the past, which holds on to "old ways of thinking" and the new, nondrinking self of the present and the future, which may or may not take on the A.A. way of thinking and acting. The alcoholic's sobriety is maintained precisely because these two selves are continually kept alive in the dialogues that occur within A.A. meetings. A temporal structure that reaches back into the past, drawing always from the vantage point of the present, thus organizes the alcoholic's recovery experiences. Because the past can always be returned to by taking the first drink, the alcoholic learns to distance herself from who she has been as an active drinker. But because who she was is kept alive in the vividness of her memories of it, and because she learns to talk about it, she comes to define herself in terms of who she no longer wants to be. A negativity structures the interaction of the two selves that coexist simultaneously in the alcoholic's mind. By knowing who she does not want to be (negatively) she is drawn to the affirmative structures of experience A.A. offers.

The Old Self

The self of the alcoholic, that structure of experience that is woven through the streams of real and unreal consciousness alcohol has produced, must be presented to the A.A. group. It is a self that has degraded itself, embarrassed itself, and lost itself within alcoholic dreams and fantasies. Divided against itself, it comes to A.A., even after treatment, in shattered pieces. It is a self that has been humbled by alcohol. This self is familiar to A.A. members, for it is a self they keep alive in the daily discourse that makes up an A.A. meeting. Consider the following statement made by a member with six years sobriety.

> When I first got here I couldn't talk. I was shaking and crying. I sat in the corner. When it came my turn to talk I mumbled something, I don't even remember what. I felt like I had just crawled out of a hole. I felt lower than a snake on the ground. I couldn't look people in the eye. I was like this for months. Finally I started to be able to talk. I started to get some self-confidence back. It used to be that I couldn't go into a room with more than two people in it without being high on drugs and alcohol. I was afraid of people. Today I feel comfortable here. I can actually talk! That's quite an accomplishment for me. It helps me to remember who I was and what I used to be like. I've come a long ways [field observation, December 4, 1984, 32-year-old female, printer].

The old and the new self of the speaker are presented in this account. The speaker reflects back on who she was, laughing as she describes her previous inability to be in a room with people without being high. Thus, an old self is presented through the voice of a new self. This reflective stance toward the past is basic to the restructuring of self that occurs within A.A. That is, recovering alcoholics, as they move forward in recovery, continually distance themselves from who they were. Yet this distancing process occurs in small increments, built upon the sobriety trajectory that accumulates one day at a time. The self that is moving forward judges the momentum of this movement in terms of where it used to be.

The following speaker is quite explicit on this point. She has been out of treatment for three months as she speaks:

> The first time I went through treatment I didn't get it. I didn't want to be there. I was there for somebody else and I wanted to be like I always was, only I wanted to be able to control my drinking. This second time something happened in about the third week. My counselor said, "You know you don't have to drink anymore. You can let go of that part of your self." I surrendered right there. I thought that in order to be who I was I had to fight alcohol and still drink. That way I could prove that I was strong and the same old self I'd always been. Since that day I've had a peace of mind you can't imagine [field conversation, 47-year-old female, field of education].

The speaker let go of her drinking self. She surrendered to her alcoholism, which is the Sixth Thesis of Recovery.

The next speaker evidences an unwillingness to let go of the drinking self.

> I love that stuff. It's my love. I love it deeply. I don't want to give it up. I love it like a man loves a woman. When I was in the Hollywood Group in L.A. I wanted those sobriety buttons. I wanted the 30-day, the three-month, and the six-month buttons. I was wearing my clean sobriety T-shirt. I was going to sew those buttons on that shirt. I was proud of my sobriety. I went out after 28 days. That's the longest I've ever had. I can't get past 28 days! [field observation, January 5, 1985].

This member sets 28 days in front of himself as a barrier that cannot be broken. This obstacle, self-imposed, yet derivative of A.A.'s sobriety markers of one, three, and six months, indicates how a member can use time and A.A. in a self-defeating fashion.

Still attached to the drinking self, the member interprets the sobriety markers he has not received as symbols of self-failure. Yet he loves alcohol like a woman and does not want to give it up.

The alcoholic's love affair with alcohol is referenced in the following statement by a counselor at Northern. She is speaking to patients four days before they are to leave treatment.

> You're all going through a grieving process. It's like losing a loved one. Except you've lost your best friend, which is alcohol. You'll have to get used to this if you want to recover. You'll cry, you'll scream for it. You'll try and do anything to get a drink when the desire returns. But you can't give in. You've got to give it up if you want to get better. You'd better all get to A.A. because they'll help you replace this loved one with something else [field conversation, April 19, 1982].

The metaphor of "loved one," standing for alcohol and the alcoholic's relationship to alcohol, personalizes alcoholism. It drives alcohol deeply into the emotional structures of the alcoholic's self. The metaphor "death of a loved one" also attaches a familiar structure of experience to the death of this relationship. That is, grieving, pain, and shows of emotion will accompany this process.

Commonsense Structures of Self

MacAndrew and Garfinkel (1962) analyzed the images of sober self, drunk self, and ideal self of 62 Caucasian male alcoholics hospitalized for treatment. The findings indicated that the alcoholics in this sample associated forcefulness, persuasiveness, and assertiveness with reasons for drinking. Drinking was seen as allowing the alcoholic to be free to pursue a valued self, which is an assertive self.

At the commonsense level, alcohol releases inhibitions, relieves loneliness, reduces fears and tensions, and creates momentary sociability with others. These motives for drinking are thus associated with self-experiences that lead alcoholics to approach an ideal self that can not be given in the sober state.

The transition in selfhood that occurs within A.A. requires that the old understandings of self that the alcoholic held to must be relinquished. A *sober self-ideal*, to use MacAndrew and Garfinkel's (1962: 254) term, must be learned. The commonsense foundations of selfhood that link self with alcohol must be broken if A.A.'s version of recovery is to be established.

A.A.'s Theory of Self

A Jamesian theory of self is embedded within A.A.'s precepts concerning being good to yourself and watching out for anger and resentment. James's self—including the "Me," or the empirical self as known by others, and the "I," or self as knower—consisted of self-feelings, actions prompted by the self, and embodied feelings felt in the body of the person (James, 1890/1950: 292). Self-feelings, which radiate through the body of the subject, define the inner meaning of lived experience as that experience is confronted by the subject. The actions, which the subject's self-feelings and self-thoughts lead him to produce and embrace, create situations in which success, failures, and pretensions interact and collide. The subject's self-esteem, James (1890/1950: 320) argued, is the ratio of success over pretensions.

These formulations are familiar to the alcoholic. By setting herself up to fail, the alcoholic lowers her self-esteem, for her pretensions will always exceed her successes. Furthermore, by failing and drinking, she diminishes the value of her empirical self, or me, in the eyes of others. At the same time, her meaning to herself—as she knows herself—after failure has been experienced is also lowered. The consequence is that the self-feelings the alcoholic experiences, including those feelings accompanying a hangover, or a drunk, are negative, hostile, and focused on anger and resentment.

Until alcohol is removed from the alcoholic's embodied consciousness, these feelings will remain and be a part of the emotional repertoire he or she brings to every empirical situation that is confronted. But more is involved. The alcoholic must learn to bring expectations of self in line with the actual accomplishments of self. By making sobriety the primary goal of the alcoholic, A.A. produces a situation in which daily success can be accomplished and hence experienced. In a self-fulfilling fashion, sobriety produces the very circumstances of self the alcoholic had previously attempted to achieve through drinking.

G. H. Mead and the A.A. Self

If A.A. fills out, in empirical detail, elements of William James's theory of self, G. H. Mead's (1934) theory of self may also be fitted to the A.A. experience. Mead's "I" and "me" are located in the A.A. group. The "sober I" learns how to be sober by taking the attitudes of sober selves who are A.A. members. The A.A. group becomes a generalized other for the member. The significant symbols of the group (the Steps) slowly come to call out in the member consensual self-understandings regarding A.A. and recovery. The symbolic meanings of the word "alcoholic" similarly come to be integrated into the member's "I"-"me" inner dialogues. A self grounded in the symbols, meanings of self, alcohol, drinking, and alcoholism thus emerges. As this new structure appears, old meanings of self, alcohol, and alcoholism are pushed aside.

These social objects assume new meanings that are given in A.A.'s languages of self.

The unstable inner "I" of the alcoholic that had previously experienced various forms of madness (Lacan, 1977) discovers a new forum for selfhood. In this inner arena of self-conversations, which flow from participation in the A.A. group, a stable inner "I" and "me" is built.

In terms of Kohut's (1971, 1977; see also Benjamin, 1981: 203) psychology of self, the member experiences two kinds of interactional relationships; idealizing ones that permit dependency, and mirroring ones that allow for autonomy. A cohesive self that merges with the selves of other A.A. members thus appears. At least the potential for that merger is present.

In order for the alcoholic to become a member of A.A. she must be able to interpret meaningfully the actions of other A.A. members. She must also be able to judge and formulate lines of action based on these interpretations. These actions, in turn, must be fitted to the ongoing actions of others in the A.A. group. The A.A. language and a process of taking the attitude of the other underlies this experience. It revolves, as argued earlier (Chapter 4), on A.A. understanding.

Stages of Becoming an A.A. Self

In becoming an A.A. member the individual can be seen as passing through three stages of selfhood. In the *preparatory stage* the individual imitates and mimics the words, actions, and feelings of other A.A. members. Deep understanding of the attitudes of others is not yet present. In the *interactional stage* the individual learns how to take the attitudes of specific A.A. members, and a process of anticipatory socialization into A.A. begins to occur. The member still, however, speaks from a self-centered point of view, and misunderstandings regarding A.A. occur. In the *participatory stage* the individual learns to take the attitudes of the A.A. group as a collectivity. The generalized A.A. attitude is learned. Socialized speech of a nonegocentric nature is produced and the member slowly begins to build up friendships that connect him or her to a network of A.A. members (see Mead, 1934; Meltzer, 1972: 9-10; Stone, 1981: 200-201).

These stages of socialization into A.A. may be depicted as follows:

(1) *Preparatory Stage*:	Imitation of others, low understandings of A.A. Few interiorizations of A.A. self-structures.	
(2) *Interactional Stage*:	Attitudes of specific A.A. members (sponsors) are taken. Learning of A.A. language begins to occur.	

(3) *Participatory Stage*:   Attitudes of the group are taken, socialized
                                A.A. speech is produced. Friendships within
                                A.A. are entered into. Member begins to lead
                                meetings, sponsor other members, and so on.

Gender and Selfhood

The three stages of socialization into A.A. relate, then, to stages in selfhood. However, the self that emerges in A.A. is not gender free. Gender, sexuality, and personal biography structure the transitions in self that occur within the A.A. social group. The morality and emotionality of A.A. interactions align males to males and females to females. An axis of value and mood (Stone, 1981), or instrumental and emotional attachment (Denzin, 1986d; Gilligan, 1982: 8-9) differentiates the interactions of the two sexes in A.A.

Two moral codes—one masculine, the other feminine (Erikson, 1950; Kohlberg, 1981)—are thus evidenced in A.A. These codes revolve around instrumentality and emotionality. The masculine code represses emotionality; the feminine code releases it. Because A.A. is a male-dominated social structure, the masculine, instrumental value dimension predominates. However, a tension is produced in this code. The heart of A.A. works through the disclosure of emotionality, which underlies A.A.'s particular form of emotional understanding (see Chapter 4). Consequently, the feminine moral code—the showing of emotion and the valuing of emotionality—undercuts the masculine code.

Two important implications follow. First, women appear to acquire the A.A. point of view more rapidly than do men. Their empathetic abilities and previous socialization experiences allow them more quickly to enter the emotional space that exists within any A.A. meeting. Second, males who reach the participatory stage of A.A. selfhood move from the masculine, repressive view of emotion to the feminine mode of mood and emotionality.

The stigma that applies to female alcoholics in American society (Gomberg, 1976) and the double standards that are applied to them often produce a suppression of emotionality on the woman's part when she first enters A.A. She acts, that is, like a man in her show of emotion. If she remains in A.A. she will move more rapidly to the participatory stage of involvement than do males. This is because, as just indicated, she has a history of emotional expression that many males in American society have not had.

A middle ground on emotion (see next section) thus appears within A.A. This involves a merger of gender-specific attitudes on emotionality. It is not that gender becomes irrelevant. Rather, a neutral emotional zone of self-disclosure appears. Either sex can enter that zone and discuss self-degrading or emotionally disruptive experiences and not be evaluated negatively by members of the opposite sex.

Such an emotional social structure thus allows for the emergence of self-structures that are grounded in emotional experiences that would otherwise be denied members of both sexes. In Kohut's (1977) terms, cohesive selves, responsive to one another but not intimidated by the authority of the other, appear in this social situation. Independent selves, differentiated from one another yet intersubjectively dependent upon each other, thus emerge within the A.A. experience. Accorded recognition by members of the opposite sex, but not dominated by them, the member learns to interact with himself or herself in ways that had not been previously possible.

Selves and Slips

The foregoing remarks suggest a way of interpreting the analysis of slips offered in the last chapter. They indicate that relapses will be most likely to occur during the preparatory and interactional stages of a member's socialization into A.A. They suggest that the situational alcoholic identity will be most likely to appear in the preparatory and early interactional stages of involvement. It might also be proposed that there will be fewer slips for those members who are able to relinquish the instrumental, masculine code of emotional expression. To the extent, however, that the moral, interactional, and emotional code of A.A. remains embedded in the white, Anglo-Saxon culture, the slips of blacks and Hispanics will be high (see Madsen, 1974: 157). That is, the self that is produced in A.A. enters an androgynous zone of emotionality that still flows from the white, Anglo-Saxon culture. This interpretation can be further examined by discussing the black experience in A.A.

Madsen (1974: 156) suggests that there is an effort to repress racial and ethnic hostility in A.A. I observed this in the A.A. community that I studied. However, over a five-year period of fieldwork I observed only two successfully recovering blacks; both were males. Perhaps 100 or more black males and females entered treatment, attended a few meetings, and then disappeared back into the black community. One of the two members who succeeded started his own version of A.A. and located it within the black community. The other member regularly attended predominantly white A.A. meetings.

Summarizing, three key factors work against the recovery of blacks and Hispanics in A.A. (see Caldwell, 1983: 91; Kane, 1981; Madsen,

1974: 157; Watts and Wright, 1983). First, A.A. is a white, Anglo-Saxon social movement; it has few if any deep roots in the minority experience. Second, the repressed racial hostility against minorities still sets a tone of interaction that is filled with suppressed tension when blacks and whites meet across the A.A. tables. Third, the emotional tone of the A.A. meeting, although tilted in the direction of emotional display, is a tone that is modulated by the white, male experience. This tone allows emotion to be expressed, but contained within an "in-control" framework. The "talking" style of whites simply differs from the "talking" style of blacks (Labov, 1971). It is more likely to occur within a restricted emotional code that does not elaborate in thick detail the history, biography, and personal experiences of the speaker (see Bernstein, 1971). A black speaker fills his or her A.A. talk with contextualized meanings that are often not understood by the white listener (see Labov, 1971).

Hence, in the basic arena of talking and storytelling the black speaker experiences an alienation from his white A.A. listeners. This is because he speaks from a different linguistic background. His talk overflows with emotionality. There are few similar spaces within white A.A. discourse for such elaborated emotional talk. The following account is typical. It is given by a black male with four years sobriety. He spoke at an "open" A.A. meeting. His audience was all white; an equal number of males and females were present.

> We was in Germany, I was in the Fifth Airborne. We was at a football game. I was dressed to the tee; I mean I was a real stud, a dude in the stands. Cool man. I had me a pint of Jack. I drank it before the first quarter was over. I pissed in my pants and passed out. Puked all over a lady in front of me. My fuckin' pants were soaked. I had puke all over my jacket. I fell down three rows and had to be taken back to the base by the MPs. Woke up hung over and started all over. I was sailin' like a bird on that Jack; higher than a cloud in the sky. Kept thinkin' of my "auntie" back home and wanted to be back in Chicago, safe and with my friends. That drunk lasted two weeks [field observation, October 23, 1982].

The speaker's story lasted one-and-a-half hours. By the time he was done, members were becoming uneasy. They cringed as he told the self-degrading portions of his story. The speaker never returned to this group.

The black emphasis on close interpersonal relationships, on an affective symbolic imagery, on verbal rhythm, and on a logic that combines opposites, does not find a comfortable place within the universe of discourse that makes up white-dominated A.A. meetings (see Caldwell, 1983: 91). Yet, A.A. works for some black alcoholics (see the case presented by Caldwell, 1983: 91). It must be noted that the community I studied has a history of a well-formed black community that is not integrated with the larger white community (see Stack, 1970).

Temporality

Within A.A., as noted earlier, progress is measured in part through length of sobriety. The medallions that are given for 30 days, 90 days, six months, and one year represent significant temporal markers in the recovery process. Transformations in self are assumed to accompany each of these temporal points.

A speaker with five years sobriety comments:

> The first year is the hardest. You deal with physical problems of the addiction. The second year is psychological, dealing with the old ways of thinking that lead to drinking. The third year is spiritual, for you finally have to confront a higher power in your life. The fourth year is the hardest because you are supposed to be better by then. I'm over five years now and the fifth year has been the hardest for me. When does it end? [field observation, October 27, 1983, 37-year-old male counselor].

Change is organized around what A.A. recognizes as the three sides to alcoholism—that is, the physical, mental or psychological, and the spiritual or moral. Hence, a transformation of self that encompasses these three dimensions is presumed to be at work during recovery (see Wholey, 1984).

As the old self of the past is relinquished, the new self of A.A. comes to speak in terms of the Steps, the program, the past, spirituality, the present, and the gifts of the program. The following speaker illustrates this point.

> I'm nothing without A.A.—nothing. Without the Steps, the higher power, my sobriety which is given on a daily basis, my sponsor, these meetings, my new friends—without all this I'd be nothing and nothing was just what I was when I got here [field observation, April 2, 1982, 48-year-old male, salesman, four years sobriety].

As A.A. gets inside the self of the recovering alcoholic, recovery is conceptualized on two levels: the abstract components of alcoholism as a physical, mental, and spiritual illness, and the specific dimensions of one's "state of mind" at the moment. Thus, although an alcoholic may be judged to have a sound and stable A.A. program, on any given day his or her "serenity" or "peace of mind" is judged to be less than acceptable to another member. The following statement by a recovering alcoholic with nearly six years of sobriety speaks to this distinction.

> I'm hangin' in there. One day at a time. I got nothin' to complain about. I got my meetings, I still go to three or four a week. I got my friends. The business is going good. My spiritual program is working. I still eat too much, but I feel good and I got peace of mind. It's O.K. today.
>
> Saw H on the street yesterday. Gave him a big wave and smile. He just lifted his hand and kept his head down. That sonofabitch. I'm not getting into his shit anymore. He pulled me down for too long. Sucked me right in. Two months ago I saw him at the Monday night meeting. I said "Hi, H" two times and he didn't say a damned thing. That's enough for me. He can have what he has. That's not what the program's all about for me. I don't care if he does have over five years. I don't care how many spiritual books he reads on a daily basis. He ain't got it. And I know I'm takin' his inventory [field conversation, January 25, 1985; recovering alcoholic, self-employed, 51 years old].

This speaker indicates how the recovering alcoholic uses the criteria of "serenity" and peace of mind to measure and judge his personal progress in the program (see discussion of serenity below; also see Denzin, 1986a: chap. 7). Hence, he moves from the abstractions of alcoholism as an illness to the specifics of lived experience that, for him, embody what the program means. These dimensions of the program become the new commonsense foundations of the recovering self.

Concomitant with the appearance of the "new self" of the recovering alcoholic emerges the ability to become a "storyteller" within the lore and language of A.A. It is to this topic that I next turn.

BECOMING A STORYTELLER

The speaker at an A.A. meeting must learn that he speaks only for himself, not for A.A. or for the A.A. group. Three processes are involved in becoming a storyteller. The first involves learning how to speak and connect one's statements to the A.A. experience. The second involves learning what a story is. The third involves learning how to tell and modify that story to any specific problem that might arise that could test one's ability to stay sober.

When the speaker makes reference to A.A. or to her own experiences, she must learn not to use the pronouns "we," "us," "they," or "our." The following exchange between two male speakers reveals this A.A. understanding. The first speaker is discussing the Third Step Prayer. With over four years sobriety, he is an established member of the group. He begins by repeating the prayer:

> God, I offer myself to thee—to build with me and to do with me as Thou wilt. Relieve me of the bondage of self, that I may better do thy will. Take away my difficulties, that victory over them may bear witness to those I would help of Thy power, Thy love and Thy way of life. May I do Thy will always!

He then states:

> This is our prayer. We say it every night before we go to sleep.

He is interrupted at this point by a speaker who also has over four years sobriety:

> You can't say "our." You can't say "we." It's your prayer. You say it. We don't say it! Speak for yourself!

The first speaker retorts:

> Shut up. Cram it up your ___ . I'm talking. You can talk when it's your turn. I know its me saying the ___ damned prayer. Do you think I'm a dummy? I'm sick and tired of your coming in here and acting so ___ damned holy! [field conversation, September 17, 1982].

This angry display of emotion between two A.A. speakers is uncommon. Yet the second speaker was making an important point. No one individual speaks for A.A.; each member speaks from individual experience. However, each member is expected to learn what the Steps are, what the Traditions are, what A.A. stands for, and what sobriety and serenity mean within A.A. More than this, the alcoholic must learn how to talk about self. He must become a storyteller, but he must become a particular kind of storyteller. He must learn how to relate events that occur within his everyday life to the language and meanings of A.A. He must learn to see that everything that happens to him could cause him to drink. When he learns this he can relate this A.A. life to his other life. Becoming an A.A. "talker" and "storyteller" thus requires that the member be able to maintain an interaction between what A.A. teaches him and what he experiences in his everyday life.

The Story

A story within A.A. is an accounting of "what it was like, what happened and what it is like now." In "How It Works" (A.A., 1976: 58) the reader is told that "our stories disclose in a general way what we used to be like, what happened, and what we are like now." This definition of a story limits the storyteller's story to her life before she became an alcoholic, to a description of what happened during her active alcoholism, and to a discussion of how she has recovered. Hence, A.A. stories are stories of recovery from alcoholism. Some are called "drunk-a-logs." They are part of each member's biography, which is shared within the A.A. community at "open" meetings.

The guide for the member's story is given in A.A.'s *Big Book*, which contains 44 life stories framed around the above-mentioned three criteria. As the member learns the *Big Book* she may find a story that is close to her own lived experiences. This story may be adapted to fit the member's life story as it is told to the A.A. group. The following story is representative. The speaker, who had 34 years of sobriety when he died at the age of 76, told the following story about himself.

Bill Wilson could have told my story. Same circumstances. Bright prospects for a prominent career in business. Good schools, loving parents, lovely wife, nice home. Everything. Heavy social drinking in the early days. The best drinks, best bars and restaurants. The good life. But the drinking got heavier. I was taking a bottle to work in my briefcase. Nips in the morning to get started. Early lunches so I could get a fix before I started to shake too much. Then I started getting home late from work. I'd stop for a few and a few would turn into all night. I became irresponsible toward my family. My work started to show it. I wasn't making the accounts like I used to. I decided I needed to switch jobs. So I did and for a while it was better. Then I started hitting the bottle more and more. Some days I'd leave at noon. Sometimes I'd call in sick on Monday. It got so I couldn't go longer than an hour without a drink. The wife left me and took the kids. I said to hell with them, and I took an expensive apartment in the city. Tried to live the bachelor life. I went down fast after that. Started ending up in the drunk tanks. Went into a sanitorium to dry out. Got drunk the day I got out. That was in the early forties. People were talking about this A.A. thing at the sanitorium. I read that Jack Alexander article. A friend got a copy of the *Big Book* and gave it to me. I looked at it and threw it away. Kept on drinking. I finally lost my job, everything. Another place to dry out but this time when I came out I was ready to stop. I got to an A.A. meeting and saw that *Big Book*. This time I read it. It fit me to a "T." I knew I was an alcoholic. They said there was hope if I followed their simple program. I started going to meetings. Got a sponsor. Dried out, got sober. Got my old job back and after a year the wife and kids came back. I've been in ever since. It turned my life around. I owe everything to A.A. and to Bill Wilson, Dr. Sam Shoemaker, Dr. Bob, and all those old-timers who held in there and kept A.A. going. In the early days we used to drive 500 miles a week just to make meetings every night. There weren't many then, you know. We all hung together and helped each other. Just like you people are today [field observation, May 2, 1982].

This speaker spoke from the historical vantage point of over 30 years in A.A.; the following speaker has been in A.A. seven months.

I read that story in the *Big Book,* "The Vicious Circle." That's me. I get sober a few days, then I drink and I can't stop. I've been here seven months and I have three months sobriety. I just couldn't stay stopped. Always something. Boss would yell at me. My mother'd be sick. The car wouldn't start. Green Bay would lose a football game. Any damned excuse to go off and get drunk. I just about lost my good job. Today the boss is happy with me and everything's goin' good. I finally got a sponsor and got me a regular set of meetings I go to. It's working for me. Last night, tho', I wanted to drink. My sister called and told me I was a quitter for stopping drinking. She's an alcoholic, too. It scares her that I've quit. She wants me to keep drinking. Three months ago I would have gone out and drank a fifth over that call. Today I don't need to [field observation, January 10, 1985; 48-year-old mechanic, single].

This man is speaking at a First Step meeting to a newcomer who is at her first meeting. Seven months earlier our speaker was a newcomer. He has learned how to tell his story and he tells it exactly as it is suggested in the *Big Book.* First step meetings (as discussed earlier) are the occasions for alcoholics to tell their stories (see also Denzin, 1986a: chap. 7). Hence, part of becoming an A.A. member involves learning how to tell one's story to newcomers and regulars at First Step meetings.

Of equal importance, however, is the ability to adjust one's story to one's daily living situation. This is what the speaker in the last statement does. By weaving the telephone call from his sister into his account, he addresses a problem of staying sober, while telling how he became sober. He has joined the problematics of living sober with the A.A. experience.

A.A. Humor

In discussing the stories and experiences of A.A. members, the reader of the *Big Book* is told that our struggles . . . are variously strenuous, comic, and tragic. . . . There is, however, a vast amount of fun about it all. I suppose some would be shocked at our seeming worldliness and levity. But just underneath there is deadly earnestness [A.A., 1976; 16].

Laughter, self-criticism, and humor are basic to the stories A.A. members learn to tell about themselves. The self-humor that A.A. promotes instances what Flaherty (1983: 75) terms *reality play*; the transformation of serious "reality work" into playful, humorous interaction that is amusing and nonserious. Reality play draws its humorousness from the seriousness of the social situation that is transformed, by means of paradox, contradictions, and laughter, into a situation that is joked about.

A.A. members laugh at themselves and joke about their escapades while drinking. They speak with humor to the seriousness of their lived experiences as practicing alcoholics. By laughing and joking about themselves they transcend the seriousness of the past and learn how to put that past in the past tense of their lives. A.A. interaction works, then, on the dialectics of reality work and reality play, as these processes have been discussed by Flaherty (1983).

But more than the past is joked about, for the present and the future supply the alcoholic with an ample supply of experiences that can be humorously defined. The following speaker is scheduled to make a speech at a professional convention in three months. She has been asked to prepare an abstract of her paper. She speaks:

I'm terrified. What if I get drunk on the plane? What if there is no A.A. there (she is going to San Francisco), what if I lose my paper on the way. Christ, I've got myself all twisted around. I got so upset this morning I forgot to make coffee. Finally, I got hold of myself and said, "Now listen. This is funny. You should be glad they asked you to give a paper. Of course they have A.A. in San Francisco. Get serious, you fool!" Then I laughed at myself and thought, "This is just how you used to think. You don't have to do this today." I had a good laugh at myself" [field observation, September 2, 1982; 29-year-old chemist].

As this speaker talked, laughter filled the meeting room (see also Maxwell, 1984: 45). As she laughed at herself others laughed with her. Through humor a serious situation was transformed into one that could be laughed about. In this move the situation was made manageable. It was brought back into the interpretive framework of A.A.. Humor thus is an integral part of A.A. talk and of A.A. storytelling.

A putting down of self in relationship to ordinary language is a form of A.A. humor. The following speaker illustrates this point:

> I don't know what the word "complacency" [the topic of the meeting] means. It's too big a word for me [group laughter]. If it means getting back in the driver's seat I can understand it. If it means taking myself too damned seriously I can understand it [laughter]. If it means taking A.A. for granted I can understand it. Is that what it means? [laughter] Now I know I'm a damned fool when it comes to big fancy thinking and talking. But I know I have to come to meetings and keep telling myself I'm an alcoholic. If I forget that I guess I must get complacent and the last time I got complacent I got drunk! [field observation, January 28, 1985, 75-year-old retired salesman].

Here the speaker plays on the meaning of the word "complacency." He works back and forth between its serious meanings and self-deprecating references to his lack of knowledge regarding the meaning of the word. He elaborates the word's meanings for him, connecting his talk to his alcoholism and to getting drunk. As he spoke A.A. members laughed at his statement, "I don't know the meaning of the word." In this act of turning back on himself and showing that he did in fact know the meaning of the word, the speaker distanced himself from the seriousness of the topic, while at the same time grounding his remarks in the last time he was complacent and drank. This ability to laminate, or layer humor alongside a serious topic, through self-distancing humorous asides, characterizes a great deal of A.A. meeting talk. Indeed, this feature of A.A. talk may be said to be its most distinguishing feature. Until the speaker can inject humor into his or her A.A. talk, he or she will not have learned the full meaning of being an A.A. speaker.

Humor and Self-Degradation

Humor is central to the alcoholic's recovery of self. Alcoholics have routinely experienced variations on the degradation ceremonies Garfinkel (1956) has described. They have been placed within an interpretive scheme that brought moral indignation and denunciations from others, usually members of their families and perhaps their employers. Their total identities have been affected by these denunciations, which have produced shame for them and perhaps group solidarity for their denouncers (Garfinkel, 1956: 421). Alcoholics overcome the shame of these experiences by learning to laugh and joke about them. Indeed a member's standing in A.A. is associated, in part, by the degree of humorous distance he can effect between his past and his present humorous understanding of that past. Humor becomes a "role-distancing" (Goffman, 1961b) or "self-distancing" social act.

Consider the following statement that might be negatively met in another social setting. The speaker just broke 11 months of sobriety.

> I bought a whore last night. Blew $450 on booze, cocaine, and sex. Also broke three windows in my house and smashed a table. Found out my old lady was a dealer and had been shacking up with the biggest dealer in town. Boy, was I dumb! I had to weasel the information out of her new old man. Christ, I was groveling on my feet, begging for coke and information at the same time. They was all laughin' at me. I ain't got nowhere to go but up today. I called my parents and told them. They were shocked. Didn't know what to say. Got a head that hurts, a pride that's broken. Feel ashamed of myself. What do you do? Laugh and get your ass to A.A.. Don't drink today. Thanks [field conversation, December 12, 1985; 36-year-old auto mechanic].

The member presents his account in a forthright manner. He discloses the humilating nature of his experience, yet distances himself from it. He placed himself outside normal society, but within A.A. as he spoke. Turning back on himself he laughed. His deviance was understandable because he had been under the influence of drugs and alcohol.

In order to incorporate the deviant and the degrading into the normal, taken-for-granted structures of recovery, the A.A. group (and the member) are led to adopt the self-distancing, nonmoralizing stances that humor provides. However, at the normative level A.A. admonishes the member. "We find it better to stick to our own stories. A man may criticize or laugh at himself and it will affect others favorably" (A.A., 1976: 125). The member is advised not to laugh at another unless he first laughs at himself.

TRANSITIONS IN SELFHOOD: FEAR AND GUILT

As the alcoholic learns how to talk and tell her story in the meetings, a transition in selfhood occurs. As she moves farther and farther away from her last drink she draws nearer to the new self that is sober. Letting loose of the old self is fraught with two problematics: fear and guilt. Fear first: Even if the old self was sick and insane, it was familiar. Furthermore, there was always the drug alcohol to dull the pain of confronting a world that had become totally problematic. The following alcoholic, sober eight months, speaks to this transition in self that occurs in the early days of recovery:

> I'm afraid a lot of the time. Afraid of what people will think. Afraid of what I say. Afraid that my hair is too long, afraid that I'm not clean shaven, afraid that my clothes aren't neat and clean, afraid that I might take that drink. At least when I was drinking the fear was dulled by the booze and the drugs. Now it's just me and the world. Sometimes I'm afraid to go forward. Some days all I do is not drink and not drug. I know these fears are unreasonable. I know I have the program and a higher power and you people, but sometimes I forget. Christ, sometimes I'm afraid to get up in the morning [field observation, January 23, 1985, recovering male alcoholic, age 34, draftsman].

Fear of self, fear of other people, fear of sobriety, fear of time; these fears grip this alcoholic as he, in his words, "white knuckles sobriety." He is caught in the gap between two selves. No longer divided against himself, as he was when he was drinking, he lingers still in the fear of moving forward into the world without the aid of alcohol or drugs. Faced with such a situation the newcomer is told to "Breathe Fear Out and Breathe In Faith."

Alcoholics in recovery distinguish several types of fear: the fear of taking the first drink, the fear of living sober, the fear of confronting the past. A fear of taking the first drink is regarded as healthy. The other fears are not so interpreted, for the program offers measures for living sober without fear. The following alcoholic speaks to the forms of these fears:

> When I was drinking I was afraid of everything. I had a deep, hollow sinking feeling of fear inside myself. Like a huge hole that you could see through. I would pour alcohol into that hole and get over some of the fear, but it was always there when I woke up. It was the fear of self, as the *Big Book* says. When I am overwhelmed by that fear today I say the Serenity Prayer and it helps the fear go away.

> My fear of taking the first drink is good. I never want to go back to drinking and those old fears that made me afraid to go outside and see people. I used to be afraid to deal with what I had done when I was drinking. The Fourth and the Fifth helped with that though. Today I see that my past is something I can learn from. It was somebody I used to be, it's not me today [field observation, February 13, 1982, 26-year-old alcoholic and addict, three years sober and clean].

This attitude toward the past, which can evoke fear, primarily turns on feelings of guilt the alcoholic feels regarding who she was when she drank and what she did when she drank. The following speaker, a female alcoholic with over four years sobriety, clarifies A.A.'s position on fear and guilt toward the past:

> My sponsor put it to me like this. You can either plead guilty for what you did in the past, or plead insanity, like the Second Step says. When I was an active alcoholic I was insane a lot of the time. The crazy things I did were done under the influence of alcohol. If I felt guilt about those things I'd go crazy again. I prefer to think of myself as having been insane when I drank and did those things. That helps take care of the fear, the guilt, and anxiety [field observation, June 23, 1983].

The Past: Regret versus Guilt

A.A. offers, as the last member's account indicates, a method for dealing with the past. The Fourth and Fifth Steps (see Chapter 3; also Denzin, 1986a: chap. 7) are explicitly addressed to the past. Of equal importance is the attitude the member is asked to take toward the past. Three processes are involved. First, the past is to be laid to rest. Second, the member is told to feel regret about the past, but not guilt or shame. Third, closely parallel to the neutralization of guilt is the attitude that those past acts that evoke guilt were in fact produced when the alcoholic was insane. Hence, to be morally accountable and guilty for past actions that were done when the member was in the active phases of alcoholism is itself regarded as an act of insanity.

In these three moves A.A. places a wedge between the member's pre-A.A. history and the experiences of recovery. Laying the past to rest, members are told to remember past mistakes, to remember how bad it was when they drank, and to keep these thoughts fresh. To do so will help keep them from drinking again. A.A. humor defuses the moral stigma of the alcoholic's past. The attitude of regret toward the past further contributes to the member's ability to neutralize the past so as to move forward in recovery.

A.A. teaches, then, a new attitude toward time, morality, guilt, and shame. Guilt is seen as being produced when the member violates a moral code of society that has been internalized and made into a personal moral standard. In order to expunge the guilt from the member's consciousness, A.A. directs the individual to a forgiving higher power. Members are told that this power has forgiven them for what they did in the past. Hence, unless they choose to play God, they should forgive themselves (Kurtz, 1979). By releasing the alcoholic from the past, A.A. puts in motion a process that locates the member in the "now" of the present. These moves reference the Six Theses of Recovery, for they produce a reconstruction in the alcoholic's temporal, emotional, and relational ways of dealing with herself and her interactional associates.

The following members speak to these points on time, morality, guilt, and shame. The first speaker is an elder member of the A.A. group. He has over 15 years sobriety.

> I'll not go to my grave with guilt. I was crazy back then. Sure, I'm ashamed of some of the things I did. But no guilt or shame. Regret, yes. That's healthy. That's good. Hell, I knew every whorehouse in three counties. Every gambler, every prostitute, every drunk. I drank and fucked with all of them. And I went to church every Sunday and asked for forgiveness. Never believed it though. Today I do because my higher power has forgiven me [field conversation, February 19, 1983].

The next speaker has four months sobriety. Divorced, she makes reference to her marriage and family:

> The first time in A.A. I couldn't let go of the past. I felt guilt about my marriage. I was guilty about my daughters and what I had done to them. I was ashamed because I became alcoholic when they were little girls. I took full responsibility for everything. I mean *everything*! Needless to say I was drunk three weeks after I got out of treatment. Today I don't look back. I can't. I can still get all stirred up. I've forgiven myself and so has God. I feel bad about what happened. But I'm not guilty or ashamed any longer. This lady's gettin' better. She's movin' forward [field conversation, December 14, 1985].

The next member speaks to not being able to deal with the past.

> Three months out of treatment I tried to take up everything that had happened to me and that I'd done when I was drunk. Family, work, everything. I got drunk in a week. I made a decision not to deal with those things until I'd had a year's sobriety. So I waited a year. By that time I'd gotten some distance. I learned that I wasn't all bad. I slowly learned to accept my alcoholism and to accept the fact that I wouldn't have done those things if I hadn't been sick, crazy, and drunk. I learned how to forgive myself. I regret that I lost those years, but I don't look back anymore. I think I'm a stronger person today because of those things. You people have shown me how to grow and get stronger and learn from my mistakes [field conversation, May 2, 1983, 51-year-old male, carpenter].

The following woman has been out of detox and in treatment for two days. She is at her second A.A. meeting. The topic of the meeting was "One Day At A Time." She speaks softly:

I've been depressed all day. All this guilt about the past. My kids, my husband, my mother. I've let everybody down. How can I stay sober for the rest of my life with all of this stuff in my head? I get so deep into this stuff. The past and the future are right next to each other. There's no room for the present in my head. I hope I can learn how to live one day at a time [field observation, December 17, 1985].

For this woman the past and the future push the present out of her thoughts. She experiences fear of the future and guilt about the past. A.A.'s theory of the past, which she has yet to learn, hinges on the disease conception of alcoholism. It also includes a theory of a higher power who is forgiving about the past. The A.A. theory makes a basic distinction between guilt, shame, and regret that she has still to learn. As the A.A. member becomes incorporated into the A.A. framework this interpretive theory becomes a part of the new self.

ACCEPTING THE ALCOHOLIC IDENTITY

Acceptance of the alcoholic identity means that the member has moved this identity to the top of his or her hierarchy of personal identities (McCall and Simmons, 1978). This identity has become a master identity (Hughes, 1951) for the alcoholic. Within the A.A. world, and perhaps his other worlds as well, there is no doubt in his mind who he is, wherever he goes. He is an alcoholic first, and then he is the other identities his other commitments in life give him. As this conception of himself is secured, his position within A.A. becomes more firm. He becomes integrated into the A.A. experience (Maxwell, 1984). He may become a GSR of a group, or a group's treasurer. He may speak before "open meetings." His name will be on the list of names that his local A.A. answering service uses when Twelve Step calls come in. His friendship network will include a large number of A.A. members and his participation in pre-A.A. social circles may diminish. He will become a sponsor of other A.A. members. He will continue to work the Twelve Steps and he will be looked upon as a stable member of his A.A. group.

The length of time it will take for these events to begin occurring in the member's life will vary from less than one year to three years. How quickly they come to pass will depend on a number of factors, including the following: (1) the size of the A.A. community; (2) contingencies that arise within that community, such as deaths, moves, and so on; (3) the number of meetings the member attends over a regular span of time; (4) the member's commitment to a particular group; (5) the desire on the part of the member to become involved; (6) other commitments the member has that restrict A.A. participation; and (7) slips.

The Stigma of Alcoholism

Beauchamp (1980), Madsen (1974), Maxwell (1984), Trice and Roman (1970), and A.A. (1975: 70) discuss the stigma of alcoholism. The belief that an alcoholic resides on Skid Row as a result of a failure of morals and self-control lies at the core of this stigma. In order for the member to move to the fully committed A.A. identity, this stigma must be overcome. A.A. is quite explicit on this point. Newcomers are told that a measure of increased self-respect will return when they are able to tell others that they are alcoholic and recovering from alcoholism (A.A., 1975: 70). Such statements, A.A. argues, help to remove the stigma of the malady of alcoholism. Hence, to speak out as an alcoholic has organizational benefits for A.A.; it spreads the understanding that alcoholism is a disease, not a failure of self-will. It also strengthens the members' self-respect and commitment to A.A.

Self-identification as "a recovering alcoholic" is a problematic that every alcoholic must deal with. Next to staying sober, it is perhaps the most difficult situation any newcomer must confront. As the alcoholic progresses through the recovery trajectory, self-attitudes toward the "stigma" of alcoholism change and take on new meanings. Like the homosexual (Boswell, 1980; Foucault, 1982), the alcoholic must, so to speak, "come out of the closet" at some point in his or her recovery career. At first, or course, this new "deviant" identity is shared in A.A. meetings, with fellow alcoholics. Then the alcoholic may share this identity with intimates, family members, and employers. Finally, strangers or brief acquaintances may be informed, as when a person is offered a drink at a cocktail party by a host and turns down the drink because of membership in A.A.

The following member accounts speak to the problematics of this self-disclosure process. The first speaker has been to one A.A. meeting and calls himself an alcoholic.

> I went to a dinner party last weekend. It was O.K. at the beginning 'cause I just got a glass of soda. Then we sat down for dinner and there was a wine glass in front of me. I didn't know what to do. The hostess filled it up and there was a toast. I drank it. I've felt guilty ever since. What should I have done? [field conversation, January 9, 1985].

The next speaker has been sober two weeks. A 40-year-old businesswoman, she states:

We went for cocktails after work last Friday. I didn't know what to say. Everybody looked at me like they expected me to take a drink. I said I wasn't drinking anymore. I could just see all their eyebrows go up. I felt like I wanted to sink under the table. What was I supposed to say? That after 10 years of hell I finally got myself to A.A. and one drink would take me right back where I was before? [field conversation, January 9, 1985].

The next speaker has been sober nine months. A 38-year-old civil servant, he was on a New Year's Eve date with three friends.

We were going to make an evening of it. When it came time to order drinks I said I wanted a Coke. My date looked at me and said, "What's wrong, don't you drink?" I said, "no, not today." She said, "That's good, my father was a drunk." Then I found out she takes every kind of drug I'd ever heard of, even some I hadn't [field conversation, January 9, 1985].

The next speaker has been sober three years. He recounts a drinking situation in the following words:

I'd gone to this Halloween party. The hostess knew I'd stopped drinking. So when I went in she announced: "Here's M, he's stopped drinking. I'm so proud of him." I could have killed her. Then everybody started talking about how they'd like to stop and didn't want to yet. I sat there in front of all that booze. Four days later I went and got drunk. I still wanted to drink. I shouldn't have gone to that party [field observation, January 9, 1985].

The following speaker has been sober 14 years. He states:

Your anonymity is precious to me. I would never disclose your identity as an alcoholic. But mine, I don't care. Everybody within four counties knew I was a drunk. I don't care who knows I'm in A.A., maybe it helped somebody come in to find out about me. That's why I have those A.A. stickers on my car. It lets people know [field observation, January 9, 1985].

This speaker announces his recovering identity with bumper stickers. He represents the opposite end of the self-disclosure continuum. The first two speakers would never announce their identities as recovering alcoholics with an A.A. slogan on their car. These accounts display, then, the differing attitudes A.A. members have toward alcoholism, drinking in social situations, and A.A.. The first four accounts represent members working through their own recovery trajectories. They reveal the heightened self-awareness and self-stigma the new member feels when sobriety is just under way.

These self-attitudes will change as the alcoholic becomes more comfortable in A.A. meetings and in sobriety. But in the early days of recovery the stigma that the alcoholic attaches to alcoholism may in fact impede sobriety. The member is afraid to go to A.A. meetings for fear of being seen by "normals." The following member speaks to this situation.

> In my early days I parked blocks away from the meeting place. I'd walk through the alleys to get there. I'd look both ways before I went in. I was afraid of who would see me. Today I don't care who sees me go in to an A.A. meeting [field conversation, January 9, 1985].

Becoming committed to the A.A. identity and to the identity of recovering alcoholic involves, as the above remarks suggest, a sequential socialization process. Beginning in the preparatory phase as a situational alcoholic, the member moves to the interactional stage where the situational identity is slowly released as the self-stigma of alcoholism is confronted. In the participatory phase the member has internalized the recovering identity, moved beyond the stigma, and accepted the alcoholism-as-a-disease understanding of A.A. The past has been dealt with; its guilt evoking feelings neutralized through A.A.'s theory of regret. In the participatory phase the member has become a fully integrated member of the A.A. group and the larger A.A. community.

As these events come to pass, the member's commitment to A.A. thickens and deepens. She invests herself (Becker, 1960) in A.A., emotionally, personally, temporally, and interactionally. As this commitment increases, her stature as an A.A. member increases. This means, in effect, that when she talks in A.A. meetings other members make it a point to listen. It also means that when they talk they know she will be listening to them. Stature, or standing in A.A., thus turns on the member's ability to talk and listen. It is to these twin topics that I now turn.

TALKING

Talking within the A.A. frame of reference requires, as noted earlier, an ability to speak to the Steps, the Traditions, and the basic A.A. texts, including the *Big Book, The Twelve and Twelve, As Bill Sees It,* and *A.A. Comes of Age.* In those A.A. groups where the *Twenty-Hour a*

Day book is read, the thought for the day is often a topic of discourse as well. That is, a member can presume, upon meeting another member during the day, that he or she has read the thought for the day.

There are two contexts for A.A. talk: in meetings, and outside meetings, including the telephone. The normative constraints that shape these two forms of talking must briefly be addressed.

Talking in Meetings

Within meetings members seldom speak longer than two or three minutes. If they speak for a longer period of time and if they are repeating themselves, or if they are not speaking on topic, the attention of other members will drift. Within meetings members may or may not direct their talk to the talk of another. Members speak, instead, to the topic of the meeting. They may, however, make reference to the talk of another, expressing agreement or disagreement with what another member has said. A member typically only speaks for one turn within a meeting, although after all members have spoken, the Chair will typically ask, "Are there any seconds?" With this invitation a member may speak again, either on or off topic.

Talk within meetings is dictated by the topic of the meeting, which may be a Step, the presence of a newcomer, the thought for the day, an emotion, or a problematic situation a member is confronting. Each member frames a statement around the topic of the meeting, speaking from personal experience and from the standpoint of the A.A. texts.

Breaking "Frame"

Two frames, or frameworks (Bateson, 1972d; Denzin, 1980; Denzin and Keller, 1981; Goffman, 1974), structure the definitions and interactions that occur within the A.A. meeting. The primary framework states, "What is happening here is an A.A. meeting." A secondary framework says, "We are alcoholics, taking turns talking at an A.A. meeting." When members who are in treatment and in treatment groups (see Chapters 3 and 4) come to A.A. meetings as a group, a clash in interpretive framework occurs. A third frame is in operation; the frame of the treatment group. This framework endorses talking at the same time, speaking out of turn, jumping into conversations, and directing advice to another member. It is a personalizing, talking framework. It is counter to the primary and secondary framev   s that structure A.A. meetings.

When members from treatment speak within the framework of the treatment group at an A.A. meeting, regular A.A. members experience what is called "breaking frame." They feel that the A.A. meeting has been turned into a treatment group. This violates their understanding of A.A. discourse. It produces discomfort, anger, and frustration.

Patients from Eastern often came to A.A. meetings as a group. A regular meeting was created in part for them. Its founders intended it as a "newcomer" meeting that would teach patients in treatment how to use A.A. to stay sober. An established A.A. member with five years sobriety became the GSR of the group. He quit after one month. He states his reasons:

> I can't take that fucking group. The members don't know how to talk. They interrupt. They talk out of turn. They gossip, they give advice. They don't stay on the topic. They talk about everything under the sun except A.A. Christ, I need my old Tuesday night group. I can't get to enough meetings as it is. I quit. Sorry, I've got to take care of me [field conversation, October 13, 1985].

The following is an example of the form of talk he found unacceptable. The topic of the meeting is how to deal with resentments.

> *First speaker:* That's a good topic for me. But I don't want to talk about it. I'm mad at my old lady. She ain't sent me any money. Course she's pregnant, got to work, and has other things on her mind. Hell, I'm worried about her and I can't seem to listen in those damned group meetings at the center.
>
> *Second speaker:* My grandmother died. My little girl's sick. I want a drink so bad I can taste it.
>
> *Third speaker:* [Interrupting second] What's your name? Your s'posed to say you're an alcoholic before you speak. We're talking about resentment, not families.
>
> *Fourth speaker:* Let N [second speaker] finish. You ain't s'posed to interrupt. Anyway, I want to talk when he's done. I'm about to do my Fourth Step. Can anybody help me?
>
> *Fifth speaker:* I can. I just finished mine. Felt great when it was done.
>
> *Second speaker:* I haven't finished yet. Can somebody tell me how to stay sober?
>
> *Sixth speaker:* I'm an alcoholic. Pay attention and listen. Let C [a regular A.A. member and Chair of the meeting] talk.

Seventh speaker: I think we should talk about N's [second speaker] problem. I had that kind of thing happen to me three months ago and I've been drunk ever since.

Chair: My name's C. I'm an alcoholic. We are talking about resentments and staying sober today. Some of these other problems we can take up after the meeting. Who wants to go next?

With this statement the meeting fell back into A.A. order, or back into the primary and secondary frameworks of an A.A. meeting. For the first 30 minutes, however, it was in the framework of a treatment group, although specific members attempted to return it to the A.A. framework.

Breaking frame is a recurring feature of A.A. meetings that combine alcoholics in treatment and alcoholics in the community. This clash of interpretive perspectives, evident in the previous account, reveals two strategies of talking in a group. As the more powerful socializing agency, A.A. quickly teaches the new member how to talk within the A.A. primary and secondary frameworks. Once the member leaves treatment this process is quickened because he or she no longer has the treatment group to draw upon within the A.A. meeting. This critical mass of talking others dissolves once its members leave treatment.

Forms of A.A. Meeting Talk

The following format underlies a typical set of utterances by an A.A. member when talking on topic:

(1) self-introduction—"My name is ___ . I'm an alcoholic";
(2) self-reference to topic of meeting, such as resentments;
(3) brief discussion of personal experience with resentments;
(4) connection of topic to an A.A. text or Step (such as the Fourth and Fifth Steps);
(5) illustration of how the topic is or has been resolved in the life of the member;
(6) brief reference to member who has introduced topic (optional); and
(7) expression of gratitude for being sober and conclusion of talk.

Each member within a meeting will be expected to follow a format something like this. When he or she does not, inappropriate talk is being produced. If the member, for example, talks about a personal problem that has no relationship to the topic at hand, or if he or she begins discussing A.A.'s relationship to religion, when spirituality is not the topic, he or she will be ignored or not listened to. While such a speaker is

talking other members will get up, go to the bathroom, get coffee, light
cigarettes, look askance at one another, or begin looking at A.A.
literature if it is on the table.

Talking Outside Meetings

The talk that occurs within A.A. meetings is only a small portion of
the talk that occurs between and among A.A. members. Although
meetings and participation in meetings constitute the focal point of the
A.A. experience, interactions that occur before, after, and between
meetings are significant as well. In these moments personal relationships
are solidified among A.A. members (see Maxwell, 1984: 10). Indeed, a
large amount of the socialization into the A.A. way of life occurs outside
the immediate confines of meetings.

The settings for the interactions that occur outside meetings will vary
by the A.A. group. Some groups have clubhouses, others have large
rooms outside meeting rooms where socializing occurs. Others select a
restaurant or cafe as a meeting place where "the meeting after the
meeting" occurs. Such public places become known as A.A. meeting
places. A member can usually expect to find other A.A. members in such
places before and after meetings.

In these settings sponsors meet with newcomers, and old-timers share
common experiences. These A.A. conversations extend beyond the
narrow "topic"-defined boundaries of the A.A. meeting. In this regard,
they are similar to the conversations that would be produced by the
members of any small group. The rules that govern such conversations
apply, as well, to A.A. conversations (see Grimshaw, 1980, on conversational rules). However, the focus of the talk is nearly always A.A.
related. The following interaction between two A.A. members in a local
cafe having breakfast is an example. The speakers are C, a middle-level
employee of a large multinational communications firm with over four
years of sobriety, and R, a self-employed businessman with over five
years of sobriety.

> C: What's happening with Friday night? Nobody comes anymore. Only six
> there last Friday. Hear they threw eight out of [a treatment center] for
> using. They ain't got any clients right now. Seems like they got more
> N.A.'s (Narcotics Anonymous) than A.A.'s right now. Where's N.A.
> meeting on Tuesdays? Hear [name of a hospital] is closing out that
> meeting. Maybe we should move Friday night [name of another meeting
> place], least we'd have the 7:00 o'clock N.A. meeting beforehand.

Hell, I don't know about this stuff. Somebody slashed all four tires on my car last Friday night. I got other problems. I'm a drunk and I could get drunk over somethin' like that. I got a short memory. Remember, it took me 20 years to get here.

R: I can't worry about other people's meetings. I got to make the meetings that I need. When people go out and use that helps me stay sober. Seems like there a lot more "duals" coming in these days with the young people. Hell, I'm just lucky I never got hooked on drugs. I could be just like them. Friday night used to be the biggest meeting in town. Over 100 people. Now we got five meetings on Friday night. That's good. Gives more people a chance to talk. Friday night will pick back up gain. It always does. Christ, that's a shame 'bout your tires. Who do you think did it? Something like that happened to me once before I got here. I went on a drunk that lasted a week! Hell, in those days I'd use any excuse. I'm just glad I haven't had to have a drink today. I got nothin' to complain about. Where's breakfast? [laughs] Who's complaining? [field observation, as reported, October 2, 1983].

This A.A. conversation weaves problematics within A.A. around the biographical experiences of the two speakers. The Friday night meeting provides a common source of experience for both individuals. C's concern about that meeting is turned by R into a personal statement about meetings. Connecting himself to that meeting, he makes a statement concerning his pattern of meeting attendance. Each speaker makes reference to sobriety, to going out, and to what it was like when they used to drink. They use the slashed tires on C's car as an instance for reflecting on what their conduct in the past would have been like, had that happened before they got to A.A.

This shared, friendly conversation is typical of A.A. interactions outside meetings. The common A.A. identity is shared. A.A. problematics are discussed. Issues from the personal lives of the members are discussed. A sharing of the past and the present is evidenced. Most important, the speakers share their mutual commitment to staying sober today. These conversations outside meetings solidify the underground network that exists between A.A. members.

Seeing another A.A. member in a public place reaffirms a commitment to the identity of recovering alcoholics. Passing as a "normal" in a public place, the member shares his or her A.A. identity with another A.A. member in these conversations that occur over breakfast, lunch, dinner, and coffee. These public meetings, then, provide a bridge between the two worlds of the alcoholic. By being a recovering alcoholic in a public place, the member achieves an interactional accomplishment that had previously been impossible. Passing as a normal (Goffman, 1963), the member presents a public self that alcohol had previously destroyed. Indeed, at the end of the member's drinking days public places may have been avoided. Now, with sobriety in hand, the member comes and goes from the public realm, attempting, as often as possible, to anchor these public appearances in the shared company of other A.A. members.

Telephone Talk

Talking over the telephone is the third major form of A.A. talk. Members share telephone numbers and develop their own A.A. telephone directories. Newcomers are encouraged to call their sponsor, day or night, if they think they may take a drink. Sponsors work with newcomers over the telephone. A.A. friends maintain daily or weekly contact with one another through telephone calls. Arrangements for rides to meetings are made over the telephone. Initial contact with A.A. may occur over the telephone, if a newcomer calls the A.A. answering service. In these several ways the A.A. network is activated and kept alive through the mediated exchanges the telephone offers.

A fully integrated A.A. member will be the recipient of many telephone calls. As a member, because of age or illness, becomes less able to attend meetings, the telephone may be the major form of A.A. contact he or she has. The following statement speaks to this situation. The speaker is 75 years old. Ill for several months, he has not been able to attend meetings. Famous for his sponsorship work within A.A., he discusses his relationship to those he works with over the telephone.

> I was on the phone for over five hours today. Three lovely ladies called me. One from Canada, one from Florida, and one here in town. They wanted to know how I was feeling. They just shared their experiences with me. I don't know what I'd do without that phone of mine. It keeps me alive and helps me stay off the self-pity pot.
>
> You know, this program gave me my life back. I have so many dear friends. I am just so grateful [field observation, June 20, 1984. This speaker died two weeks later].

The use of the telephone and learning how to use the telephone are two major measures of how the recovering alcoholic becomes, in a fuller sense, an A.A. member. Indeed, it may be said that next to the meeting, the telephone is the most important form of interaction members have with one another. To not use the telephone is, then, to restrict severely one's participation in the A.A. world. There are, of course, members who do not have telephones and there are A.A. "loners" who are located in settings where telephones cannot be used. In these situations A.A.'s *Grapevine* becomes an important medium of A.A. interaction, as are the few meetings that the member is able to attend. The next speaker speaks to this situation.

> I was in North Africa. Ain't no meetings there. Can't call your sponsor back home, either. I read my *Big Book* and some old *Grapevines* I took with me. Then they had a flight come up to Morocco. I got myself on it. Plane stopped three times. Picked up three A.A.'s on the way. I didn't know that 'till I got to Morocco and to the A.A. meeting place. Them three guys were there, too. That meeting cost me $500. Cheap [field observation, as reported, April 2, 1983; 41-year-old Marine sergeant, over seven years sobriety].

LISTENING

In addition to learning how to talk within the A.A. frame of reference, the member must learn how to become a listener. This requires an ability to identify with the person who is speaking and to locate the central problematic the speaker is attempting to discuss. An A.A. saying, often repeated, goes as follows: "Take the cotton out of your ears and put it in your mouth. You can't learn to speak until you learn to listen." A.A. newcomers are told to listen. They are told that they will hear their stories around the tables. They are also told that they are not unique. They are told that before they can understand their problems they have to learn what A.A. is all about. This involves a loss of ego, or a loss of self-centeredness. Told to "eat your ego" and be quiet, the newcomer may be chastised for speaking too much.

The following speaker makes this point. Sober over 14 years, he has been the director of a treatment center. He is talking to a newcomer who has talked for 15 minutes, repeating himself several times:

> Learn to keep your mouth shut. Listen, don't talk. The answers are here. You don't have them. That's why you are here. Your way didn't work. Learn to swallow your pride and listen. I had to. When I first got here I thought I had all the answers. I didn't. I'm not sure I do today. But I know I had to learn to keep quiet and listen [field observation, June 20, 1983].

If listening involves learning how to keep quiet in a meeting and not "over-talking," it also involves an ability to speak to the problems of another.

The next speaker describes her sponsor:

She's a good listener. I call her. I'm all messed up, saying a thousand
things at the same time, nothin' making sense. Just confused. I can go on
like this for 10 minutes and she won't say anything. Then I'll stop and
she'll say something like, "Do you think you are getting in the way of your
program? Have you turned it over today?" That's all she'll say, oh, maybe
a little more. Like "be good to yourself." And that's exactly what I need to
hear. She knows how to listen [field observation, June 20, 1982].

BRINGING PROBLEMS TO THE TABLES

Having discussed the major "forms" of A.A. talk, I now turn to the
"content" of the talk that occurs around the A.A. tables. As the
member learns how to talk and listen, he or she learns to bring "sobriety
problems" to the tables for discussion.

Told to "talk about it in here so you don't drink about it out there,"
the member learns that anything can be a sobriety problem. He or she
learns this in two ways. First, by listening to the topics that are discussed
at the tables the member comes to understand what the other members
regard as sobriety problems in their lives. Second, by inspecting her own
biography, the member can discover what events she is using, or could
use, as excuses to drink again. Reminded by old-timers that "anybody
can get sober, but not everybody can stay sober," the new member is
admonished to bring her problems to the meetings. She is told that she
must be able to go to any length to achieve and maintain her sobriety.

Sobriety Problems

The problems of living sober are, in a sense, the same problems that
stand in the way of obtaining sobriety. The new member who listens at
meetings will learn that any of the following topics of discussion
represent "sobriety problems": anger, resentment, depression, conflicts
in the workplace or at home, confusions over sexual identity, disputes
with A.A. members (including sponsors), broken anonymity, dry
drunks that turn into wet drunks, slips that aren't returned from,
temptations to drink from friends, amends that go wrong, loneliness,
feelings of guilt and shame about the past, inabilities to meet high
standards set by self or others, using drugs other than alcohol,
frustrations with Twelve Step Calls, problems with the "spiritual" part
of A.A., false pride, lack of patience, tolerance or acceptance of others,

attempts to control others, criticisms of A.A. by friends, divorces, deaths, close friends in the program "going out," living too far in the past or the future, money problems, debts, loss of a driver's license, being sent to prison, jail, or a mental hospital, envy of others with more sobriety, envy of others who can still drink, promotions at work, being fired or terminated from a job, being given more choices than one can deal with, or being sober, but having no peace of mind, or serenity. In short anything can be a sobriety problem. It is not necessary, nor is it possible, to discuss all of the "sobriety" problems that are brought to the A.A. meetings. The preceding list is representative.

There are two levels to the content of the topics that are discussed at A.A. meetings: (1) the directly personal and (2) the A.A. concept that would fit the personal. In a sense, this distinction reflects Schutz and Luckmann's (1973) distinction between first-order and second-order concepts. First-order concepts, derived from lived experience, are filtered in A.A. meetings through the second-order conceptual structure of the A.A. philosophy.

The following is a depiction of these two conceptual structures:

A Problem from Lived Experience:	A.A.'s Conceptual Re-Interpretation:
(1) feeling lonely, fearful, wanting to drink;	(1) self-pity, faith, gratitude, primary purpose;
(2) anger with family;	(2) powerlessness, emotional sobriety;
(3) guilt about the past;	(3) Fourth and Fifth Steps;
(4) depression;	(4) get involved in A.A.; chapter 7 *Big Book*;
(5) resentments;	(5) Fourth and Fifth Steps;
(6) failing to meet standards;	(6) Easy Does It, First Things First;
(7) slips;	(7) spiritual program, First and Third Steps;
(8) impatience with work;	(8) gratitude;
(9) confused, anxious;	(9) Turning It Over, One Day At A Time; and
(10) relationships.	(10) primary purpose, Third Step, prayer and meditation.

As a member presents a problem to the A.A. group when the call for topics is made, the chairperson will if possible reinterpret that problem within the A.A. framework. The following exchange is typical, and it indicates how the above list of two topics works.

Chair: Does anyone have a topic or problem they would like to discuss?
Speaker: I do. I don't know how to put it exactly. I guess it's work. There's this guy. I used to drink a lot with him. I know he's got a problem. I've said something to him. He doesn't want help. I think I secretly hate him. Anyway he controls what I do, he's head of my division. This morning he called me in and I got so mad I could have screamed. I've been upset ever since. I'm glad I'm here. Thank you.
Chair: Sounds like resentment to me. Anybody want to start? [field observation, November 2, 1983]

The speakers that followed discussed resentments, powerlessness, anger, emotional sobriety, turning it over at work, being grateful for a job, and First Things First. Each speaker drew upon a personal instance in his or her life where the problematics presented by the second speaker had appeared. In this way this meeting addressed the specific problems one member had on that day living sober and not drinking. This is how A.A. works in the meetings.

SELVES, TALKING, AND STORYTELLING

In Denzin (1986a: chap. 8) I suggested that the recovering alcoholic experiences four forms of self-awareness. I termed these (1) self-as-loss, (2) self-as-false-subjectivity, (3) self-as-transcendent, and (4) self-as-social-critic. Every alcoholic, I proposed, moves from experiences of feeling that life is empty and lacking in meaning (self-as-loss), to attempts to locate self in material things (false subjectivity), to feelings of transcendence, which are located in alcohol and drugs and in the A.A. experience. As a social critic the alcoholic believes that he sees things about his culture and his times that other persons are unable to see.

Self as a Double
Structure of Experience

Once alcoholics reach the participatory stage of A.A. selfhood and fully commit themselves to the recovering alcoholic identity, they are able to look back on their lived experiences and find a "center" to their life that was previously not present. A doubling of self occurs (see Booth, 1961/1983: 71-76, 83, 109, 151-152, 172; Dostoevski, 1846; Lacan, 1977: 3-4). That is, the individual is able to turn back on himself, see himself as subject and object, and distance himself from who he previously was (see Mead, 1934).

This doubling occurs within the stories the alcoholic tells. She sees herself reflected in the looking-glass of her past experiences. Her new self is also reflected back to her in the faces of her fellow A.A. members (Cooley, 1902/1956: 183-185). She becomes a second self within the texts of the stories she tells (Booth, 1961/1983: 83, 109). Through a variety of narrative stances toward herself and her past she tells a multitude of stories and tales about "what it was like, what happened and what it is like now" (A.A., 1976: 58).

In this process the alcoholic relives her past. She seizes it anew, retrieves it, and recenters it within her recovery experience. As she goes through her old experiences she does so from the vantage of a new recovering self. She exorcises herself from her past in retelling stories of it. In this process she becomes a different kind of self. She objectifies her past, gets outside of it, and turns it into a social object that now takes on new meanings. She locates her past within a new structure of experience, which is given by A.A..

The Stories

It is in the alcoholic's stories that the doubling of self is most frequently displayed. The A.A. member reveals two selves when speaking. The first is the self of the storyteller. The second is the self of the recovering alcoholic who is reflecting on the past, the present, and the future. These two selves merge and double back on one another. As the member speaks, the voice of the storyteller is heard. This voice provides facts, pictures, and images about events that the other members have not witnessed. The speaker molds a picture of himself that joins him to the group. He socially constructs himself as he talks.

When the member talks he offers others a privileged access to inner thoughts and past experiences. However, as a dramatic narrator of life events, the speaker may be a reliable or unreliable storyteller. He or she may be comic, serious, satiric, ironic, truthful, overly emotional, deadpan, deceptive, direct, or indirect. But as the member talks, a narrative structure of events unfolds. When speaking the A.A. narrator controls the distance between himself, the story he tells, and his audience. He may say, as does the following speaker, the following to preface his story:

> You may not like me for what I'm about to say. You may hate me. But that's all right. This is what I have to say. I've lied. I've cheated, I've stolen things. I've been violent to people, once I broke a man's back because he wouldn't give me a hit. I don't care what you think, I'm here for me [field

observation, as reported, January 14, 1985; 28-year-old recovering alcoholic and addict, third week in treatment; salesman].

As this speaker distances himself from his A.A. audience, he challenges that audience to draw near to his story. He evokes sympathy and dislike in the same breath. In this process emotion is controlled, and attempts to present a realistic, if not glossed over, view of lived experience is given. The speaker's voice, then, as he acts out his part as a storyteller, speaks the words of a self that is recovering. Direct or indirect, objective, subjective, compassionate, or neutral, personal or impersonal, humorous, pompous, ministerial, therapeutic, philosophical, fatherly or motherly, this is the voice of recovery. And it is the voice of a speaker who is able to double back on himself, reflect himself in his talk, distance himself from his experiences, and talk about himself in a way that seemingly only requires his voice in order for the talk to be accomplished. *That is, he has become a storyteller.* He is no longer a suffering alcoholic unable to speak, nor is he a lost self. He has obtained an objective view of his own subjectivity. He has discovered that his subjectivity is interactional, reflective and *in* the stories he tells to the A.A. group.

The member has become the producer of the oral text he speaks. This is the text of his life. But this work is always unfinished, for his story will never be completely told. There are too many ways to tell it. Furthermore, the meaning of these stories he tells resides in the telling, for he creates meaning as he speaks. He must, as Booth (1961/1983: 83) suggests of all authors, literally put "his self on the table" in some form or another.

The alcoholic speaker, as he experiences the doubling of self, is firmly rooted in the oral tradition of Western culture. He is the storyteller par excellence. He has learned how to define himself through his talk. However, the language of A.A. speaks, not the alcoholic. The alcoholic is the language he speaks (Heidegger, 1976). His talk, as a spoken text, produces him (Derrida, 1978). And this is his ultimate paradox: In order to find himself he has to learn to speak a language that others before him have produced. He can only learn that language by listening to others who are also learning how to talk and think within the same set of meanings. But by learning how to speak this language he finds a new image and understanding of himself. The alcoholic finds himself, in part, in the external signs and significations of A.A.. He does this by telling his story over and over again, for he resides in these stories. He knows, too, that he will always have an audience for his stories. All he needs to do is go to the next A.A. meeting. For at the A.A. meeting he will be given his turn to talk and in that talk he can accomplish what he cannot do by himself. He can, that is, double back on himself, reflect on himself, hear himself talk, and locate himself within a structure of experience in which he is both object and subject to himself. In so doing he provides the context for others who seek the same ends for themselves.

Doris Lessing (1969) provides a fitting conclusion to this discussion for she speaks directly to the doubling of self that the alcoholic experiences.

> How very extraordinary it was . . . being the person who ran and managed and kept going. . . . It was as if more than ever one was forced back into that place in oneself where one watched; whereas all around the silent watcher were a series of defences, or subsidiary creatures, on guard, always working, engaged with—and this was the point—earlier versions of oneself.

CONCLUSIONS

I have examined the relationship between A.A. and the changing self of the recovering alcoholic. I have shown how A.A. gets inside the self of the alcoholic. In this process the alcoholic moves from being a situational alcoholic to a committed member of A.A. A socializing process organizes this experience, moving the member through three stages of A.A. selfhood. I have shown how gender and race structure this process, which involves a radical restructuring of the commonsense foundations of the individual's self. Central to the recovery of self is learning how to become a storyteller about one's life, before and after A.A. membership. The self is recovered in and through the stories the member learns to tell. Talking and listening thus become the key processes that structure the member's new senses of A.A. selfhood. "Breaking frame," or talking outside the primary and secondary interpretive frameworks of an A.A. meeting, reveals how individuals in the preparatory stages of becoming members socialize one another into and away from the A.A. point of view.

Fully committed A.A. members learn how to deal with the self and societal stigmas of being alcoholic. They accept the disease conception of alcoholism, and see themselves as members of an organization that is changing their life for the better. Learning how to let go of the past and the guilt it carries for them, A.A. members live into existence the Six Theses of Recovery. In so doing they transform themselves and the worlds they live in.

7

INTERPRETING ALCOHOLISM
AND RECOVERY

The desire [to drink] will return [A.A. member].

The task of offering an interpretive framework for the understanding of alcoholism and the recovery process remains. This requires a reflection on the contents of this volume and its companion, *The Alcoholic Self.* It is not my intention to offer a *theory* of alcoholism and recovery; however, the outline of an interpretation may be set forth. This will involve a reconsideration of the Six Theses of Alcoholism, and a discussion of selfhood, desire, drinking, and alcohol in American society.

THE SIX THESES

I have repeatedly examined the two sides of alcoholism, asking in a variety of ways the same two questions: "How do ordinary men and women live into existence that dis-ease of conduct called alcoholism, and then, having been labeled alcoholics, recover from this form of experience?" The center of my work has moved outward from the self of

195

the active and recovering alcoholic. My analysis has shown that it is impossible to separate alcoholism from group, interactional, and cultural contexts. Alcoholism and recovery are group phenomena. In its active phases, alcoholism involves families, drinking groups, and interactional associates. In the recovery phases, treatment centers and Alcoholics Anonymous play central parts in restructuring the alcoholic's self. In both phases the alcoholic develops situational adjustments to the problematics her alcoholism has produced for her. These adjustments lead to situational and committed self-definitions that identify the individual as an alcoholic.

The Six Theses of Alcoholism map the interpretive structures of self, time, emotion, and social relationship that the active alcoholic develops and lives out. Alcoholism involves a denial process that leads the alcoholic to live a mode of existence that is rooted in bad faith. Committed to the belief that each individual should be the "captain of his soul," the alcoholic denies the facts of his alcoholic existence. Willful self-pride leads her to drink when the likelihood of success is minimal and the probability of failure is high (Bateson, 1972a). Alcoholism becomes a form of self risk-taking in which the alcoholic tests her will power against the drug alcohol. Only when the problematics of her life become subjectively insurmountable is the alcoholic likely to surrender to her dis-ease of alcoholism and admit that she cannot drink like "normal" social drinkers. This act of commitment may bring her into a treatment center for alcoholism where she will learn that she suffers from what her society calls a disease. Her disease of alcoholism is emotional, her drinking but a symptom of an underlying emotional disorder. Treatment and A.A. offer the languages and situations for a restructuring of self that incorporates the alcoholism-as-disease conception into the alcoholic's view of herself.

The insanity of the alcoholically divided self has been compared to the new senses of self that A.A. and treatment offer. My lengthy study of the treatment process disclosed how old structures of self are cleared away through a "stripping" process that lays bare an empty inner self that has lost itself to alcoholism.

I have shown that once the world of recovery is entered, both in treatment and in A.A. meetings, the alcoholic finds a new structure of experience that rests on "alcoholic understanding" and a dialectical group process. A new self rises out of the languages, rituals, and interactions that A.A. groups and meetings offer. As this new self appears, and as the alcoholic learns how not to drink, the old self of the past slips away, to be replaced by a radically transformed sense of selfhood.

The recovering alcoholic discovers a new interpretive theory of self, meaning, alcohol, and alcoholics. This theory replaces the system of denial and bad faith that his or her self-system had previously clung to. This theory, which is A.A.'s, blends a pragmatic understanding of conduct with a practical, spiritual ethic that has a single purpose— staying sober today.

In telling this story I have repeatedly focused on the universal singularity of each alcoholic's recovery experience. I have assumed that each alcoholic's experience is unique, particular to his or her lived situation. Hence, there are as many stories of recovery as their are alcoholics who are recovering. However, it can be argued that there is only one recovery story, the story that is given in the Twelve Steps of A.A., and in A.A.'s *Big Book*. That is, alcoholics who recover through A.A. learn and tell the same basic recovery story, the one that is given in the basic texts of A.A. Hence, recovery becomes a story-telling process involving socialization into the language and lore of A.A. (Thune, 1977).

DRINKING, ALCOHOL, AND AMERICAN SOCIETY

The schools, laws, peer groups, families, work groups, and agencies of social control in American society teach individuals how to drink, how to use alcohol, and how to act when under the influence of alcohol (Jellinek, 1962; Lemert, 1967; MacAndrew and Edgerton, 1979). American society, like other societies, ritually integrates the beverage and drug called alcohol into its interactional and moral orders. The drinking of alcohol is a symbolic ritual and interactional act in our society. Americans connect the drinking of alcohol with the occasioned release of tension and anxiety. They drink so as to solidify lines of sociable identification with one another. They utilize certain alcoholic beverages as status markers of self-worth. They connect the drinking of alcohol with the pursuit and interactional realization of a valued social self. They learn to drink so as to celebrate the good times and they drink to drown the sorrows of failures and bad times.

Accepted normal drinking is symptomatic of our culture's attitudes toward the drinking act; that is, all drinkers, when they stay within the boundaries of acceptable "drinking comportment," are culturally symptomatic drinkers (Jellinek, 1962; MacAndrew and Edgerton, 1969). The drinking act connects the drinker's self to the culture's values regarding alcohol and social drinking. However, some "symptomatic drinkers" become occasional, symptomatic excessive drinkers. They transfer alcohol from its status as a beverage to its use as a drug. They use alcohol as a means of relieving major individual stresses that are social in nature. Within this group of occasional symptomatic excessive drinkers emerge those individuals for whom alcohol becomes a "mode of living" (Jellinek, 1962: 359). These drinkers become addictive alcoholics. They lose control over the amount they drink on any given occasion and they are unable to abstain from drinking for any continuous period of time. Their use of alcohol causes them and society problems. It is this category of drinker that I have studied in this volume and in *The Alcoholic Self*.

Alcoholics appear to emerge in those social groups, families, and cultural settings where heavy drinking is permitted and where the temporary euphoria of the alcoholic "high" is valued over its dysfunctional and negative psychological effects; indeed, these negative effects are often defined as part of the cost of the high that the drinking of alcohol produces (see Cahalan, 1970: 151-154; Jellinek, 1960). Alcoholics create and seek out social spaces that legitimate heavy, regular alcohol consumption. The "drinking spaces" alcoholics live in place a high premium on the selfhood that is achieved through the drinking act. These places are also filled with sufficiently justifiable reasons for drinking. These reasons, which become motives for drinking, may include unemployment, marital or relational disruptions, loneliness, financial pressures, anxiety, and the desire to escape from the demands of ordinary life. *The core problematic that organizes the "pre-alcoholic" drinking situation is the desire to escape from self through the use of alcohol.* The inner structure of the pre-alcoholic's self tends, as Tiebout (1949) suggested, toward self-centeredness, narcissism, loneliness, and a fearfulness of self and other.

Ressentiment and Alcohol

Particular social groups, by virtue of their structural location in American society, are more likely to adopt the previously outlined definitions regarding self and alcohol. Members of such groups are characterized by the emotional attitude Scheler (1912/1961: 39-40) termed *ressentiment*. Ressentiment is a backward-looking emotionality. It is a form of self-hatred that is located in the real and imagined actions another has taken toward the person. It is a self-poisoning emotion that colors all of the interactions the subject has with others, particularly those in authority positions. Ressentiment is characterized by two key features. First, it involves the repeated experiencing and reliving of a particular emotional reaction against someone else. Second, the quality of this emotional reaction is negative, often involving hostility, anger, wrath, and a vengeful joy in the other's misfortunes. Scheler suggests that for the man or woman of ressentiment, this cluster of emotional feelings comes to form the center of their personality. Such persons look out on the world of interaction through the negative framework that ressentiment offers. Each time the subject acts toward the other for whom ressentiment is felt, a sense of inferiority and repressed rage is experienced. Because of their structural relation to the other for whom they feel this hatred, the subject is unable to express the feelings that are felt. Hence, ressentiment becomes a repressed or buried emotional attitude. Holding in these feelings, which are then turned inward, subjects come to undermine their own senses of self-worth. They feel inferior in the eyes of the other. The desire to strike out is repressed, leading to a feeling of impotence, which is surrounded by an inner seething rage.

Scheler argues that certain social structures regularly produce the emotion of ressentiment (also see Denzin, 1984a: 226). Social democracies that espouse equality of rights for all but allow wide variations to exist between expectations and what is in fact received engender ressentiment on the part of the "young, the elderly, women, the handicapped, the stigmatized, and members of racial and ethnic minorities" (Denzin, 1984a: 226). These special populations are especially prone to alcohol abuse and to higher rates of alcoholism within American society (see Gomberg, 1982: 337-343, 351-352). Certain occupational groups also experience greater degrees of ressentiment, including the military, civil servants, academic professionals, certain clergy groups, other members of the educational establishment (including students), professional athletes, the unemployed, and those on welfare. Ressentiment is greatest when self- or group-injury is experienced as destiny and as being beyond one's control. When powerlessness is great, ressentiment increases, as does alcohol use and abuse.

The man or woman of ressentiment fuels these negative emotional feelings with alcohol; indeed, drinking may be the only socially legitimate escape persons in such situations feel is available to them. When the economic, interactional, gender, moral, political, legal, and religious structures of a society regularly produce large categories of persons who experience the emotions of ressentiment, then such structures lay the foundation for higher rates of alcoholism among the members of these special populations who come to feel that ressentiment is in fact their destiny. The dis-ease of alcoholism thus becomes a structural phenomenon, attached to the emotional experiences of large categories of persons in contemporary American life. It may be argued that the structures of society produce the emotions and forms of emotionality that turn back on the very structures that produced them (Denzin, 1984a: 227). In this sense the dis-ease of alcoholism becomes a poisoning emotional attitude that reflects an inner dis-ease of self in the central social institutions of American society. Basic to this dis-ease conception are the negative attitudes toward time and emotion that I have located at the heart of the alcoholic's alcoholism. The backward-looking, temporal nostalgia that typifies much of the postmodern period (Habermas, 1985), which combines with a negative emotional reading of current social relationships (Baudrillard, 1983b, 1983c) is thus symptomatic of a contemporary version of ressentiment. Such conditions create the basis for the violent, repressed, distorted emotion-ality so characteristic of alcoholism and related drug abuses.

Motives, Desire, and Drinking

For individuals of ressentiment a functional autonomy of drinking motives (Allport, 1964: 29; Cahalan, 1970: 153; Jellinek, 1960: 74; Wexberg, 1951) develops. This joins the drinking of alcohol with (a) the euphoric pleasures of drinking and (b) the inner emptiness of self the individual feels on a regular basis. The reasons and purposes for drinking extend beyond the original contexts in which the individual drank for social reasons. He or she now drinks so as to relieve the stress of self that is continually felt. Drinking becomes a functionally autonomous act. It is inscribed in the basic and primary self-images the person commits to. Because alcoholics carry this picture of themselves into every situation they enter, they always have a reason to drink or to think about drinking.

The functional autonomy of the drinking motive is layered through the basic self-structures of the individual. As the alcoholic moves from the pre-alcoholic to the prodomal and then crucial and chronic stages of alcoholism, the drinking act produces a second layer of emotions and negative experiences that are woven into the underlying negative emotions the person already holds about himself (Jellinek, 1962). The individual literally produces an "alcoholic personality" for himself.

The drinking motives of the individual are driven by the "desire" to escape and then to find self. The alcoholic's desire for self seeks realization in a mode of consciousness that is in control of itself and free from fear and anxiety. Alcoholic desire is that mode of self-consciousness that desires itself through the altered streams of experience alcohol produces. Alcoholic desire is consciousness aimed at its own fulfillment. It is self- and body centered, for it is felt throughout the drinker's body as he or she drinks. In this desire the objects of the alcoholic's consciousness are under her control, for she brings them into existence as she drinks. Her desire links her to a world of others that is primarily imaginary, distorted, and inward based. The alcoholic's drug-induced desire brings her up against relations with others, which she often demolishes through alcoholic and emotional violence. Her desire shuts her off from the very world she wishes to be a part of (Denzin, 1985c: 49).

Desire and the Self

When alcoholics tell newcomers that "the desire to drink will return," they are referencing the double aspect of alcoholic desire. That is, the desire that returns is aimed at a form of selfhood that alcohol produces. Hence, the desire to drink is a desire to return to a self of the past in which alcoholic desire dominated the drinker's consciousness.

The self that the alcoholic seeks in the drinking act is a ritual, sacred self that will join him with his fellows, who may also share his ressentiment. He desires a mode of self-experience that will ratify his wholeness to himself and to others; never mind that this is a fictional wholeness based on alcohol. By producing a fictional unity with self and other he molds a sacred, ritual image of himself that purportedly allows him to pass as "normal" in the company of other "normal" interactants, with and toward whom he may share or feel ressentiment.

However, the alcoholic's fellow interactants find a valued mode of selfhood in "normal" social drinking that is filtered through social interaction. The alcoholic, on the other hand, understands that he can only find his ritual, sacred self in the privateness of alcoholic drinking. Once he finds that self in alcohol he can then bring it to the occasions of social interactions his fellows take for granted. Literally overflowing with selfhood, the alcoholic finds that his cherished, sacred, inner ritual self is unwanted in civil, social society.

The Inner, Alcoholic Self

The inner self of the alcoholic, nourished on alcohol, has been wounded, perhaps since childhood. The sources of these wounds are interactional and interpersonal. They derive from the formative matrix of interactional experiences that brought the alcoholic into the drinking cultures of his or her society. At the center of these experiences stand unstable inner self-feelings, faulty understandings of the other, emotional loneliness, a lack of trust in the others, and an inability to enter into fully consensual "I-me" dialogues with others. An "anxiety" of relating to the other (Sullivan, 1953), a preponderance of negative emotional experiences that detach the individual from close relations with others, and a failure to achieve full recognition in the "eyes" of the other contribute to the inner instability of the pre-alcoholic's self.

Distorted, unbalanced, and uneven emotional relations with "fathering" and "mothering" others lead the pre-alcoholic to place an emotional wedge between self and figures of authority. Fearful of abuse, shame, or experiencing a lack of subjectively defined proper recognition from the other, the pre-alcoholic enters the world of interaction from the vantage point of an imaginary self that has found its own center in its self. Unable to love the other fully, the alcoholic exaggerates self-love, becoming narcissistic, self-centered, and resentful. But because the other cannot or will not furnish the recognition and love that is desired, the alcoholic's self-love is tainted with insecurity, guilt, and egocentric uncertainty.

If the alcoholic's significant others are (or were) alcoholic (as was the case for nearly every alcoholic I studied), then two self interactional patterns are set in motion. First, the pre-alcoholic learns alcoholic emotions and learns how to drink alcoholically. Second, the pre-alcoholic sets out to prove that he or she *will not* become alcoholic. A battle with alcohol, which is a battle with self, follows. In an attempt to regain a measure of status and recognition in the eyes of the significant other, the pre-alcoholic sets out to drink more than the other, and yet not become alcoholic. Perhaps genetically doomed to failure, the individual becomes an alcoholic in the process.

Alcoholic Self-Comportment

Hence, those same social agencies, social groups, and individuals who taught the alcoholic how to drink so as to bring a valued social self into existence now turn against her and brand her a problem drinker, or an alcoholic. These labels, which apply to selfhood and interactional comportment, serve to undercut the drinker's standing in her social groups. She finds herself with a self that has no place to go. She has acquired the stigmatizing label of "alcohol." As a recovering alcoholic she will work to remove this stigma of self.

The foregoing suggests that those agencies and groups that teach individuals how to drink normally also teach them how to identify problem drinkers. Alongside these agencies exists a social structure that has been created to deal with problem drinkers. Alcoholism researchers, treatment centers for alcoholism, and A.A. study and teach problem drinkers how to become recovering alcoholics.

These structures remind us that although any society apparently finds some utility in having deviants who define the outer limits of normal conduct, they also need agencies that bring these deviants back in line (Durkheim, 1912/1961). So it is with the active and recovering alcoholic. He or she traverses both edges of the sacred and the profane in American society. Once a flagrant drinker, the alcoholic who recovers in A.A. becomes abstinent. The alcoholic's career thus highlights the two moral extremes American society takes toward drinking and alcohol. Yet, by learning how not to drink, but by discovering a new sense of selfhood in A.A., the alcoholic presents a dilemma to society. That is, the resources for discovering a nonalcoholic, serene self lie in interactions with one's fellows; just as it supposedly rests in the drinking groups that make up our society. Hence, either way he looks, the alcoholic finds that the foundations of his self rest in structures that are outside the mainstream interactional worlds of modern American life.

RECAPTURING SELF

The recovering alcoholic recaptures a sense of selfhood that was lost to alcoholism. A new, sacred, ritual self is given by virtue of sobriety and participation in the storytelling rituals and traditions of A.A. It must be remembered that 7 of 10 alcoholics who undergo treatment relapse. These persons adopt the situational identity of alcoholic. Those who do commit themselves to recovery assume committed, recovering alcoholic identities. In Rudy's (1986) terms they become pure, converted, and committed alcoholics. It is these alcoholics that I now speak to. Their social experiences are sociologically important because they reveal how a new social self, which flows from the sacred, collective structures of group life, may be created.

With Mead (1934), Durkheim (1912/1961), Sullivan (1953), and Wiley (1985) the following process for recapturing self may be sketched. As previously argued (Denzin, 1986a), the recovering alcoholic experiences four modes of self-awareness: self-as-loss, self located in material things, self-as-transcendent, and self-as-social-critic. The recovering alcoholic learns a new mode of selfhood that locates self in the interactional structures of the A.A. experience (Maxwell, 1984). This structure is larger than the alcoholic. It has collective, ritual properties, given in the A.A. Steps and Traditions. These properties are also evidenced in A.A. storytelling and in the other interactions that occur around the A.A. tables.

Four levels, or structures, of experience connect the self of the individual to A.A.: the personal, the dyadic, the group, and the collective. The personal level is given in the member's daily meditations with the texts of A.A. The dyadic level is given in the sponsor relationship and in the friendships that develop in A.A. In the sponsor relationship (Denzin, 1986a) the member reenacts a relationship to authority figures from the past. In this relationship members find social recognition, self-esteem, and a sense of identification that was previously lacking in their lives. They learn how to identify with and through the emotional experiences of another who has the valued, sober, sacred self they seek.

The sponsor relationship objectifies the new self that is sought. It anchors that self in the experiences of an older, more knowledgeable member, who becomes a coaching, socializing agent for the new A.A. member (see Strauss, 1959).

Within the A.A. group the member learns how to enact and present this new, sober self. Members learn how to talk about the self of the past that is slipping away as they become sober. They learn how to allow this self to become a part of the past. The old self of the past, filled with not-me and bad-me social experiences (Sullivan, 1953), is absorbed into the archetypical past (Thune, 1977) A.A. offers. As this self becomes a part of the past, the new sober self, grounded in the rituals and languages of A.A., takes its place. This self is located in the "good-me" experiences (Sullivan, 1953) that the sponsor and the A.A. group make available to the member. It becomes a storytelling, sober self that enters into the collective structures of the A.A. community.

That is, as the member becomes and stays sober, his or her biography becomes a part of the collective A.A. consciousness. The member's recovery story is shared by others. His or her home group becomes common knowledge within the A.A. social world, for instance, Jane of the Monday Night Group. At this collective level, the new, sacred self of the member becomes part of a collective group self. It enters into the group's collective understanding of itself as a group that has regular, sober members.

A.A. symbolizes the sacredness of the member's self at each of the previously stated four levels: the individual, the dyadic, the group, and the collective. This is seen in the principle of anonymity that is the spiritual foundation of the A.A. traditions (A.A., 1953). By stripping each individual of any sense of uniqueness, and by transforming each member into an anonymous member of a collective whole that is governed by spiritual principles, A.A. creates a society of co-equal selves. Each self is sacred in its own right, but sacred only because of its membership in the collectivity as a whole. Each part of that collective whole (the personal, dyadic, group) is necessary in order for the collective level to exist. A.A. cannot be reduced to the selves of its individual members. These selves are part of and produced by something that is larger than any given individual. Hence, a collective, ritual self enters the self of each member; that ritual self in turn contributes to and becomes part of something larger than it is.

By taking individuals with ruined, distorted, disorganized selves and giving them a new, sacred, whole self, A.A. reveals how the collective creates the individual. At the same time, the individual creates the collective, for without members there would be no A.A. groups. Without groups there would be no society of preexisting sober selves. Such a society, which exists *sui generis*, is necessary for the emergence of a new sober self that learns how to take the attitudes of sober, previously drinking alcoholic selves (see Mead, 1934). Mead's principle of sociality, which involves the ability to take the attitude of the other, thus organizes the key processes through which A.A. works. As Mead noted, significant symbols, meaningful social objects, and a universe of shared discourse are all requirements for the genesis and emergence of self in the social situation. A.A. makes these essential ingredients available through its texts, Traditions, Steps, and meetings.

But to Mead must be added Durkheim's insights on the ritual sacredness of the self that emerges out of the collective structures of social groups. The self that is recaptured in A.A. is a sacred, ritual self. It is a self that flows out of and into the A.A. group. Its moral significance lies in its symbolic capacity to activate and stand for the fundamental principles of sobriety and anonymity that A.A. values. This moral self becomes, as Goffman (1967) argued, a god. But it is not an isolated god; it is an intersubjectively produced, sacred, social object. Each A.A. self thus symbolizes the totality of the A.A. experience. For in each sober self lies the residues of the A.A. past that holds this society of recovering selves together.

In this manner, a ritual yet commonsense structure of self-feelings is produced in the person of the new member. These feelings and self-understandings come into existence as the member learns to fit himself or herself into the taken-for-granted meaning structures of the A.A. cultural structure. When the member slips and relapses, he or she relapses into a previously learned mode of self and cultural under-standing. That is, the member draws away from the meaning structures of A.A. and seeks an old ritual self in the standardized understandings that his drinking culture has given him.

In so doing he seeks a privatized, ritual self that turns its back on the collective, ritual self of the A.A. social structure. This self is repositioned within the competitive, dualistic divisions of the broader society in which "being captain of one's soul" is paramount. Hence, in order to find the new ritual A.A. self the member must give herself to the collective structures A.A. offers. These collective structures, as Bateson (1972a) argued, following Durkheim, are outside the person, immanent in a system greater than the person, and based on a noncompetitive, nonnegotiative, nonconflictual mode of self and social interaction. This collective whole is a Durkheimian religion. As Bateson (1972a: 333) observes and Wiley (1985) suggests, this religion sacretizes the person at every level of interaction. It joins the member to a transcendent group structure that is stronger than he or she is. It envelopes the member. It gives a sense of sacred, ritual selfness that cannot be given in the solitary drinking act, or in drinking groups, which are predicated in a competitive, individualistic model of person and interaction.

The sociological foundations of this view of persons, selves, and groups thus derives, as Durkheim observed, from the sacred, symbolic impulse that organizes all human societies. By deifying the personhood of the recovering alcoholic self, A.A. symbolizes this sacred impulse that some contend has been lost in the modern, secular world. But A.A.'s move is collective, not individualistic. Hence, the A.A. self finds its locus in a cultural structure that stands to the side, if not outside, the mainstream of modern group life.

CONCLUSION

Our society, however, has created a space for the alcoholic. This can be seen in the expanding social worlds of recovery. As a social critic the alcoholic's life stories record the effects of our society upon the "civilized individual" (Spender, 1947/1984: ix). This cultural member shows possibilities of existence that would otherwise not be present if our attitudes toward drinking and alcohol were not as they are. This individual symbolizes, through his or her experiences, the fate of all persons who wish to control their own lives and live into existence a mode of selfhood that is shareable, sociable, assertive, and pleasurable. Yet, alcoholics remain outsiders to this culture, which still does not understand them. This is the alcoholic's dilemma, and the culture's, too.

Glossary

A.A. member   Any person who calls himself or herself an A.A. member.

A.A. meeting   Two or more alcoholics meeting together for the purposes of sobriety. Types: *Closed*, attended only by individuals who have a desire to stop drinking; *Open*, attended by those who have an interest in alcoholism and A.A.; *Speaker*, where one A.A. member tells his or her story to others in an open meeting; *Discussion*, where a topic of discussion (such as resentment, anger) is discussed by each member, in turn. *First Step*: a meeting (usually closed) devoted to a discussion of A.A.'s First Step, by tradition any meeting attended by a "newcomer" or a person at their first meeting becomes a First Step Meeting. *Step Meeting*: a meeting devoted to a discussion of each of A.A.'s Twelve Steps.

A.A. motives   Reference reasons for attending A.A., including attempts to resolve situational problematics that have arisen in the member's life, for instance, a DUI. Such motives may become functionally autonomous. The person continues to attend A.A. after the original problem has been solved. In the process they move from situational to committed, recovering alcoholics.

A.A. calendar   Any 12-month calendar hung in an A.A. meeting place upon which group members write the date of their last drink.

A.A. preamble   (Read at the beginning of every A.A. meeting): "Alcoholics Anonymous is a fellowship of men and women who share their experience, strength and hope with each other that they may solve their common problem and help others to recover from alcoholism. The only requirement for membership is a desire to stop drinking. There are no dues or fees for A.A. membership; we are self-supporting through our own contributions. A.A. is not allied with any sect, denomination, politics, organization or institution; does not wish to engage in any controversy, neither endorses nor opposes any causes. Our primary purpose is to stay sober and help other alcoholics to achieve sobriety."

A.A. ritual   The Steps, Traditions, opening and closing ceremonies (such as Serenity Prayer, Lord's Prayer), and birthdays.

A.A. selfhood   Becoming a self within A.A. Stages: (1) preparatory, (2) interactional, (3) participatory.

A.A. talk   Meeting talk that is dialogic; the speaker engages the group in a self-dialogue.

Abstinent alcohol culture   (Pittman, 1967): The cultural attitude is negative and prohibitive toward any type of ingestion of alcoholic beverage.

Addict   In this study, refers to a person who calls himself or herself a member of Narcotics Anonymous.

Adult child of an alcoholic parent   An adult with a parent that is an alcoholic.

Alcoholic rhythm   A regular pattern of drinking, established in the critical and chronic phases of alcoholism, usually involving drinking on a four-hour cycle.

Alcoholic   A person who defines himself or herself as alcoholic. Characterized by an inability to control drinking once the first drink is taken, and an inability to abstain from drinking for any continuous period of time.

Alcoholism I   A self-destructive form of activity involving compulsive, addictive drinking, coupled with increased alcohol tolerance and an inability to abstain for long periods of time from drinking. Phases: pre-alcoholic, prodomal, crucial, chronic. Types: alpha, beta, gamma, delta (see Jellinek, 1960).

Alcoholism II   American Medical Association definition: An illness characterized by preoccupation with alcohol and loss of control over its consumption such as to lead usually to intoxication if drinking is begun; by chronicity; by progression; and by tendency toward relapse. It is typically associated with physical disability and impaired emotional, occupational, and/or social adjustments as a direct consequence of persistent and excessive use of alcohol.

Alcoholism III   Alcoholics Anonymous definition: The manifestation of an allergy, coupled with the phenomenon of craving for alcohol, producing an illness that is spiritual, mental and physical.

Alcoholic aphasia and amnesia   Thought disorders associated with the crucial and chronic stages of alcoholism. Wernicke's disease and Korsakoff's psychosis are types.

Alcoholic-as-social critic   A mode of self-transcendence in which the alcoholic locates himself or herself outside society, seeing in society a sickness or illness that no one else sees.

Alcoholic-centered relationship   A relationship between an alcoholic and an other in which alcohol has become the center or focus of interaction. Alcohol displaces intimacy, love, or conversation as the previous focus or center of the relationship.

Alcoholic dreams   Dreams reported by alcoholics involving drinking, slips, and relapses.

Alcoholic identity   Coming to define one's self as alcoholic. There are 10 types: (1) *transient alcoholic*—assuming the alcoholic identity so as to overcome a problematic situation. This is a situational adjustment to the problems alcoholism produces; (2) *committed alcoholic*—investing and committing one's self in the identity of recovering alcoholic as defined by A.A. This identity is produced by a transformation of self, whereas a transient identity is produced by an alternation of identity; (3) *neutralized*; (4) *helplessly alcoholic*; (5) *situational; (6) transsituational*; (7) *newcomer*; (8) *old-timer*; (9) *regular*; and (10) *alcoholic in treatment*.

Alcoholic other   An emotional-interactional associate of the alcoholic; may be spouse, friend, relative, employer, fellow drinker. This other becomes a member of an alcohol-centered relationship.

Alcoholic pride   (Bateson): Also called false pride, which is mobilized behind the alcoholic's belief that alcohol can be controlled. Leads to "risk taking" in drinking.

Alcoholic problematic situation   A situation that produces sobriety problems, typically flowing from work, family, and relational settings. Faced with such problematics, alcoholics develop situational adjustments and identities that may or may not lead them to drink again.

Alcoholic risk taking   (Bateson): Taking a drink when the probabilities of success are minimal and the likelihood of failure is high.

Alcoholic self   A self divided against itself, trapped within the negative emotions that alcoholism produces. Key emotions are ressentiment and self-pride. Characterized by denial, bad faith, and emotional and physical violence.

Alcoholic situation   (1) Act One of the three-act play called "A Merry-Go-Round-Named Denial"; (2) descriptive term used to reference four interactional drinking patterns the alcoholic and his or her other become embedded in: open-drinking context, closed-drinking context, sober context, in control, normally intoxicated context.

Alcoholic understanding   The process of interpreting, knowing, and comprehending the meaning intended, felt, and expressed by another alcoholic. Types: (1) authentic; (2) A.A.; (3) insincere; (4) spurious.

Alcoholic violence   Attempts by the alcoholic to regain through emotional and physical violence a sense of self that has been lost to alcohol and his or her other. The five types are emotional, playful, spurious, real, and paradoxical.

Alternation of identity   Changes in identity that do not require transformations or a radical restructuring of self. Evidenced in alcoholics who do not remain in A.A. and in the self-changes the alcoholic's other often experiences.

Ambivalent alcohol culture   (Pittman, 1967): The cultural attitude toward alcohol usage conflict between use and nonuse.

Bad faith   A lie to oneself in an attempt to escape responsibility for one's actions. A denial of one's situation and one's place in it. A fleeing from what one is—alcoholic.

Big Book   A.A.'s name for *Alcoholics Anonymous: The Story of How Many Thousands of Men and Women Have Recovered from Alcoholism: The Basic Text of Alcoholics Anonymous*.

Birthday (A.A. or N.A.)   Measured in years, but the first year is measured by one, three, six, and nine months sobriety, or clean intervals, which must be continuous.

Blackout   Amnesia, not associated with loss of consciousness, for all or part of the events that occurred during or immediately after a drinking session (Keller and McCormick, 1968).

Bottom   Confronting one's alcoholic situation, finding it intolerable, and surrendering to alcoholism. Accompanied by collapse and sincerely reaching out for help. May be high or low.

Circuit of selfness   The moving field of experience that connects the person to the world.

Clean date   The date of one's last use of a drug (N.A.).

Codependent   An alcoholic other who has become dependent on the alcoholic's alcoholism.

Confronting   Telling another how you see and feel about him or her.

Craving   Overwhelming desire for alcohol. Two forms: (1) *physiological*, or *nonsymbolic*, located in the withdrawal effects felt as the body detoxifies alcohol, and (2) *psychological, symbolic,* or *phenomenological*, felt as a compelling need for alcohol in the absence of any withdrawal symptom.

Culturally symptomatic drinker   An individual whose use of alcohol (1) conforms to the ritual drinking patterns of the culture, (2) does not go beyond the boundaries of acceptable drinking comportment for the culture, and (3) does not become excessive, which (4) could produce occasional or regular excessive drinking, in which case (5), alcohol becomes a drug and no longer functions as a ritual beverage.

Denial   Refusing to accept one's alcoholism; closely akin to being in "bad faith."

Desire (alcoholic)   That mode of self-consciousness that seeks freedom from fear and anxiety through the altered streams of experience alcohol produces. It is self- and body centered.

Dis-ease   An uneasiness, or disorder in health, body, or manner of living. Alcoholism is a dis-ease of conduct in the world, involving an uneasiness with self, time, emotion, and relations with others.

Drinking motive   Reasons alcoholic gives for drinking; motive becomes *functionally autonomous*, that is, freed from the original ritual situations where drinking was learned.

Drunk-a-log   Story told at an "open" A.A. meeting.

Drunken comportment   (McAndrew and Edgerton, 1969): Culturally and socially patterned forms of behavior that occur after an individual has been drinking. Situationally, culturally, and historically determined and defined.

Dry   Not drinking, but not working the A.A. program.

Dry date   The date of one's last drink.

Dry drunk   When an A.A. member displays all of the characteristics of being drunk, or hung over—self-centered, emotional, self-pitying, angry, resentful—he or she is said to be in a dry drunk.

DUI   Driving under the influence of alcohol.

Emotion   Self-feeling.

Emotionality   The process of being emotional.

Emotionality I. Normal: A balance of emotional experiences, in which extreme negativity or exaggerated exhilaration are absent. An emotional ideal alcoholics seek to attain.

Emotionality II. Alcoholic   Contrasted to normal emotionality, includes extreme negativity (ressentiment) and exaggerated exhilaration produced by alcohol. Tends toward emotional violence.

Emotional account   Justification of a self-feeling.

Emotional associate   A person who is implicated in the subject's emotional world of experience.

Emotional practice   An embedded practice that produces anticipated and unanticipated alterations in the person's inner and outer streams of emotional experience.

Emotional understanding   Knowing and comprehending through emotional means—including sympathy and imagination—the intentions, feelings, and thoughts expressed by another.

Emotionally divided self   A self turned against itself, disembodied, characterized by self-loathing and ressentiment.

Enabler   An alcoholic other who enables, or assists, the alcoholic in his or her drinking career.

Family Week   Occurs during the fourth, or last, week of treatment. The alcoholic's family and significant others come to the treatment center for group and individual counseling. The alcoholic is confronted by and confronts his or her family during this week. Leveling also occurs.

Field of experience   The temporal structure of meanings, definitions, and feelings that surround and situate the person in the world.

Field research   Phrase used by recovering alcoholics to describe their experiences when they return to drinking.

First-Step assessment   Occurs during the first week of treatment, done in the context of the First-Step Group, involving the alcoholic's answering a series of questions concerning alcohol use and abuse prior to treatment. Intended as a measure that produces a surrendering to the First Step of A.A.

First-Step group   A non-sex, non-age stratified group formed within the first week of treatment. The alcoholic does a First-Step assessment before this group.

Frame   An interpretation that structures the definition of a situation. Types within A.A.: (1) primary, "This is an A.A. meeting"; (2) secondary, "We are talking at an A.A. meeting, taking turns"; (3) treatment group, counter to A.A. frames, "We give advice to each other, talk out of turn, and do not focus on a single topic of discussion."

Functional autonomy   An action organized as an adjustment to a situational problematic that becomes dislodged from the original situation and takes on an autonomous life of its own.

Fused group   A newly formed group opposed to seriality, or separateness. Initially unstructured, yet fused, or drawn to a common purpose. The first A.A. group (or meeting) between Wilson and Smith was a fused group that later became a pledged group, and hence the archetype of all subsequent A.A. groups.

Gamma alcoholic   Jellinek's term: involves excessive drinking, acquired increased tissue tolerance to alcohol, withdrawal symptoms, craving due to physical dependence on alcohol, and an inability to stop drinking once it is begun. This type is most like A.A.'s alcoholic.

Grapevine   A.A.'s international monthly magazine.

Group conscience   The will of an A.A. group expressed through a vote on any matter brought before the group, such as moving the group to another meeting place, changing the format of the group, or electing a GSR.

GSR   Group Service Representative for an A.A. group. Such persons are responsible to the group for collecting contributions at meetings, keeping rent paid, seeing to it that coffee and supplies are available for meetings and for chairing, or securing chairpersons for the group's meetings. GSRs may move on to represent groups within A.A. districts and become delegates to national conventions. A person is assumed to have a lengthy period of sobriety before being elected to the GSR position.

Home group   The A.A. group an A.A. member calls his or hers. Often the first group ever attended, but not necessarily. The member will become a regular in this group.

"How It Works"   Portion of the *Big Book*, pp. 58-60 through point (c) which is read at many A.A. meetings as it contains A.A.'s Twelve Steps.

Ideal self   Self-ideal individual selects for self, but often fails to achieve.

Imaginary   The inner world of symbolic, imaginary conversations the person locates himself or herself within.

Integration hypothesis   (Ullman): A social group will have lower rates of alcoholism when it has clear rules concerning how alcohol is to be used, that is, when drinking is ritually integrated into the group's way of life.

Johari Window A four-celled window that addresses the problem of self-awareness, covering the self that is open, unknown, hidden, and blind to self and others. This model is presented to alcoholics in treatment.

Languages of treatment There are three: (1) meta-language of emotionality; (2) language of direct feeling and emotion; and (3) the language and terms of A.A.

Lay-theory of alcoholism A threefold interpretive structure that contains theories of time, causality, denial, and successful drinking.

Leveling Spontaneously sharing one's feelings with another during treatment.

Loss of control Any drinking of alcohol starts a chain reaction that is felt as a physical and psychological demand for alcohol. Typically experienced as (a) an inability to stop drinking after one drink, and (b) an inability to predict one's behavior once drinking begins.

"Merry-Go-Round-of-Trouble" A continuous circuit of negative symbolic interaction, involving the alcoholic and his or other in an endless round of problems and troubles, such as DUIs, unpaid bills, loss of work, divorce, violence, and so on.

N.A. Narcotics Anonymous.

Narcissism The individual acts as if he were in love with himself. The state of self-love and admiration of oneself. In A.A. the phrase "his or her majesty" is taken to refer to this form of narcissism, which alcoholics believe they suffer from.

Negative symbolic interaction An interaction process characterized by violence, contrasting, negative emotions, and destructive schismogenesis.

Newcomer A person early in A.A.'s program of recovery; usually with less than three months sobriety.

Normal social drinker A drinker who can control alcohol and not become alcoholic.

Old-timer An A.A. regular with 10 years or more continuous sobriety and A.A. membership.

Overpermissive alcohol culture (Pittman, 1967): The cultural attitude is permissive toward drinking, to behaviors that occur when drinking, and to drinking pathologies.

Paradoxes of treatment Five dilemmas the alcoholic must confront in treatment, including learning how to become a therapist for the dis-ease of alcoholism.

Permissive alcoholic culture (Pittman, 1967): Cultural attitude toward ingesting alcohol is permissive, but negative toward drunkenness and other drinking pathologies.

Pigeon   An A.A. term for a newcomer an old-timer is working with.

Pledge   A historical act that connects individuals to a group or joint activity. A pledge produces a mediated reciprocity between members, as with A.A.'s pledge of "Responsibility."

Pledged group   A group pledged to or committed to a single purpose. The A.A. group is a pledged group. Such groups share a common perspective, and are organized around an agreed-upon distribution of rights and duties enforced by a pledge.

Program   An A.A. reference to the Twelve Steps and the Twelve Traditions and the spiritual program contained in the Steps. Alcoholics in treatment must develop their own program for recovery, which is not the same as the A.A. program.

Recovering alcoholic   An individual who (1) incorporates the identity of recovering alcoholic into his or her self-conception; (2) having once been an active drinking alcoholic, becomes a nondrinker, and (3) calls himself or herself a member of Alcoholics Anonymous.

Recovering self   A form of selfhood involving a validated program of self-indications that exercise a regulatory function over other actions of the person, including not drinking. This transsituational self is learned in A.A. meetings and in treatment.

Relapse   The return to drinking by a recovering alcoholic, also called *slip*. Types: (1) paired, (2) sequential, (3) solitary, (4) planned, (5) unplanned, (6) short term, (7) long term, (8) of old-timer, (9) of regular, (10) of newcomer.

Responsibility slogan (A.A.)   "I am responsible. When anyone, anywhere, reaches out for help, I want the hand of A.A. always to be there. And for that: I am responsible."

Ressentiment   The repeated experiencing and reliving of a particular emotional reaction against another. The emotion is negative, hostile, and includes a cluster of interrelated feelings—anger, wrath, envy, intense self-pride, and desire for revenge.

Ritual   Conventionalized joint acts, given to ceremony, that convey special emotion and sacred meaning for performers.

Ritual self   New, sacred self acquired by the recovering alcoholic. Sobriety is the key feature. It is learned through interactions at the personal, sponsor, group, and collective levels of A.A. It is a moral, sacred self that flows from and into the A.A. group.

Schismogenesis   (Bateson): The genesis of divisions and conflicts within a relationship such that more of one kind of behavior by one member produces more of a counterbehavior by the other member; attempts to control the alcoholic's drinking produce more drinking.

Self That process that unifies the stream of thoughts and experiences the person has about herself around a single pole or point of reference; not a thing, but a process. It is consciousness conscious of itself, referring always to the sameness and steadiness of something always present to the person in her thoughts, as in "I am here, now, in the world, present before and to myself." Involves moral feelings for self, including all the subject calls hers at a particular moment in time, such as material possessions, self-feelings, and relations to others. Also includes the meaning the person gives to herself as a distinct object and subject at any given moment, involving the meaning of the person to herself as she turns back on herself in reflection. The self is not in consciousness, but in the world of social interaction. It haunts the subject.

Self-account A member's story of self in relation to a problematic event.

Self-as-double Doubling of self within A.A., involving telling stories about self that transform the self into a subject and an object of recovery.

Self-as-false-subjectivity Living self through material things and experiencing a loss of self as a result.

Self-as-loss Experiencing the absence of an inner sense of selfness, or positive being.

Self-as-narrator The A.A. storytelling self.

Self-as-transcendent Seeking a mode of self-understanding and awareness that is located in a structure outside the self. May be produced by drugs and alcohol or by interaction in a group.

Self-feelings Sequences of lived emotionality having self-referents, including a feeling for self, a feeling of this feeling, and a revealing of the moral self to the person through this feeling.

Self-ideal Ideal self set before person by others.

Serenity A.A. term for peace of mind, emotional sobriety, and the absence of negativity in one's life.

Serenity Prayer Said at the beginning of every A.A. meeting: "God grant me the serenity to accept the things I cannot change, courage to change the things I can, and wisdom to know the difference."

Six Theses of Alcoholism Six points of interpretation in the structures of experience that constitute the alcoholic circle. They refer, in turn, to temporality, self, relations with others, emotionality, denial, bad faith, self-control, and surrender.

Slip A return to drinking by a recovering alcoholic. May be planned or unplanned. Also called relapse. It is a slip away from the A.A. program into drinking.

Sober Not drinking and working the A.A. program.

Sobriety date   The date of an A.A. member's last drink, often written on the Group's Sobriety Calendar.

Social phenomenological method   That mode of inquiry that returns to the things of experience and studies them from within. Involves five phases: deconstruction of previous theories of the phenomenon, capture, reduction, construction, and contextualization.

Social world of recovery   The network of social experiences wherein recovery from alcoholism occurs, including treatment centers and A.A.

Sponsor   An older A.A. member who assists a newcomer in getting sober and working the Steps.

Steps   A.A.'s Twelve Steps (see A.A., 1976): (1) We admitted we were powerless over alcohol—that our lives had become unmanageable; (2) Came to believe that a power greater than ourselves could restore us to sanity; (3) Made a decision to turn our will and our lives over to the care of God *as we understood Him*; (4) Made a searching and fearless moral inventory of ourselves; (5) Admitted to God, to ourselves, and to another human being the exact nature of our wrongs; (6) Were entirely ready to have God remove all these defects of character; (7) Humbly asked Him to remove our shortcomings; (8) Made a list of all persons we had harmed, and become willing to make amends to them all; (9) Made direct amends to such people wherever possible, except when to do so would injure them or others; (10) Continued to take personal inventory and when we were wrong promptly admitted it; (11) Sought through prayer and meditation to improve our conscious contact with God *as we understood Him*, praying only for knowledge of His will for us and the power to carry that out; (12) Having had a spiritual awakening as the result of these Steps, we tried to carry this message to alcoholics, and to practice these principles in all our affairs (italics in original).

Stigma (of alcoholism)   Accepting the belief that alcoholism is a failure of self-will, and not a disease.

Story   Self-accounting, or self-story, told by an A.A. member involving "what it was like, what happened, and what it is like now."

Surrender   A threefold process: (1) admitting alcoholism, (2) accepting alcoholism, and (3) surrendering in the inner self to alcoholism.

Tables   A.A.'s name for the tables around which all A.A. meetings occur.

Temporality I. Normal   Time experienced reflectively, merging the past, present, and future in a nonthreatening fashion. Making time a nonproblematic in everyday experience.

Temporality II. Alcoholic   Time experienced through the altered consciousness alcohol creates. Characterized by a fearfulness of time and its passage, including a tendency to dwell in the past and to feel guilt about past deeds.

Therapy (treatment) group   An age- and sex-stratified group that the alcoholic moves into after the first week of treatment. The Fourth and Fifth Steps were taken with this group at Northern.

Third party An individual or a concept that unifies a group by observing or commanding it. Within A.A., the Steps, the higher power, and the traditions act as third parties, as does the collective history of A.A.

Time-out period (McAndrew and Edgerton, 1969): A universal societal phenomenon in which the everyday demands for accountability over one's actions are suspended, or set aside. Drunken comportment is typically structured within these moments, as drinking is commonly associated with time-out periods of experience.

Traditions A.A.'s Twelve traditions (see A.A., 1953). (1) Our common welfare should come first; personal recovery depends upon A.A. unity. (2) For our group purpose there is but one ultimate authority—a loving God as He may express Himself in our group conscience. Our leaders are but trusted servants; they do not govern. (3) The only requirement for A.A. membership is a desire to stop drinking. (4) Each group should be autonomous except in matters affecting other groups or A.A. as a whole. (5) Each group has but one primary purpose— to carry its message to the alcoholic who still suffers. (6) An A.A. group ought never endorse, finance, or lend the A.A. name to any related facility or outside enterprise, lest problems of money, property, and prestige divert us from our primary purpose. (7) Every A.A. group ought to be fully self-supporting, declining outside contributions. (8) Alcoholics Anonymous should remain forever nonprofessional, but our service centers may employ special workers. (9) A.A., as such, ought never be organized; but we may create service boards or committees directly responsible to those they serve. (10) Alcoholics Anonymous has no opinion on outside issues; hence the A.A. name ought never be drawn into public controversy. (11) Our public relations policy is based on attraction rather than promotion; we need always maintain personal anonymity at the level of press, radio, and films. (12) Anonymity is the spiritual foundation of all our Traditions, ever remaining us to place principles before personalities.

Transformation of self Radical restructuring of self and its basic beliefs, evidenced in recovery from alcoholism.

Twelve and Twelve A.A.'s name for its second basic text, *The Twelve Steps and the Twelve Traditions.*

Universal singular (alcoholic) A single instance of a process that is experienced by any alcoholic who seeks to recover from the dis-ease of alcoholism.

Victim An alcoholic other who becomes victimized by the alcoholic's alcoholism.

Working the Steps A phrase used by A.A. members when they are in the process of going through the Twelve Steps or focusing on a particular Step.

References

Ablon, Joan
    1976   "Family structure and behavior in alcoholism: a review of the literature," pp. 205-242 in Benjamin Kissin and Henri Begleiter (eds.) The Biology of Alcoholism, Vol. 4. Social Aspects of Alcoholism. New York: Plenum.

Adler, A.
    1927   The Practices and Theory of Individual Psychology. New York: Harcourt.

Al-Anon Family Groups
    1977   Lois Remembers. New York: Al-Anon Family Group Headquarters, Inc.
    1985   Al-Anon Faces Alcoholism. New York: Al-Anon Family Group Headquarters, Inc.

Alcoholics Anonymous
    1953   Twelve Steps and Twelve Traditions. New York: Alcoholics Anonymous World Services, Inc.
    1957   Alcoholics Anonymous Comes of Age: A Brief History of A.A. New York: Alcoholics Anonymous World Services, Inc.
    1963   "The Bill W.-Carl Jung letters." Grapevine (January): 26-31.
    1967   As Bill Sees It: The A.A. Way of Life. Selected Writings of A.A.'s Co-Founder. New York: Alcoholics Anonymous World Services, Inc.
    1973   Came to Believe: The Spiritual Adventure of A.A. as Experienced by Individual Members. New York: Alcoholics Anonymous World Services, Inc.
    1975   Living Sober: Some Methods A.A. Members Have Used for Not Drinking. New York: Alcoholics Anonymous World Services, Inc.
    1976   Alcoholics Anonymous. New York: Alcoholics Anonymous World Services, Inc.
    1980   Dr. Bob and the Good Oldtimers: A Biography with Recollections of Early A.A. in the Midwest. New York: Alcoholics Anonymous World Services, Inc.
    1983   "Treatment centers for alcoholism." Grapevine (March): 62
    1983-1984 The A.A. Service Manual combined with Twelve Concepts for World Service by Bill W. New York: Alcoholics Anonymous World Services, Inc.
    1984   "Pass It On": The Story of Bill Wilson and How the A.A. Message Reached the World. New York: Alcoholics Anonymous World Services, Inc.

Allport, G. W.
    1964   Personality and Social Encounter. Boston: Beacon.

American Medical Association
    1968   Manual on Alcoholism. New York: Author.

American Psychiatric Association
    1980   Diagnostic and Statistic Manual of Mental Disorders (DSM-III). Washington, DC: Author.

Armor, D. J., J. M. Polich, and J. B. Stambul
    1976   Alcoholism and Treatment. Report R-1739-NIAAA. Santa Monica, CA: Rand
            Corporation.
Bacon, M. K., H. Barry, III, and I. L. Child
    1965   A cross-cultural study of drinking. II: Relations to other features of culture."
            Quarterly Journal of Studies on Alcohol Supplement 3, pg. 29.
Baekeland, Frederick
    1977   "Evaluation of treatment methods in chronic alcoholism," pp. 385-440 in
            Benjamin Kissin and Henri Begleiter (eds.) The Biology of Alcoholism, Vol. 5.
            Treatment and Rehabilitation of the Chronic Alcoholic. New York: Plenum.
Baekeland, Frederick and Lawrence K. Lundwall
    1977   "Engaging the alcoholic in treatment and keeping him there," pp. 161-196 in
            Benjamin Kissin and Henri Begleiter (eds.) The Biology of Alcoholism, Vol. 5.
            Treatment and Rehabilitation of the Chronic Alcoholic. New York: Plenum.
Baldwin, John W.
    1984   "Comment on Denzin's 'Note on Emotionality, Self and Interaction.' " Ameri-
            can Journal of Sociology 90: 418-421.
Bales, Robert F.
    1946   "Cultural differences in rates of alcoholism." Quarterly Journal of Studies on
            Alcohol 6: 480-499.
Bandura, Albert
    1977   Social Learning Theory. Englewood Cliffs, NJ: Prentice-Hall.
Barnes, Gordon E.
    1983   "Clinical and prealcoholic personality characteristics," pp. 113-196 in Benjamin
            Kissin and Henri Begleiter (eds.) The Biology of Alcoholism, Vol. 6 Psychosocial
            Factors. New York: Plenum.
Bateson, Gregory
    1972a   "The cybernetics of 'self': a theory of alcoholism," pp. 309-337 in Steps to an
            Ecology of Mind. New York: Ballantine.
    1972b   "The logical categories of learning and communication," pp. 279-308 in Steps
            to an Ecology of Mind. New York: Ballantine.
    1972c   "Double bind," pp. 271-278 in Steps to an Ecology of Mind. New York:
            Ballantine.
    1972d   "A theory of play and fantasy," pp. 177-193 in Steps to an Ecology of Mind.
            New York: Ballantine.
    1972e   "Toward a theory of schizophrenia," pp. 201-227 in Steps to an Ecology of
            Mind. New York: Ballantine.
Baudrillard, Jean
    1983a   "The ecstasy of communication," pp. 126-134 in Hal Foster (ed.) The Anti-
            Aesthetic: Essays on Postmodern Culture. Port Townsend, WA: Bay Press.
    1983b   In the Shadow of the Silent Majorities. New York: Semiotext.
    1983c   Simulations. New York: Semiotext.
Beauchamp, Dan E.
    1980   Beyond Alcoholism: Alcohol and Public Health Policy. Philadelphia: Temple
            University Press.
Becker, Howard S.
    1960   "Notes on the concept of commitment." American Journal of Sociology 66:
            32-40.
    1964   "Personal change in adult life." Sociometry 27: 40-53.
    1967   "History, culture and subjective experience." Journal of Health and Social
            Behavior 8: 163-176.
    1973   Outsiders. New York: Free Press.

Becker, Howard S., Blanche Geer, Everett C. Hughes, and Anselm L. Strauss
1961   Boys in White. Chicago: University of Chicago Press.

Beecher, Henry K.
1959   Measurement of Subjective Responses: Quantitative Effects of Drugs. New York: Oxford University Press.

Bellah, Robert, N. (ed.)
1973   Emile Durkheim on Morality in Society. Chicago: University of Chicago Press.

Bellah, Robert, N. et al.
1985   Habits of the Heart: Individualism and Commitment in American Life. Berkeley: University of California Press.

Benjamin, Jessica
1981   "The Oedipal riddle: authority, autonomy and the new narcissism," pp. 195-224 in J. P. Diggins and M. E. Kann (eds.) The Problem of Authority in America. Philadelphia: Temple University Press.

Berger, Peter and Thomas Luckmann
1967   The Social Construction of Reality. New York: Doubleday.

Berk, Richard A., Sarah Fenstermaker Berk, Donileen R. Loseke, and David Rauma
1983   "Mutual combat and other family violence myths," pp. 197-212 in David Finkelhor et al. (eds.) The Dark Side of Families: Current Family Violence Research. Beverly Hills, CA: Sage.

Bernstein, B.
1971   Class, Codes and Control, Vol. 1. Theoretical Studies Toward a Sociology of Language. London: Routledge & Kegan Paul.

Bertaux, Daniel
1981   "Introduction," pp. 1-22 in D. Bertaux (ed.) Biography and Society. Beverly Hills, CA: Sage.

Berryman, John
1973   Recovery: A Novel. New York: Farrar, Straus and Giroux.

Biegel, Allan and Stuart Ghertner
1977   "Toward a social model: an assessment of social factors which influence problem drinking and its treatment," pp. 197-234 in Benjamin Kissin and Henri Begleiter (eds.) The Biology of Alcoholism, Vol. 5. Treatment and Rehabilitation of the Chronic Alcoholic. New York: Plenum.

Blane, H. T.
1968   The Personality of the Alcoholic: Guises of Dependency. New York: Harper & Row.

Blane, H. T.
1977   "Psychotherapeutic approach," pp. 105-160 in Benjamin Kissin and Henri Begleiter (eds.) The Biology of Alcoholism, Vol. 5. Treatment and Rehabilitation of the Chronic Alcoholic. New York: Plenum.

Blumer, Herbert
1946   "Collective behavior," pp. 166-222 in A. M. Lee (ed.) New Outline of the Principles of Sociology. New York: Barnes & Noble.
1969   Symbolic Interactionism. Englewood Cliffs, NJ: Prentice-Hall.

Booth, Wayne C.
1983   The Rhetoric of Fiction. Chicago: University of Chicago Press. (originally published in 1961)

Boss, M.
1958   The Analysis of Dreams. New York: Philosophical Library.
1963   Psychoanalysis and Daseinsanalysis. New York: Basic Books.
1977   "I Dreamt Last Night . . . ": A New Approach to the Revelations of Dreaming and its Uses for Psychotherapy. New York: Gardner.

Boswell, John
    1980   Christianity, Social Tolerance and Homosexuality: Gay People in Western
            Europe from the Beginning of the Christian Era to the Fourteenth Century.
            Chicago: University of Chicago Press.
Burke, Kenneth
    1954   Permanence and Change. Los Altos, CA: Hermes.
Caddy, G. R., H. J. Addington, and D. Perkins
    1978   "Individualized behavior therapy for alcoholics: a third year independent
            double-blind follow-up." Behavior Research and Therapy 16: 345-362.
Cahalan, Don
    1970   Problem Drinkers: A National Survey. San Francisco: Jossey-Bass.
Cahalan, Don and Robin Room
    1972   "Problem drinking among American men aged 21-59." American Journal of
            Public Health 62: 1473-1482.
    1974   Problem Drinking Among American Men. New Brunswick, NJ: Rutgers
            Center of Alcohol Studies.
Cahalan, Don and I. H. Cisin
    1976   "Drinking behavior and drinking problems in the United States," pp. 77-115 in
            Benjamin Kissin and Henri Begleiter (eds.) The Biology of Alcoholism, Vol. 4.
            Social Aspects of Alcoholism. New York: Plenum.
Caldwell, Fulton J.
    1983   "Alcoholics Anonymous as a viable treatment resource for black alcoholics,"
            pp. 85-99 in T. S. Watts and R. Wright, Jr. (eds.) Black Alcoholism: Toward a
            Comprehensive Understanding. Springfield, IL: Charles C Thomas.
Cappell, H. and C. P. Herman
    1972   "Alcohol and tension reduction—a review." Quarterly Journal of Studies on
            Alcohol 33: 33-64.
Carpenter, J. A. and N. P. Armenti
    1972   "Some effects of ethanol in human sexual and aggressive behavior," pp. 509-
            543 in Benjamin Kissin and Henri Begleiter (eds.) The Biology of Alcoholism,
            Vol. 2. Physiology and Behavior. New York: Plenum.
Carver, Raymond
    1983   "The Paris Review interview," pp. 187-216 in Raymond Carver (ed.) Fires,
            Essays, Poems, Stories. New York: Vantage Books.
Catanzaro, Ronald J.
    1967   "Psychiatric aspects of alcoholism," pp. 31-44 in David J. Pittman (ed.)
            Alcoholism. New York: Harper & Row.
Cavan, Sheri
    1966   Liquor License: An Ethnography of Bar Behavior. Chicago: Aldine.
Chafetez, Morris E. and Robert Yoerg
    1977   "Public health treatment programs in alcoholism," pp. 593-614 in Benjamin
            Kissin and Henri Begleiter (eds.) The Biology of Alcoholism, Vol. 5. Treatment
            and Rehabilitation of the Chronic Alcoholic. New York: Plenum.
Charmaz, K. C.
    1980   "The social construction of self-pity in the chronically ill," pp. 123-146 in
            Norman K. Denzin (ed.) Studies in Symbolic Interaction, Vol. 3. Greenwich,
            CT: JAI.
Chomsky, N.
    1967   "A review of B. F. Skinner's Verbal Behavior," pp. 142-171 in L. A. Jakobovitz
            and M. S. Miron (eds.) Readings in the Psychology of Language. Englewood
            Cliffs, NJ: Prentice-Hall.

Cicourel, A. V.
　1974　Cognitive Sociology. New York: Free Press.
　1981　"The role of cognitive-linguistic concepts in understanding everyday social interaction," pp. 87-106 in R. H. Turner and J. F. Short, Jr. (eds.) Annual Review of Sociology, Vol. 7. Palo Alto, CA: Annual Reviews, Inc.
Clough, Patricia T.
　1979　"Sociability and public behavior in a mid-sized city," pp. 359-376 in Norman K. Denzin (ed.) Studies in Symbolic Interaction, Vol. 2. Greenwich, CT: JAI.
Collins, R.
　1975　Conflict Sociology. New York: Academic Press.
　1981　Sociology Since Midcentury. New York: Academic Press.
Conger, J. J.
　1951　"The effects of alcohol on conflict behavior in the albino rat." Quarterly Journal of Studies on Alcohol 12: 1-29.
　1956　"Alcoholism: theory, problem and challenge. II: Reinforcement theory and the dynamics of alcoholism." Quarterly Journal of Studies on Alcohol 17: 291-324.
Cooley, C. H.
　1956　The Two Major Works of C. H. Cooley. New York: Free Press. (originally published in 1902)
Corsini, R. J.
　1984　"Innovative psychotherapies," pp. 223-225 in R. J. Corsini (ed.) Encyclopedia of Psychology, Vol. 2. New York: John Wiley.
Couch, Carl J., Stanley L. Saxton, and Michael A. Katovich (eds.)
　1986　Studies in Symbolic Interaction: The Iowa School. Greenwich, CT: JAI.
Davies, D. L.
　1962　"Normal drinking in recovered alcoholics." Quarterly Journal of Studies on Alcohol 23: 94-104.
Davis, Fred
　1961　"Deviance disavowal: the management of strained interaction by the visibly handicapped." Social Problems 9: 120-132.
Denzin, Norman K.
　1968　"The self-fulfilling prophecy and patient therapist interactions," pp. 349-358 in S. P. Spitzer and Norman K. Denzin (eds.) The Mental Patient: Studies in the Sociology of Deviance. New York: McGraw-Hill.
　1977a "Notes on the criminogenic hypothesis: a case study of the American liquor industry." American Sociological Review 42: 905-920.
　1977b Childhood Socialization. San Francisco: Jossey-Bass.
　1978　"Crime and the American liquor industry," pp. 87-118 in Norman K. Denzin (ed.) Studies in Symbolic Interaction, Vol. 2. Greenwich, CT: JAI.
　1979　"On the interactional analysis of social organization." Symbolic Interaction 2: 59-72.
　1980　"Towards a phenomenology of emotion and deviance." Zietschrift für Soziologie 9: 251-261.
　1982　"Notes on criminology and criminality," pp. 115-130 in H. E. Pepinsky (ed.) Rethinking Criminology. Beverly Hills, CA: Sage.
　1983a "A note on emotionality, self and interaction." American Journal of Sociology 88: 943-953.
　1983b "Interpretive interactionism," pp. 129-146 in G. Morgan (ed.) Beyond Method. Beverly Hills, CA: Sage.
　1984a On Understanding Emotion. San Francisco: Jossey-Bass.

1984b "Toward a phenomenology of domestic, family violence." American Journal of Sociology 90: 483-513.

1984c "Reply to Baldwin." American Journal of Sociology 90: 422-427.

1984d "Ritual behavior," pp. 246-247 in R. J. Corsini (ed.) Encyclopedia of Psychology, Vol. 3. New York: John Wiley.

1985a "Review essay: Signifying Acts: Structure and Meaning in Everyday Life." American Journal of Sociology 91: 432-434.

1985b "Emotion as lived experience." Symbolic Interaction 8: 223-239.

1985c "On the phenomenology of sexuality, desire and violence," pp. 39-56 in S. McNall (ed.) Current Perspectives in Social Theory, Vol. 6. Greenwich, CT: JAI.

1986a The Alcoholic Self. Beverly Hills, CA: Sage.

1986b Treating Alcoholism. Beverly Hills, CA: Sage.

1986c "A phenomenology of the emotionally divided self," in Krysia Yardley and Terry Honess (eds.) Self and Identity: Psychosocial Perspectives. New York: John Wiley.

1986d "A phenomenological analysis of social referencing," in S. Feinman (ed.) Social Referencing in Infancy. New York: Academic Press.

Denzin, Norman K. with Charles Keller

1981   " 'Frame Analysis' reconsidered." Contemporary Sociology 10: 52-59.

Derrida, Jacques

1972   "Structure, sign, and play in the discourse of the human sciences," pp. 247-272 in Richard Macksey and Eugenio Donato (eds.) The Structuralist Controversy: The Languages of Criticism and the Sciences of Man. Baltimore, MA: Johns Hopkins University Press.

1973   Speech and Phenomena. Evanston, IL: Northwestern University Press.

1976   Of Grammatology. Baltimore, MA: Johns Hopkins University Press.

1978   Writing and Difference. Chicago: University of Chicago Press.

1981   Positions. Chicago: University of Chicago Press.

Dewey, J.

1922   Human Nature and Conduct: An Introduction to Social Psychology. New York: Henry Holt.

Dostoevski, Fyodor

1846   "The double," in The Short Novels of Dostoevski [Constance Garnett, trans.]. New York: Dell.

Duhman, Bob

1984   "The curse of the writing class." Saturday Review (January-February): 27-30.

Durkheim, Emile

1951   Suicide. Glencoe, IL: Free Press. (originally published in 1897)

1961   The Elementary Forms of Religious Life. New York: Collier.

1964   The Division of Labor in Society. Glencoe, IL: Free Press. (originally published in 1893)

1982   The Rules of Sociological Method. New York: Free Press. (originally published in 1895)

Edel, Leon

1984   Writing Lives: Principia Biographica. New York: Norton.

Erikson, Erik H.

1950   Childhood and Society. New York: W. W. Norton.

Erikson, Kai T.

1966   Wayward Puritans. New York: John Wiley.

Fagerhaugh, S. Y. and A. Strauss
  1977 Politics of Pain Management: Staff-Patient Interaction. Menlo Park, CA: Addison-Wesley.
Faulkner, William
  1981 "Mr. Acarius," pp. 435-448 in Joseph Blotner (ed.) *Uncollected Stories of William Faulkner*. New York: Vantage.
Flaherty, M.
  1983 "A formal approach to the study of amusement in social interaction," pp. 71-82 in Norman K. Denzin (ed.) Symbolic Interaction, Vol. 5. Greenwich, CT: JAI.
Foucault, M.
  1970 The Order of Things: An Archaeology of the Human Sciences. New York: Random House.
  1977 Discipline and Punishment. New York: Pantheon.
  1980 Power/Knowledge: Selected Interviews and Other Writings 1972-1977. [C. Gordon, ed.; C. Gordon, L. Marshall, J. Mepham, K. Soper, trans.]. New York: Pantheon.
  1982 "Afterword: the subject and power," in H. Dreyfus and P. Rabinow (eds.) Michael Foucault: Beyond Structuralism and Hermeneutics. Chicago: University of Chicago Press.
Foulkes, D.
  1978 A Grammar of Dreams. New York: Basic Books.
Fox, R.
  1957 Treatment of alcoholism," pp. 163-172 in H. E. Himwich (ed.) Alcoholism: Basic Aspects and Treatment. Washington, DC: American Association for the Advancement of Science.
Franks, David
  1984 "Role-taking, social power and imperceptiveness: the analysis of rape," pp. 123-147 in Norman K. Denzin (ed.) Studies in Symbolic Interaction, Vol. 6. Greenwich, CT: JAI.
Franks, Lucinda
  1985 "A new attack on alcoholism." New York Times Magazine (October 29): 46-48, 50, 61-65, 69.
Freedman, Samuel G.
  1984 "Fugard traces a dark parallel on film." New York Times Section 2: 1, 19.
Freud, S.
  1938 The Basic Writings of Sigmund Freud. New York: Random House.
  1954 The Standard Edition. London: Hogarth.
  1960 Group Psychology and the Analysis of the Ego. New York: Bantam Books (originally published in 1921)
  1965 The Interpretation of Dreams. New York: Avon Books. (originally publishd in 1900)
  1968 The Interpretation of Dreams. In The Standard Edition of the Complete Psychological Works of Sigmund Freud, Vols. 4 and 5. London: Hogarth.
Gadamer, H. G.
  1975 Truth and Method. London: Sheed and Ward.
  1976 Philosophical Hermeneutics. [D. E. Linge, ed. and trans.]. Berkeley: University of California Press.
Garfinkel, H.
  1956 "Conditions of successful degradation ceremonies." American Journal of Sociology 61: 420-424.

1967   Studies in Ethnomethodology. Englewood Cliffs, NJ: Prentice-Hall

Geertz, C.
1973   The Interpretation of Cultures. New York: Basic Books.
1983   Local Knowledge: Further Essays in Interpretive Anthropology. New York: Basic Books.

Gelles, Richard J.
1972   The Violent Home: A Study of Physical Aggression Between Husbands and Wives. Beverly Hills, CA: Sage.
1979   Family Violence. Beverly Hills, CA: Sage

Glaser, Barney and Anselm Strauss
1964   Awareness of Dying. Chicago: Aldine.
1967a   "Awareness contexts and social interaction." American Sociological Review 29: 669-679.
1967b   The Discovery of Grounded Theory. Chicago: Aldine.

Glasser W.
1965   Reality Therapy: A New Approach to Psychiatry. New York: Harper & Row.

Goffman, E.
1956   "Embarrassment and social organization." American Journal of Sociology 67: 264-271.
1959   The Presentation of Self in Everyday Life. New York: Doubleday.
1961a   Asylums. New York: Doubleday.
1961b   Encounters. Indianapolis, IN: Bobbs-Merrill.
1963a   Behavior in Public Places. New York: Free Press.
1963b   Stigma. Englewood Cliffs, NJ: Prentice-Hall.
1967   Interaction Ritual. New York: Doubleday.
1971   Relations in Public. New York: Basic Books.
1974   Frame Analysis. New York: Harper.
1981   Forms of Talk. Philadelphia: University of Pennsylvania Press.
1983   "The interaction order." American Sociological Review 48: 1-17.

Gomberg, Edith Lisansky
1976   "Alcoholism in women," pp. 117-166 in Benjamin Kissin and Henri Begleiter (eds.) The Biology of Alcoholism, Vol. 4. Social Aspects of Alcoholism. New York: Plenum.
1982   "Special populations," pp. 337-354 in Edith L. Gomberg et al. (eds.) Alcoholic, Science and Society Revisited. Ann Arbor, MI: The University of Michigan Press.

Gomberg, Edith, L., Helene R. White, and John A. Carpenter
1982   Alcohol, Science and Society Revisited. Ann Arbor: University of Michigan Press.

Goodstein, L.
1984   "Human relations training," p. 161 in R. Corsini (ed.) Encyclopedia of Psychology, Vol. 2. New York: John Wiley.

Goodwin, Donald
1976   Is Alcoholism Hereditary? New York: Oxford University Press.
1979   "Alcoholism and heredity: a review and hypothesis" Archives of General Psychiatry 36: 57-61.

Goodwin, Donald W. and Samuel B. Guze
1974   "Heredity and alcoholism," pp. 37-52 in Benjamin Kissin and Henri Begleiter (eds.) The Biology of Alcoholism, Vol. 3. Clinical Pathology. New York: Plenum.

Goshen, Charles E.
1973   Drinks, Drugs, and Do-Gooders. New York: Free Press.

Greil, A. L. and D. R. Rudy
1984   "What have we learned from process models of conversion? An examination of ten case studies." Sociological Focus 17: 305-323.

Grimshaw, Allen D.
1981   "Talk and social control," pp. 200-234 in M. Rosenberg and R. H. Turner (eds.) Social Psychology: Sociological Perspectives. New York: Basic Books.

Gross, Milton M., Eastlyn Lewis, and John Hastey
1974   "Acute alcohol withdrawal syndrome," pp. 191-264 in Benjamin Kissin and Henri Begleiter (eds.) The Biology of Alcoholism, Vol. 3. Clinical Pathology. New York: Plenum.

Grove, William M. and Remi J. Cadoret
1983   "Genetic factors in alcoholism," pp. 31-56 in Benjamin Kissin and Henri Begleiter (eds.) The Biology of Alcoholism, Vol. 7. Biological Factors. New York: Plenum.

Gusfield, Joseph R.
1981   The Culture of Public Problems: Drinking-Driving and the Symbolic Order. Chicago: University of Chicago Press.

Guze, S. B., V. B. Tuasvon, M. A. Stewart, and B. Picken
1963   "The drinking history: a comparison of reports by subjects and their relatives." Quarterly Journal of Studies on Alcohol 24: 249-260.

Habermas, Jürgen
1983   "Modernity—an incomplete project," pp. 3-15 in Hal Foster (ed.) The Anti-Aesthetic: Essays on Postmodern Culture. Port Townsend, WA: Bay Press.
1985   "Neoconservative culture criticism in the United States and West Germany: an intellectual movement in two political cultures," pp. 78-94 in R. J. Bernstein (ed.) Habermas and Modernity. Cambridge, MA: MIT Press.

Hall, C. S.
1966   The Meaning of Dreams. New York: McGraw-Hill. (originally published in 1953)

Hall, C. S. and V. J. Nordby
1972   The Individual and His Dreams. New York: New American Library.

Hall, C. S. and R. L. Van de Castle
1966   The Content Analysis of Dreams. New York: Appleton-Century-Crofts.

Hall, Peter M. and John P. Hewitt
1973   "The quasi-theory of communication and the management of dissent." Social Problems 18: 17-27.

Hazelden Foundation, Inc.
1956   Twenty-Four Hours a Day. Center, MN: Author.
1982   Each Day a New Beginning. Center City, MN: Author.
1983   The Promise of a New Day. Center City, MN: Author.
1985   Today's Gift. Center City, MN: Author.

Hegel, G.W.F.
1980   The Phenomenology of Mind. [J.B. Braillie, trans.]. London: Allen & Unwin.

Heidegger, Martin
1962   Being and Time. New York: Harper & Row. (originally published in 1927)
1982   The Basic Problems of Phenomenology. Bloomington, IN: Indiana University Press.

Hetherton, E. M. and N. P. Wray
    1964   "Aggression, need for social support and human preferences." Journal of
            Abnormal Social Psychology 68: 685-689.
Hewitt, John P. and Peter M. Hall
    1973   "Social problems: problematic situations and quasi-theories." American
            Sociological Review 38: 367-374.
Hewitt, John P. and Randall Stokes
    1975   "Disclaimers." American Sociological Review 40: 1-11.
Hochschild, Arlie
    1973   The Unexpected Community. Englewood Cliffs, NJ: Prentice-Hall.
    1983   The Managed Heart: Commercialization of Human Feeling. Berkeley: Uni-
            versity of California Press.
Horton, Donald
    1943   "The functions of alcohol in primitive societies: a cross-cultural study."
            Quarterly Journal of Studies on Alcohol 4: 199-320.
Hughes, E.
    1951   Men and Their Work. Glencoe, IL: Free Press.
Husserl, E.
    1962   Ideas: General Introduction to Pure Phenomenology. New York: Collier
            Books. (originally published in 1913)
Hymes, Dell
    1974   Foundations in Sociolinguistics: An Ethnographic Approach. Philadelphia:
            University of Pennsylvania Press.
Isbell, H.
    1955   "Craving for alcohol." Quarterly Journal of Studies on Alcohol 16: 38-42.
Jackson, Joan
    1962   "Alcoholism and the family," pp. 472-493 in David J. Pittman and C. R. Snyder
            (eds.) Society, Culture, and Drinking Patterns. New York: John Wiley.
Jakobson, Roman
    1956   "Two aspects of language and two aspects of aphasic disturbances," pp. 69-96 in
            Roman Jakobson and Morris Halle (eds.) Fundamentals of Language. The
            Hague: Mouton.
    1962   Selected Writings, Vol. 1. Phonological Studies. The Hague: Mouton.
James, Henry
    1920   "Letter to Mrs. Humphry Ward," pp. 332-336 in Percy Lubbock (ed.) Henry
            James: Letters. London: Hogarth.
James, W.
    1950   The Principles of Psychology in Two Volumes. New York: Henry Holt.
            (originally published in 1890)
    1955   Pragmatism and Four Essays from the Meaning of Truth. New York:
            Humanities. (originally published in 1910)
    1961   The Varieties of Religious Experience: A Study in Human Nature. New York:
            Collier. (originally published in 1904)
Jameson, Fredric
    1983   "Postmodernism and consumer society," pp. 111-125 in Hal Foster (ed.) The
            Anti-Aesthetic: Essays on Postmodern Culture. Port Townsend, WA: Bay
            Press.
Jellinek, E. M.
    1960   The Disease Concept of Alcoholism. New Haven, CT: Hillhouse.

1962 "Phases of alcohol addiction," pp. 356-368 in David J. Pittman and C. R. Synder (eds.) Society, Culture, and Drinking Patterns. New York: John Wiley.

Jessor, R., T. D. Graves, R. C. Hanson, and S. L. Jessor
1968 Society, Personality and Deviant Behavior: A Study of a Tri-ethnic Community. Holt, Rinehart, and Winston.

Johnson, Bruce Holley
1973 "The alcoholism movement in America: a study in cultural innovation." Doctoral dissertation, University of Illinois, Urbana-Champaign.

Johnson, Dianne
1983 Dashiell Hammett: A Life. Boston: Little, Brown.

Jung, C. G.
1939 The Integration of Personality. New York: Farrar and Rinehart.
1961 Memories, Dreams, Reflections. New York: Pantheon.

Kane, Geoffrey P.
1981 Inner-City Alcoholism: An Ecological Analysis and Cross-Cultural Study. New York: Human Sciences Press.

Keller, Mark
1976 "The disease concept of alcoholism revisited." Quarterly Journal of Studies on Alcohol 37: 1694-1717.
1978 "A nonbehaviorist's view of the behavioral problem with alcoholism," pp. 381-398 in Peter E. Nathan et al. (eds.) Alcoholism: New Directions in Behavioral Research and Treatment. New York: Plenum.

Keller, Mark and Mairi McCormick
1968 A Dictionary of Words About Alcohol. New Brunswick, NJ: Publications Division, Rutgers Center of Alcohol Studies.

Kellerman, Joseph L.
1969 Alcoholism: A Merry-Go-Round Named Denial. New York: Al-Anon Family Group Headquarters, Inc.

Kemper, T. D.
1978 A Social Interactional Theory of Emotions. New York: John Wiley.
1981 "Social constructionist and positivist approaches to the sociology of emotions." American Journal of Sociology 86: 336-362.

Kissin, Benjamin
1977 "Theory and practice in the treatment of alcoholism," pp. 1-52 in Benjamin Kissin and Henri Begleiter (eds.) The Biology of Alcoholism, Vol. 5. Treatment and Rehabilitation of the Chronic Alcoholic. New York: Plenum.

Knight, R. P.
1937 "The psychodynamics of chronic alcoholism." Journal of Nervous and Mental Diseases 86: 538-548.

Kohlberg, L.
1981 The Philosophy of Moral Development. San Francisco: Harper & Row.

Kohut, H.
1971 The Analysis of the Self. New York: International Universities Press.
1977 The Restoration of the Self. New York: International Universities Press.
1984 How Does Psychoanalysis Cure? Chicago: University of Chicago Press.

Kristeva, Julia
1974 La Révolution du Langage Poétique. Paris: Editions du Seuil.

Kuhn, Manford H. and C. Addison Hickman
1956 Indiviudals, Groups and Economic Behavior. New York: Dryden Press.

Kurtz, Ernest
    1979   Not-God: A History of Alcoholics Anonymous. Center City, MN: Hazelden
            Educational Materials.
Labov, W. and D. Fanshel
    1977   Therapeutic Discourse: Psychotherapy as Conversation. New York: Academic
            Press.
Lacan, J.
    1949   "The mirror stage as formative of the function of the I as revealed in
            psychoanalytic experience," pp. 1-7 in Ecrits: A Selection. New York: W. W.
            Norton
    1957   "The agency of the letter in the unconscious or reason since Freud," pp. 146-178
            in Ecrits: A Selection. New York: W. W. Norton.
    1966   Ecrits. Paris: Editions de Seuil.
    1968   Speech and Language in Psychoanalysis. [A. Wildon, trans.]. Baltimore, MD:
            Johns Hopkins University Press.
    1977   Ecrits: A Selection. [A. Sheridan, trans.]. New York: W. W. Norton.
    1978   The Four Fundamental Concepts of Psycho-Analysis. New York: Norton.
    1982   Feminine Sexuality. New York: Norton.
Lasch, C.
    1979   The Culture of Narcissism: American Life in an Age of Diminished Expecta-
            tions. New York: Norton.
    1984   The Minimal Self: Psychic Survival in Troubled Times. New York: Norton.
Leach, Barry and John L. Norris
    1977   "Factors in the development of Alcoholics Anonymous (A.A.)," pp. 441-519 in
            Benjamin Kissin and Henri Begleiter (eds.) The Biology of Alcoholism, Vol. 5,
            Treatment and Rehabilitation of the Chronic Alcoholic. New York: Plenum.
Laing, R. D.
    1965   The Divided Self: An Existential Study in Sanity and Madness. Harmonds-
            worth, England: Penguin.
Lemert, Edwin M.
    1958   "The use of alcohol in three Salish Indian tribes." Quarterly Journal of Studies
            on Alcohol 19: 90-107.
    1964   "Drinking in Hawaiian plantation society," Quarterly Journal of Studies on
            Alcohol 25: 689-713.
    1967   Human Deviance, Social Problems and Social Control. Englewood Cliffs, NJ:
            Prentice-Hall.
Lessing, Doris
    1969   The Four-Gated City. New York: Knopf.
Levine, Harry Gene
    1978   "The discovery of addiction." Journal of Studies on Alcohol 39: 143-174.
Lewontin, R. C., Steven Rose, and Leon J. Kamin
    1984   Not in Our Genes: Biology, Ideology, and Human Nature. New York:
            Pantheon.
Lifton, R. J.
    1961   Thought Reform and the Psychology of Totalism. New York: W. W. Norton.
Lindesmith, Alfred R.
    1947   Opiate Addiction. Bloomington, IN: Principia Press.
    1968   Addiction and Opiates. Chicago: Aldine.
    1975   "A reply to McAuliffe and Gordon's 'Test of Lindesmith's Theory of
            Addiction.' " American Journal of Sociology 81, 1: 147-153.
Lindesmith, Alfred R., Anselm L. Strauss, and Norman K. Denzin
    1975   Social Psychology. New York: Holt, Rinehart and Winston.

1977 Social Psychology. New York: Holt, Rinehart and Winston.

Lisansky, E. A.
1960 "The etiology of alcoholism: the role of psychological predisposition." Quarterly Journal of Studies on Alcohol 21: 314-324.

Lofland, John
1977 Doomsday Cult: A Study of Conversion, Proselytization, and Maintenance of Faith. New York: Irvington Publishers.

Lofland, John and Rodney Stark
1965 "Conversion to a deviant perspective." American Sociological Review 30: 862-875.

Lowry, Malcolm
1984 Under the Volcano. New York: New American Library. (originally published in 1947)

Ludwig, Arnold M.
1983 "Why do alcoholics drink?" pp. 197-214 in Benjamin Kissin and Henri Begleiter (eds.) The Biology of Alcoholism, Vol. 6. Psychosocial Factors. New York: Plenum.

Luft, J.
1961 "The Johari Window: A graphic model of awareness in interpersonal behavior." Human Relations Training News 5, 1: 6-7.

Lynch, R.
1982 "Play, creativity, and emotion," pp. 45-62 in N. K. Denzin (ed.) Studies in Symbolic Interaction, Vol. 4. Greenwich, CT: JAI.

Lyotard, Jean-Grancois
1984 The Postmodern Condition: A Report on Knowledge. Minneapolis, MN: University of Minnesota Press.

MacAndrew, Craig and Robert B. Edgerton
1969 Drunken Comportment: A Social Explanation. Chicago: Aldine.

MacAndrew, Craig and Harold Garfinkel
1962 "A consideration of changes attributed to intoxication as common-sense reasons for getting drunk." Quarterly Journal of Studies on Alcohol 23: 252-266.

Madsen, William
1974 The American Alcoholic: The Nature-Nurture Controversy in Alcoholic Research and Therapy. Springfield, IL: Charles C Thomas.

Maisto, Stephen A. and Janice Boon McCollam
1980 "The use of multiple measures of life health to assess alcohol treatment outcome: a review and critique," pp. 15-76 in Linda Carter Sobell et al. (eds.) Evaluating Alcohol and Drug Abuse Treatment Effectiveness. New York: Pergamon.

Malinowski, B.
1962 Sex, Culture and Myth. New York: Harcourt. (originally published in 1913)

Mandall, Wallace and Harold M. Ginzburg
1976 "Youthful alcohol use, abuse and alcoholism," pp. 167-204 in Benjamin Kissin and Henri Begleiter (eds.) The Biology of Alcoholism, Vol. 4. Social Aspects of Alcoholism. New York: Plenum.

Mann, Marty
1968 New Primer on Alcoholism. New York: Holt, Rinehart and Winston.

Mark, V. H. and F. R. Ervin
1970 Violence and the Brain. New York: Harper & Row.

Marshall, Shelly
    1978   Young, Sober and Free. Center City, MN: Hazelden Foundation.
Marx, G. T. and J. I. Wood
    1975   "Strands of theory and research in collective behavior," pp. 363-428 in I. Inkeles
            et al. (eds.) Annual Review of Sociology, Vol. 1. Palo Alto, CA: Annual
            Reviews, Inc.
Marx, Karl
    1983   "From the eighteenth Brumaire of Louis Bonaparte," in E. Kamenka (ed.) The
            Portable Karl Marx. New York: Penguin. (originally published in 1852)
Maxwell, Milton A.
    1984   The Alcoholics Anonymous Experience: A Close-up View for Professionals.
            New York: McGraw-Hill.
McAuliffe, William E. and Robert A. Gordon
    1974   "A test of Lindesmith's theory of addiction: the frequency of euphoria among
            long-term addicts." American Journal of Sociology 77: 795-840.
McCall, G. J. and J. Simmons
    1978   Identities and Interactions. New York: Free Press.
McClearn, Gerald E.
    1983   "Genetic factors in alcohol abuse: animal models," pp. 1-30 in Benjamin Kissin
            and Henri Begleiter (eds.) The Biology of Alcoholism, Vol. 7. Biological
            Factors. New York: Plenum.
McClelland, David C., William N. Davis, Rudolf Kalin, and Eric Wanner
    1972   The Drinking Man. New York: The Free Press.
Mead, G. H.
    1899   "The working hypothesis in social reform." American Journal of Sociology 5:
            369-371.
    1934   Mind, Self and Society. Chicago: University of Chicago Press.
    1964   "A pragmatic theory of truth," pp. 320-344 in Andrew J. Reck (ed.) George
            Herbert Mead: Selected Writings. Indianapolis: The Bobbs-Merrill Company.
Mello, Nancy K.
    1972   "Behavioral studies of alcoholism," pp. 219-292 in Benjamin Kissin and Henri
            Begleiter (eds.) The Biology of Alcoholism, Vol. 2. Physiology and Behavior.
            New York: Plenum.
    1983   "A behavioral analysis of the reinforcing properties of alcohol and other drugs
            in man," pp. 133-198 in Benjamin Kissin and Henri Begleiter (eds.) The Biology
            of Alcoholism, Vol. 7. Biological Factors. New York: Plenum.
Meltzer, Bernard M.
    1972   "Mead's social psychology," pp. 4-22 in J. G. Manis and B. N. Meltzer (eds.)
            Symbolic Interaction: A Reader in Social Psychology. Boston: Allyn and
            Bacon.
Menninger, Karl A.
    1938   Man Against Himself. New York: Harcourt, Brace and World.
Merleau-Ponty, M.
    1963   The Structure of Behavior. [A. L. Fisher, trans.]. Boston: Beacon. (originally
            published in 1942)
Merryman, Richard
    1984   Broken Promises, Mended Dreams. Boston: Little, Brown.
Merton, Robert K.
    1957   Social Theory and Social Structure. Glencoe, IL: Free Press.

Mills, C. W.
  1940   "Situated actions and vocabularies of motive." American Sociological Review
         5: 904-913.
  1959   The Sociological Imagination. New York: Oxford University Press.
Mulford, Harold A.
  1969   "Alcoholics," "Alcoholism," and "Problem Drinkers": Social Objects In-The-
         Making. Report to the National Center for Health Statistics, U.S. Department
         of Health, Education and Welfare, Washington, DC. (mimeo.)
  1970   Meeting the Problems of Alcohol Abuse: A Testable Action Plan for Iowa.
         Cedar Rapids, IA: Iowa Alcoholism Foundation.
Mulford, Harold A. and Donald E. Miller
  1964   "Measuring public acceptance of the alcoholic as a sick person." Quarterly
         Journal of Studies on Alcohol 25: 314-323.
Nathan P. E., N. A. Titler, L. A. Lowenstein, P. Solomon, and A. M. Rossi
  1970   "Behavioral analysis of chronic alcoholism." Archives of General Psychiatry
         22: 419-428.
Newsweek
  1984a "Getting straight: how Americans are breaking the grip of drugs and alcohol."
         (June 4): 62-69.
  1984b "Alcoholism and the recovering generation." (September 10): 71-80.
New York Times
  1983   "Alcohol abuse in the United States." (October 23): 1.
Nietzsche, Friedrich
  1887   A Geneology of Morals: Vol. 2. [William A. Hausemann, trans.]. New York:
         Macmillan.
O'Neill, Eugene
  1955   Long Day's Journey into Night. New Haven, CT: Yale University Press.
Oscar-Berman, M.
  1984   "Central nervous system disorders," pp. 190-191 in Raymond J. Corsini (ed.)
         Encyclopedia of Psychology, Vol. 1. New York: John Wiley.
Parsons, Talcott [ed.].
  1978   "The sick role and the role of the physician reconsidered," pp. 11-16 in Action
         Theory and the Human Condition. New York: Free Press.
Pattison, E. Mansell
  1966   "A critique of alcoholism treatment concepts." Quarterly Journal of Studies on
         Alcohol 27: 49-71.
Pattison, E. Mansell, E. B. Headley, G. C. Gleser, and L. A. Gottschalk
  1968   "Abstinence and normal drinking: an assessment of changes in drinking
         patterns in alcoholics after treatment." Quarterly Journal of Studies on
         Alcohol 29: 610-633.
Pattison, E. Mansell, Mark B. Sobell, and Linda C. Sobell
  1977   Emerging Concepts of Alcohol Dependence. New York: Springer.
Pendery, Mary L., Irving M. Maltzman, and L. Jolyon West
  1982   "Controlled drinking by alcoholics: new findings and a reevaluation of a major
         affirmative study." Science 217: 169-175.
Pernanen, Kai
  1976   "Alcohol and crimes of violence," pp. 351-444 in Benjamin Kissin and Henri
         Begleiter (eds.) The Biology of Alcoholism. Vol. 4, Social Aspects of
         Alcoholism. New York: Plenum.

Pittman, David
    1967   "International overview: social and cultural factors and nonpathological,"
           pp. 3-20 in David J. Pittman (ed.) Alcoholism. New York: Harper & Row.
Pittman, David J. and C. W. Gordon
    1958   "Criminal careers of the chronic drunkenness offender." Quarterly Journal of
           Studies on Alcohol 19: 255-268.
Radcliffe-Brown, A. R.
    1922   The Adaman Islanders. Glencoe, IL: Free Press.
Redd, William H., A. L. Porterfield, and Barbara L. Anderson
    1979   Behavior Modification: Behavioral Approaches to Human Problems. New
           York: Random House.
Robbins, Lee N.
    1980   "Alcoholism and labelling theory," pp. 35-46 in W. R. Gove (ed.) The Labeling
           of Deviance: Evaluating a Perspective. Beverly Hills, CA: Sage.
Robinson, David
    1979   Talking Out of Alcoholism: The Self-Help Process of Alcoholics Anonymous.
           Baltimore, MD: University Park Press.
Roebuck, Julian B. and R. G. Kessler
    1972   The Etiology of Alcoholism: Constitutional, Psychological and Sociological
           Approaches. Springfield, IL: Charles C Thomas.
Roman, Paul M. and Harrison M. Trice
    1976   "Alcohol abuse and work organization," pp. 445-519 in Benjamin Kissin and
           Henri Begleiter (eds.) The Biology of Alcoholism, Vol. 4. Social Aspects of
           Alcoholism. New York: Plenum.
Room, Robin
    1982   "Alcohol, science and social control," pp. 371-384 in Edith L. Gomberg et al.
           (eds.) Alcohol, Science and Society Revisited. Ann Arbor: University of
           Michigan Press.
    1983   "Region and urbanization as factors in drinking practices and problems," pp.
           555-604 in Benjamin Kissin and Henri Begleiter (eds.) The Biology of
           Alcoholism, Vol. 6. Psychosocial Factors. New York: Plenum.
Roth, J.
    1963   Timetables. Indianapolis, IN: Bobbs-Merrill.
Royce, James E.
    1981   Alcoholic Problems and Alcoholism: A Comprehensive Survey. New York:
           Free Press.
Rubington, Earl
    1977   "The role of the halfway house in the rehabilitation of alcoholics," pp. 351-384
           in Benjamin Kissin and Henri Begleiter (eds.) The Biology of Alcoholism, Vol.
           5. Treatment and Rehabilitation of the Chronic Alcoholic. New York: Plenum.
Rudy, David
    1986   Becoming an Alcoholic. Carbondale: Southern Illinois University.
Ryan, Christopher and Nelson Butters
    1983   "Cognitive deficits in alcoholics," pp. 485-538 in Benjamin Kissin and Henri
           Begleiter (eds.) The Biology of Alcoholism, Vol. 7. Biological Factors. New
           York: Plenum.
Sagarin, E.
    1969   Odd Man In: Societies of Deviants in America. Chicago: Quadrangle.
Sartre, Jean-Paul
    1956   Being and Nothingness. New York: Philosophical Library. (originally pub-
           lished in 1943).

1976   Critique of Dialectical Reason. London: NLP. (originally published in 1960)

1981   The Family Idiot, Gustave Flaubert, Vol. I: 1821-1857.Chicago: University of Chicago Press.

Scheff, Thomas J.

1979   Catharsis in Healing, Ritual and Drama. Berkeley: University of California Press.

Schegloff, E. A., G. Jefferson, and H. Sacks

1977   "The preference for self-correction in the organization of repair in conversation." Language 53: 361-382.

Scheler, M.

1961   Ressentiment. [L. A. Coser, ed.; W. W. Holdeim, trans.]. New York: Free Press. (originally published in 1912)

1970   The Nature of Sympathy. [P. Heath, trans.] Hamden, CT: Archon Books. (originally published in 1913).

1973   Formalism in Ethics and Non-Formal Ethics of Values: A New Attempt Toward the Foundations of an Ethical Personalism. Evanston, IL: Northwestern University Press. (originally published in 1916)

Schenkein, J. [ed.]

1978   Studies in the Organization of Conversational Interaction. New York: Academic Press.

Schuckit, Marc A. and Jane Duby

1983   "Alcoholism in women," pp. 215-242 in Benjamin Kissin and Henri Begleiter (eds.) The Biology of Alcoholism, Vol. 6. Psychosocial Factors. New York: Plenum.

Schutz, A.

1962   Collected Papers, Vol. I. The Problem of Social Reality. [M, Natanson, ed.]. The Hague: Martinus Nijhoff.

1964   Collected Papers, Vol. II. Studies in Social Theory. [A. Brodersen, ed.]. The Hague: Martinus Nijhoff.

1967   The Phenomenology of the Social World. Evanston, IL: Northwestern University Press.

1968   Collected Papers, Vol. III. Studies in Phenomenological Philosophy [I. Schutz, ed.]. The Hague: Martinus Nijhoff.

Schutz A. and T. Luckmann

1973   The Structures of the Life World. Evanston, IL: Northwestern University Press.

Scott, M. B. and S. M. Lyman

1968   "Accounts." American Sociological Review 33: 46-62.

Searle, John

1970   Speech Acts. Cambridge: Cambridge University Press.

Shils, E.

1976   Center and Periphery: Essays in Macrosociology. Chicago: University of Chicago Press.

Shott, Susan

1979   "Emotion and social life: a symbolic interactionist analysis." American Journal of Sociology 84: 1317-34.

Silkworth, William D.

1976   "The doctor's opinion," pp. xxiii-xiv in Alcoholic Anonymous. New York: A.A. World Services, Inc.

Skinner, B. F.

1953   Science and Human Behavior. New York: Macmillan.

Smith, Bernard B.
  1957   "A friend looks at alcoholics anonymous," pp. 273-283 in Alcoholics Anonymous Comes of Age: A Brief History of A.A. New York: Alcoholics Anonymous World Services, Inc.
Snow, D. A. and C. L. Phillips
  1980   "The Lofland-Stark conversion model: a critical reassessment." Social Problems 27: 430-447.
Sobell, Linda Carter, Mark B. Sobell, and Elliot Ward
  1980   Evaluating Alcohol and Drug Abuse Treatment Effectiveness: Recent Advances. New York: Pergamon.
Sobell, Mark B. and Linda C. Sobell
  1978   Behavioral Treatment of Alcohol Problems: Individualized Therapy and Controlled Drinking. New York: Plenum.
Solomon, Joel
  1983   "Psychiatric characteristics of alcoholics," pp. 67-112 in Benjamin Kissin and Henri Begleiter (eds.) The Biology of Alcoholism, Vol. 6. Psychosocial Factors. New York: Plenum.
Spender, Stephen
  1984   "Introduction," pp. vii-xxiii in Malcolm Lowry, Under the Volcano. New York: New American Library. (originally published in 1947)
Spinoza, Benedict
  1888   The Ethics [R.H.M. Elwes, trans.]. London: George Bell and Sons.
Spradley, James P.
  1970   You Owe Yourself a Drunk: An Ethnography of Urban Nomads. Boston: Little, Brown.
Stack, Carol
  1974   All Our Kin: Strategies for Survival in a Black Community. New York: Harper.
Stark, R. and W. S. Bainbridge
  1980   "Networks of faith: interpersonal bonds and recruitment to cults and sects." American Journal of Sociology 85: 1376-1395.
Steinglass, Peter
  1977   "Family therapy in alcoholism," pp. 259-300 in Benjamin Kissin and Henri Begleiter (eds.) The Biology of Alcoholism, Vol. 5. Treatment and Rehabilitation of the Chronic Alcoholic. New York: Plenum.
Steinglass, Peter and Anne Robertson
  1983   "The alcoholic family," pp. 243-307 in Benjamin Kissin and Henri Begleiter (eds.) The Pathogenesis of Alcoholism, Vol. 6. Psychosocial Factors. New York: Plenum.
Stivers, Richard
  1976   A Hair of the Dog: Irish Drinking and American Stereotype. University Park, PA: Pennsylvania State University Press.
Stone, Gregory P.
  1962   "Appearance and the self," pp. 86-118 in A. M. Rose (ed.) Human Nature and Social Process. Boston: Houghton Mifflin.
  1981   "Appearance and the self: a slightly revised version," pp. 187-202 in Gregory G. P. Stone and Harvey A. Faberman (eds.) Social Psychology Through Symbolic Interaction. New York: John Wiley.
Straus, Robert
  1974   Escape from Custody. New York: Harper & Row.
Strauss, A.
  1959   Mirrors and Masks: The Search for Identity. New York: Free Press.

1978 "A social world perspective," pp. 119-128 in Norman K. Denzin (ed.) Studies in Symbolic Interaction, Vol. 1. Greenwich, CT: JAI.

1982 "Social worlds and legitimation processes," pp. 171-190 in Norman K. Denzin (ed.) Studies in Symbolic Interaction, Vol. 4. Greenwich, CT: JAI.

Stryker, Sheldon

1981 "Symbolic interactionism: themes and variations," pp. 3-29 in M. Rosenberg and R. Turner (eds.) Social Psychology: Sociological Perspectives. New York: Basic Books.

Sullivan, H. S.

1953 The Interpersonal Theory of Psychiatry. New York: Norton.

Sykes, G. M. and D. Matza

1959 "Techniques of neutralization: a theory of delinquency." American Sociologial Review 22: 664-670.

Szasz, Thomas

1961 The Myth of Mental Illness. New York: Dell.

1975 Ceremonial Chemistry: The Ritual Persecution of Drugs, Addicts and Pushers. New York: Doubleday.

Thomas, W. I. and D. S. Thomas

1982 The Child in America. New York: Knopf.

Thorndike, E. L.

1913 The Psychology of Learning: Educational Psychology, Vol. 2. New York: Teacher's College Press of Columbia University.

Thune, Carl E.

1977 "Alcoholism, and the archetypical past: a phenomenological perspective on Alcoholics Anonymous." Quarterly Journal of Studies on Alcohol 38: 75-88.

Tiebout, Harry M.

1944 "Therapeutic mechanisms in Alcoholics Anonymous." American Journal of Psychiatry 100: 468-473.

1949 "The act of surrender in the therapeutic process with special reference to alcoholism." Quarterly Journal of Studies on Alcohol 10: 48-58.

1953 "Surrender versus compliance in therapy.' Quarterly Journal of Studies on Alcohol 14: 58-68.

1954 "The ego factors in surrender in alcoholism." Quarterly Journal of Studies on Alcohol 15: 610-621.

Time Magazine

1985 "Cocktails '85: America's new drinking habits." (May 20): 68-73, 76-78.

Travisano, Richard

1981 "Alternation and conversion as qualitatively different transformations," pp. 237-248 in Gregory P. Stone and Harvey A. Faberman (eds.) Social Psychology Through Symbolic Interaction. New York: John Wiley.

Trice, Harrison M.

1957 "A study of the process of affiliation with Alcoholics Anonymous." Quarterly Journal of Studies in Alcohol 18: 39-43.

1966 Alcoholism in America. New York: McGraw-Hill.

1984 "Alcoholism in America revisited." Journal of Drug Issues 14: 109-123.

Trice, Harrison, M. and Paul M. Roman

1970 "Delabeling, relabeling and Alcoholics Anonymous." Social Problems 17: 468-480.

Ullman, Albert D.

1958 "Sociocultural backgrounds conducive to alcoholism." Annals of the American Academy of Political and Social Science 315: 48-55.

United States Government Printing Office
    1976   Comprehensive Alcohol Abuse and Alcoholism Prevention, Treatment, and Rehabilitation Act Amendments of 1976. Washington, DC: Author.

Updike, John
    1984   "Modernist, postmodernist, what will they think of next?" *New Yorker* (September 10): 136-137, 140-142.

Urbina, S. P.
    1984   "Amnesia," pp. 56-57 in Raymond J. Corsini (ed.) Encyclopedia of Psychology, Vol. 1. New York: John Wiley.

Valliant, George
    1983   The Natural History of Alcoholism: Causes, Patterns and Paths to Recovery. Cambridge, MA: Harvard University Press.

Vander Mey, Brenda J. and Ronald L. Neff
    1986   Incest as Child Abuse Research and Implications. New York: Praeger.

Victor, M.
    1965   "Observations on the amnestic syndrome in man and its anatomical basis," pp. 311-340 in M.A.B. Brazier (ed.) Brain Functions: Vol. 2. Berkeley: University of California Press.

Wallace, John
    1982   "Alcoholism from the inside out: a phenomenological analysis," pp. 1-23 in Nada J. Estes and M. Edith Heinemann (eds.) Alcoholism: Development, Consequences and Interventions. St. Louis, MO: Mosby.

Wallace, P. M.
    1984   "Aphasia," p. 80 in Raymond J. Corsini (ed.) Encyclopedia of Psychology, Vol. 1. New York: John Wiley.

Warner, W. L.
    1962   American Life: Dream and Reality. Chicago: University of Chicago Press.

Watts, Thomas D. and Roosevelt Wright, Jr.
    1983   Black Alcoholism: Toward Comprehensive Understanding. Springfield, IL: Charles C Thomas.

Weber, M.
    1946   From Max Weber: Essays in Sociology [H. Gerth and C. W. Mills, eds.]. New York: Oxford University Press.

Wexberg, L. E.
    1951   "Ursachen und Symptome der Arzneimittelsucht und des Alkoholismus." Z. Psychother Stuttgart 1: 227-235.

White, R. W.
    1956   The Abnormal Personality. New York: Ronald Press.

Whitney, Elizabeth D.
    1865   The Lonely Sickness. Boston: Beacon Press.

Wholey, Dennis [ed.]
    1984   The Courage to Change: Hope and Help for Alcoholics and Their Families. Personal Conversations with Dennis Wholey. Boston: Houghton Mifflin.

Wilden, Anthony
    1968   "Lacan and the discourse of the other," pp. 86-222 in J. Lacan (ed.) Speech and Language in Psychoanalysis. [A. Wilden, trans.]. Baltimore, MD: Johns Hopkins University Press.

Wiley, Norbert
    1985   "Durkheim on religion: a revision." Unpublished manuscript, Department of Sociology, University of Illinois, Urbana.

Williams, Allan F.
    1976   "The alcoholic personality," pp. 243-275 in Benjamin Kissin and Henri Begleiter (eds.) The Biology of Alcoholism, Vol. 4. Social Aspects of Alcoholism. New York: Plenum.

Wiseman, Jacqueline P.
    1970   Stations of the Lost: The Treatment of Skid Row Alcoholics. Englewood Cliffs, NJ: Prentice-Hall.

Wittgenstein, L.
    1954   Philosophical Investigations. London: Blackwell.

Woititz, Janet Geringer
    1983   Adult Children of Alcoholics. Rutgers, NJ: Health Communications, Inc.

Zald, M. and R. Ash
    1966   "Social movement organizations: growth, decay and change." Social Forces 44: 327-341.

Zurcher, Louis A. and David A. Snow
    1981   "Collective behavior and social movements," pp. 447-482 in M. Rosenberg and R. H. Turner (eds.) Social Psychology: Sociological Perspectives. New York: Basic Books.

Zuriff, G. E.
    1985   Behaviorism: A Conceptual Reconstruction. New York: Columbia University Press.

Zwerling, Israel and Milton Rosenbaum
    1959   "Alcoholic addiction and personality," pp. 624-644 in S. Arieti (ed.) American Handbook of Psychiatry. New York: Basic Books.

Name Index

Subject Index

About the Author

Norman K. Denzin is professor of sociology and humanities at the University of Illinois at Urbana Champaign. He received his B.A. degree (1963) and his Ph.D. degree (1966) in sociology from the University of Iowa. Denzin's main research activities and interests have been in childhood socialization, the study of language, the self, interaction, interpretive theory, and phenomenology. He has been vice-president of the Society for the Study of Symbolic Interaction (1976-1977), secretary of the Social Psychology Section of the American Sociological Association (1978-1980), and was recently elected president of the Midwest Sociological Society (1987). Denzin is the author and editor of several books, including *Social Psychology* (1978, with A. Lindesmith and A. Strauss, 5th ed.), *Sociological Methods* (1978), *The Research Act* (1978, 2nd ed.), *Childhood Socialization* (1977), *Children and Their Caretakers* (1973), *The Values of Social Science* (1973), and *The Mental Patient* (1968, with S. P. Spitzer), and *On Understanding Emotion* (1984). He is the editor of *Studies in Symbolic Interaction: A Research Annual* and the author of over 50 articles, which have appeared in such journals as *American Journal of Sociology, American Sociological Review, British Journal of Sociology, Semiotica, Social Forces, Social Problems,* and *Sociological Quarterly.*

NOTES